MONSTROUS

2010
VOL. 1
NO. 1

THE OVERLOOK CONNECTION
BOOKSTORE OF THE FANTASTIC

STEPHEN KING CATALOG

The MIST Special Issue!!!

INSIDE: Everything Stephen King !
Books ! Video ! Audio ! Ephemera !
StephenKingCatalog.com !

DARK FORCES

FORCES

THE **25**TH
ANNIVERSARY EDITION

EDITED BY KIRBY McCAULEY

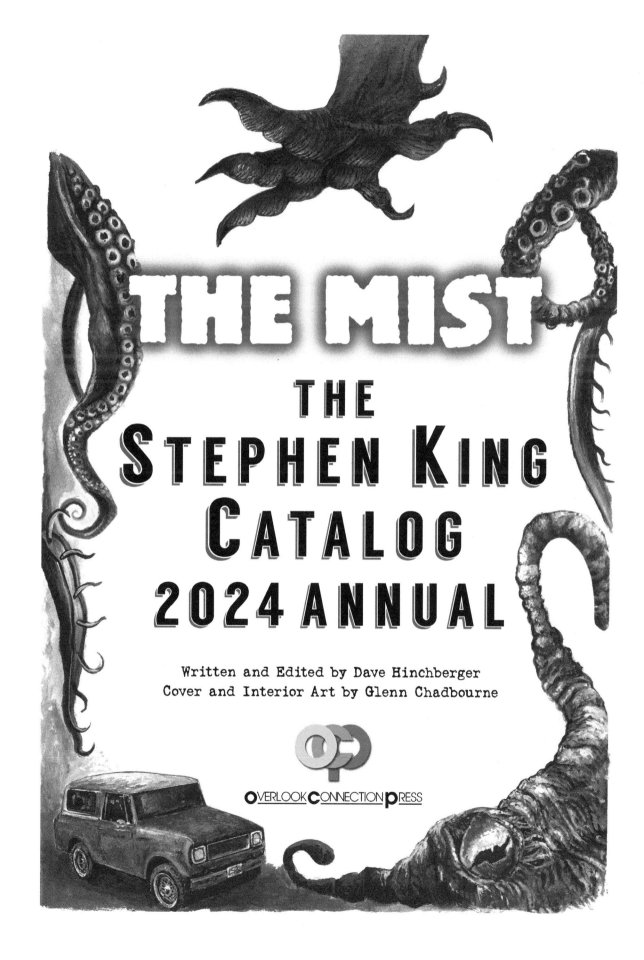

THE MIST

THE STEPHEN KING CATALOG 2024 ANNUAL

Written and Edited by Dave Hinchberger
Cover and Interior Art by Glenn Chadbourne

OVERLOOK CONNECTION PRESS

Holly - Original Book Cover Wraparound Art

From the New *Stephen King Cover Series* by artist Glenn Chadbourne.

This original art featured here is part of an original dust jacket, a complete wraparound cover, signed / numbered by artist Glenn Chadbourne. Also features original art on the front and back flaps. These original covers will fit on your copy of *Holly* by Stephen King. Measures 9 ½" x 21" Discover all the New Stephen King Covers in this exclusive series under the Glenn Chadbourne category on any web page at: **StephenKingCatalog.com**

TABLE OF TENTACLES

"The Storm is Coming"

"People began screaming again, and there was a stampede toward the back of the store. Then there was a more piercing scream, one of pain, and Ollie said, "Oh my God, that old lady fell down and they just ran over her." – **Stephen King**, *The Mist*

When *The Mist* was first published in the *Dark Forces* anthology it took his readers by (ahem), storm. It was a big hit and propelled the anthology to become an award-winner and lead a wider interest in horror fiction. At 51,000 words it was a hefty sized novella and finally became its own mass-market paperback in 2007, as a tie-in to the film release. I knew *The Mist* would eventually be a theme for a Stephen King Annual and last year it coalesced and was apparent that 2024 was the time.

The Mist read like a *Twilight Zone*, *Outer Limits*, or *Night Gallery* scenario. The influence of 50's mutant horror, sci-fi flicks, and Lovecraft's Cthulu Mythos are very evident in this tale With Stephen King's prose brings *The Mist* to life like a movie in our minds, often the case in his writing. *The Mist* is cinematic in its delivery and vision.

I was primed for this kind of story when I read this in *Dark Forces* back in 1980. I had grown up attracted to sci-fi, horror, films, and TV. This story pushed all those buttons of outrageous scenarios of mutated monsters, time travel, and other worldly dimensions. I was a senior in high-school and the sky was the limit for this fiction. *The Mist* was an exciting adventure that faded out. Not really an ending, but more than that I didn't want it to end, I needed more!

The core of *The Mist* is more about the human monsters than about the creatures themselves. The human monsters that rear their ugly minds when put in an impossible situation they can't handle, ready to throw you under the bus to save themselves. When in fact they've shown what sanity they had left is lost, themselves getting sucked under the bus they're so desperately trying to evade.

"Maple Street, U.S.A., late summer. A tree-lined little world of front porch gliders, barbecues, the laughter of children, and the bell of an ice cream vendor. At the sound of the roar and the flash of light, it will be precisely 6:43 P.M. on Maple Street.

This is Maple Street on a late Saturday afternoon. Maple Street in the last calm and reflective moment –before the monsters came."

– "The Monsters Are Due on Maple Street," Rod Serling's opening monologue,

The Twilight Zone episode, "The Monsters Are Due on Maple Street," was a definite precursor to *The Mist*. When folks are put in an impossible situation that is quite out of the norm, what extremes people will go to, to save their sanity, their very lives, in an extreme situation. Written by Rod Serling this is episode 22 in the first season of the series. It originally aired on March 4, 1960. When it aired Stephen King would have been almost thirteen.

The Mist, the film: We all received a gut punch of an ending we didn't see coming. It disturbed most, if not all, its viewers. Done with Stephen King's permission of course, and with the studio's reluctance, it was an ending which made it all that more potent in its delivery. I was very upset, enough so that I had two shots at the bar right after we saw the film. Frank Darabont took a chance and this has been discussed for the past fifteen years, ad nauseum I'm sure. Creating this kind of ending was going to upset a lot of people. No one wants to be put in that situation, yet everyone who sees it questions themselves. What's the right thing to do? I've talked to many people who didn't like

STEPHEN KING'S THE MIST

The Mist because of the ending. That's the point. We make our own luck, until that drunk driver runs you off the road. Life isn't always what you expect it to be, and that things can turn when you least expect it. Good or bad. One thing's for sure, you'll never forget this ending. Ever.

See, I've already said too much if you haven't read *The Mist* yet. Read the story, watch the film. Moments and scenes will be discussed within and it's best you've had your own opportunity to experience these before continuing. If you're familiar with the story, and film, you'll enjoy what we have gathered here of *The Mist*.

I discover, sometimes trip over, inspiration for topics and guest authors are invited from many avenues for our Stephen King Annuals. I'm fortunate to get to work with writers, directors, and many folks in these creative fields. This year's edition of articles, guests, and reviews has exceeded my expectations. Comic artist / writer legend (*Swamp Thing*, *Constantine*, etc.) Stephen Bissette's response to *Hellboy* creator, Mike Mignola's Facebook Mist post in 2022, prompted me to invite him into this year's edition, and fortunately for our readers, he gladly accepted. Stephen's response in the post said: "*The Mist* was one of a few key genre works (*Frailty* among them) that clearly dramatized where we, as a culture, were at the time and where we were going" and voila! I knew we needed his view, a valid scale about *The Mist*.

Pete Von Sholly, has worked in film for decades as a storyboard artist (and then some) and on every Frank Darabont/Stephen King adaptation, as well as creating the art for PS Publishing's *Skeleton Crew* King anniversary edition. He's even worked with a comic book hero of mine, Jack Kirby! Pete has also let us publish for the first time anywhere his comic, *The Missed!* It's time for our readers to meet "the man of many hats."

Constantine Nasr has been working alongside Frank Darabont films for decades. He's shared his wonderful memories and personal insight working on *The Mist* film. You're in for a treat!

Stephen Spignesi, one of the top Stephen King bibliophiles of the last thirty-five years, (author of *The Lost Work of Stephen King*) continues his look at Stephen King's rare and uncollected work in "The New Lost Work of Stephen King". His introduction will give readers insight and the opportunity to seek them out if they can't wait for them to be collected someday.

The Shining opera had it's East Coast premiere in Atlanta with a sold-out two week run! We were there to experience a new vision to Stephen King's opus. Check out the review and photos to see what they delivered (hint: I was impressed).

I am thoroughly amazed at what our team of writers have come up with this year. I'd like to welcome a few new annual columns: The "Dollar Baby" by Anthony Northrup looks at *The Monkey*, and will annually report on Stephen King's unique film series. "Extreme King" is a collector's corner of Stephen King limited and rare releases that Diana Petroff and Noah Mitchell will showcase for us every year. L.L. Soares is joining us for the first time with his look at *The Mist* – film and TV series — and I expect he'll be back serving up more cinematic musings for us in the future.

Our team of annual columnists are back: Bev Vincent, Tyson Blue, Kevin Quigley, Stephen Spignesi, Andy Rausch, and guest reviewer, Ariel Bosi. Their collective insights are invaluable in the King world of Constant Readers. Thank you, Annual Team King!

Until next time… in the words of Alice Cooper… "Nothing severed, nothing gained"

Keep Shining!

– Dave Hinchberger

Screaming from Ear to Ear:
The Mist in 3-D Sound

by *Kevin Quigley*

You're lying on your bed in a dark room. It's overcast outside; full dark, no stars. Slipping in your ear buds, you select *The Mist in 3-D Sound* and close your eyes. You're familiar with the story. It's scary but you know what's going to happen. And yet, this audio show is unusually adept at ramping up tension. Slowly, inexorably, you are drawn into the hell at the center of *The Mist*, your muscles growing taut, your eyes squeezing shut even tighter, as if you can block out the images in your head as well as your ears. Then, suddenly, something *slithers* from one wall to the other, and it's right in the room, it's *right next to you*, and then you're screaming and you rip out the ear buds and hurl them away at the speed of sound.

That's the experience of *The Mist in 3-D Sound*. Here's how it got from the page to the scream:

In *Danse Macabre*, King talks about his early years of being scared to pieces by thrillers on the radio, programs like *Inner Sanctum Mysteries*, *Lights Out*, and especially *Quiet Please*. He also talks about the demise of the format: "I am of the last quarter of the last generation that remembers radio drama as an active force – a dramatic art form with its own set of reality." By 1970, even the sundowning era was decades in the past. A man who went by the terrific name Meatball Fulton (aka Thomas Manuel Lopez) was trying to revive the format, forming an audio drama troupe called the ZBS Foundation (also terrific: ZBS stands for "Zero Bull Shit"). Employing top-notch acting talent and electronic musician Tim Clark, Meatball familiarized himself with state-of-the-art sound effects to support the fantastic radio plays he was writing. As it turned out, radio plays weren't quite as dead as most people thought: the format tends to re-emerge on the scene like a particularly entertaining revenant every few years. National Public Radio (NPR)

broadcast ZBS's programs throughout the 1980s, a variety of science fiction and mystery and comedy, calling them "audio stories for the soul."

But Meatball was always on the lookout for innovation, and in 1984, he discovered the utterly bizarre Kunstkopf binaural microphone, a device that most closely resembles a Rick Baker fever dream. For one thing, it's in the shape of a nearly featureless human head: a sloping forehead with concave angles suggesting an eyeline, from which juts a long, sharply rectangular nose. Beneath that: the alarming absence of a mouth, horrifyingly recalling the haunted, mouthless woman from *Twilight Zone: The Movie*, desperate to but unable to scream. But the most hellish – if most important – features are the human-like black

The Mist 3-D Sound, ZBS Cassette 1984

8

Stephen King's
The Mist in
3-D Sound
Double Black Vinyl
Record Set in a
gatefold cover
ZBS 1984

plastic ears, grotesquely realistic in contrast with the smooth humanesque head, growing seemingly organically from the sides of this bizarre Dr. Moreau experiment. Horrorshow or not, this microphone would revolutionize Meatball's and ZBS's futures in radio.

Because it mimics the shape of a human head, and "hears" like a person hears, this microphone – dubbed Mr. Fritz, because Meatball was a man of whimsy – could record sound "above, below, and all around." Put on headphones or earbuds, and a recording by Mr. Fritz would surround you on all sides. If people are walking across the room, you hear their footfalls on a floor from a distance, approaching your right, then walking away on your left. Main dialog sounds like it's right in front of you, while you can hear and sense people murmuring in a corner, quieter and further away. Overlapping dialog in either ear offers a sense of greater realism, as in a Robert Altman film. And if there's an otherworldly spider dangling from a poisonous, gossamer string, its unnatural hisses and clicks sound like they're coming right above your head.

In 1984, ZBS had the rights to produce an adaptation of "The Mist." Noted horror author Dennis Etchison, whom King had consulted extensively during the writing of *Danse Macabre*, had written an unproduced screenplay based on the novella. In a way, he was perfect for the job; previously, he had written a novelization of John Carpenter's *The Fog*. Small towns enveloped by otherworldly water vapor is a niche subject matter, but Etchison seemed to have sewn it up. Meatball adapted this script, and assembled a full cast led by Stephen King film regular Willam Sadler (in fact, Sadler appears in all Frank Darabont King adaptations: *The Shawshank Redemption*, *The Green Mile* … and *The Mist*. People associated with Stephen King seem to enjoy involving themselves with low-lying clouds time and again.)

The Mist in 3-D Sound was first serialized on public radio as part of the ZBS program *The Cabinet of Dr. Fritz* on October 2, 9, and 16 – smack dab in the middle of spooky season. Accompanying the broadcast was a longplay record edition put out by ZBS that offered the entire audioplay as a seamless hour-and-a-half-long presentation. Later cassette and CD versions followed, slightly abridged; interestingly, these were produced by Simon

& Schuster Audioworks, over a decade before King switched publishers from Viking to S&S. Like the mist itself, those releases were harbingers of a future full of scares.

In 2023, you can access *The Mist in 3-D Sound* wherever fine audiobooks are sold. The Audible presentation is unabridged, and as with the original broadcast, it is just as likely to make your skin crawl, your mind reel, your ears try to cringe away from the horrors unfolding. Nowadays, you can listen to *The Mist* anywhere – on the subway, in a car, maybe even in a brightly lit supermarket. It doesn't have to be pitch black to terrify you; just put on your headphones and try not to shriek out loud. Because while all your other senses try to tell you otherwise, you can't help but be convinced that that thing from the other side of a hole in the world feels – *is?!* – right behind you. Any second now, it will touch the back of your neck, grab, and drag you into the black nothing of itself. Of course it will. Your ears don't lie.

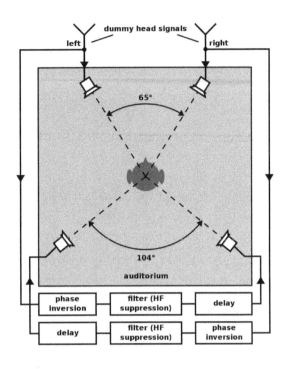

KU 100 reference microphone, also known as "Fritz," to support various binaural audio and music projects. Fritz is an artificial head microphone and one of Neumann's most valuable microphones. Recordings made with the KU 100 are incredibly realistic and precise, with a three-dimensional spatial imaging effect that can greatly enhance music and radio productions. With Fritz, anyone can create immersive recordings without any prior technical knowledge.

"The Mist", features 35 actors… Monsters were created by putting various live animal sounds into the computer of a Synclavier II digital synthesizer and then playing them on its keyboard. The meow of a Siamese cat became the sound of spiders the size of large dogs, which dropped down on the unsuspecting listener from directly above. The chirp of a parakeet was turned into the shriek of a pterodactyl." – by John Sunier,
A History of Binaural Sound (Mar. 1986)

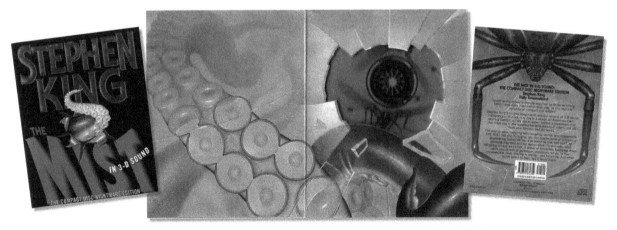

"The Mist" 3-D gatefold First Edition. Simon & Schuster 1993 Compact Disc. Illustration by Vince Natale.

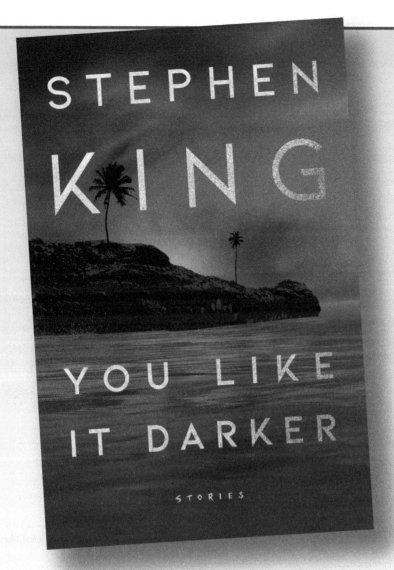

Release Date:
May 21, 2024

Includes the first publications of:

Two Talented Bastids
Danny Coughlin's Bad Dream
The Turbulence Expert
Rattlesnakes
The Dreamers
The Answer Man
Plus six more!

You Like it Darker, a new story collection that Stephen King says will feature "mostly new stories – long stories, for the most part," with the hardcover coming in at close to 600 pages!

He says it will include a Lovecraftian tale that called "The Dreamers" – dedicated to Cormac McCarthy - which will feature a character accessing a reality that exists beyond dreams, "a reality that's huge, you know apocalyptic, some huge darkness that's sentient"...

Pre-order from **StephenKingCatalog.com** and you will receive:

- **FREE** bookplate of Stephen King, with art currently featured here by Cortney Skinner with all pre-order purchases!
- **FREE** Acid-Free Book Cover placed on your copy with every purchase.
- **First Printing guaranteed!** We analyze every book to make sure it is As New before sending out.
- **Shipped in a well-packed box for complete Protection.**

Who Wants To Play In *The Mist*?

by *Dave Hinchberger*

When I first saw *The Mist* computer game sitting on a retail shelf back in 1985 I immediately picked it up. A game about one of my favorite King stories, *The Mist*? I was elated and it was the first time I'd seen any kind of artwork for this story. When *The Mist* was released it had only appeared in the *Dark Forces* anthology (no illustrations) and the J.K. Potter Scream/Press edition of *Skeleton Crew* wasn't out yet. I picked up this glossy casebound hardcover, read all the info and discovered what was inside: a floppy disc with the game, a fold-out map of the town, showing the mist encroaching toward it, a booklet about the game, and some random cards. Since the game was sealed I could only see the photo illustration on the outside of these items. The fold out map was considerable in size and could be framed. They didn't skimp on the look of the production, it was impressive. The set cost fifty bucks ($49.95), so that was a lot of dough for a curious oddity. Oh, I wanted

it, but here's the thing: I didn't own a computer (until 1988). Sure, they were around, but it's not like today where you have the world at your fingertips. There was no internet, no hookup to the outside world, everything had to be entered by a disc, literally. My first computer had… wait for it… 20 MB of hard drive space! Yes, megabytes! It was a glorified typewriter, but it changed how I could write, I could save my articles, print it out, repeatedly. And if I wanted… I could play that *Mist* game, but first I'd have to buy it, and a computer. That didn't come until much later.

I eventually found a copy of *The Mist* game second-hand, only 15 bucks. It was in perfect shape and had all the extras. I did try my hand playing the game. It's an interactive text adventure where you ask questions try to find the correct path to evade the mist full of creatures, etc. It's literally text on the screen, it's wasn't an action game, a bit of tension maybe. It didn't matter. Stephen King was now part of the "game world" and I thought that was one the coolest things to happen. Everyone who read Stephen King then (and frankly, now) was glad to see other forms of media

working to bring us more opportunities to spend time with one of our favorite writers. I've reprinted the cover of the game for you here, as it isn't something you'd usually see almost forty(!) years later (I did see it on Ebay for a few hundred bucks). I mean, did many of you even know this existed? We'll we're going to go down memory lane and look at the history of the game and even show you some of the art and screens featured in the monochromatic world that is, *The Mist* game.

When I began researching *The Mist* game for this edition I came across a lot of interesting information, including the fascinating origins of how it came to be. In 1984, American children's author Mercer Mayer, along with his business partner John Sansevere founded Angelsoft, in White Plains, New York. They were looking to create an adventure game software for home-based computers, but using only licensed properties that might attract PC gamers. They weren't having much luck so Mercer reached out to the owner of a St. Bernard... his name was *Cujo*. As you Constant Readers know, *Cujo* is a grim tale of what happens when a good dog goes bad. The story culminates with Donna Trenton and her young son Tad being attacked in their car by a rabid St Bernard. During the attack, Donna wishes that Tad was back at home, tucked up in bed reading "one of his Mercer Mayer books". Ah hah! Talk about your "in" with Stephen King. "I called King and we chatted for a while," he says, "then I asked him what he could offer us. It turned out that every one of his books had already been optioned by movie studios, ruling them all out. He went to speak to his people then came

back and told me there was actually one story available – The Mist."

Stephen King's "The Mist" first appeared in *Dark Forces*, a collection of horror stories from various authors. It tells the tale of Bridgton, Maine, a small town that is slowly taken over by an unnatural fog that unleashes terrible creatures from within it. Most of the action takes place inside a supermarket where several survivors, including the story's narrator David Drayton, hole up from the horrors outside – only to discover that evil also walks among them. Angelsoft licensed "The Mist" in late 1984 and that deal with Stephen King suddenly had folks interested. "*The Mist* deal was significant to us," says Mercer. "It opened the

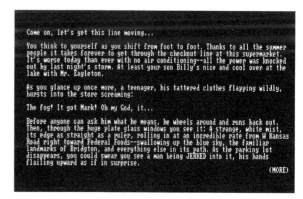

door to other deals, James Bond being next."

Angelsoft hired programmers to develop a custom adventure game system. The framework was in place – it just needed someone to fill it with locations, people, and puzzles. Enter Raymond Benson, an author who happened to be both a keen gamer and an expert on all things 007.

"My book *The James Bond Bedside Companion* had just been published in November 1984," says Raymond. "I was living in New York City at the time and I had an agent who knew I enjoyed games. I was a huge Infocom fan – I was really into *Zork* and its sequels. Angelsoft needed a writer for "The Mist" and *A View To A Kill*, and my agent immediately thought of me. I was hired as a freelance writer and designer to do both games."

They began with "The Mist" in January 1985; Raymond joined a small team that consisted of a producer and several programmers. The first thing he did was give Stephen King a call. "I spoke with Stephen on the phone. It was a short conversation. "I asked him if he cared if I invented things that weren't in his story or deleted stuff, and asked his opinion on a couple aspects. He basically said, 'Do whatever

> ❝ "The Mist" was moody and spooky – it was a good story for the medium ❞
>
> – **Raymond Benson**

you want'." Raymond decided the only changes to make were to aid in the interactive experience.

In the story "The Mist" begins slowly, with Drayton and his family surveying the after effects of a freak storm that batters their lakeside home. When Drayton and his young son Billy travel into town for supplies the story

shifts into high gear. The game begins with just Drayton – or more specifically, 'you' – inside the supermarket at the precise moment when the mist rolls in and all hell breaks loose. The original novella paints an increasingly bleak picture in which Drayton's only hope is to somehow keep himself and his son alive. The game instead introduces a clear goal – return home and rescue Billy (who sensibly didn't tag along to the supermarket).

"I figured the main point of the game would be to escape the town and kill as many of the creatures as you could," says Raymond. "The biggest challenge was to make it scary. I'm not sure if I succeeded at that – it's kind of hard for a text adventure to be scary – but I think the story came across as interesting and compelling. It's always the goal of an adapter to create something that complements the source and yet expands on it."

They developed the game for about three months, with basically no issues. Raymond does remember frustration with Angelsoft's adventure scripting language (codenamed ASG). "Angelsoft's parser was nowhere near as sophisticated as Infocom's, and I was

The map of *The Mist* with the town of Bridgeton, Maine. Illustration by Matthew Fisher, The Garden Studio, Angelsoft Inc. 1985.

disappointed that I couldn't do some of the things that Infocom did with its games. But it turned out okay in the end." The game, *The Mist*, was published by Mindscape in 1985.

The 007 games they produced were more sophisticated than *The Mist*, but not necessarily better says the author. "For Bond, you needed more than just a text adventure, you needed graphics," he says. "It didn't translate well. *The Mist* was moody and spooky – it was a good story for the medium. It just worked better." These days, Raymond is best known as an award-winning author of more than 25 books, including six original James Bond novels. He hasn't worked directly on a computer game for many years now, yet he still has a strong interest in gaming, in particular the adventure genre.

"In the late Eighties I got into the gaming industry full-time and worked for some companies like Origin Systems and MicroProse. I especially like *The Mist*, but I think the best game I ever did was *Dark Seed II* for Cyberdreams. It's too bad that text and graphic adventures have gone out of fashion. I've always enjoyed games with interactive stories. "It seems to me like Stephen King's *The Stand* would make a great game…"

I'm with Raymond Benson on that one, but how long would *The Stand* game be? Considerably! You'd never be bored that's for sure.

An item of interest that I stumbled upon was *The Mist* game actually gave life to another game. Well, *Half-Life*, fifteen years later. The creators of that video game, *Half-Life* (1998), have acknowledged that *The Mist* helped inspire their game: "The team was initially inspired by the Stephen King story, 'The Mist' and refined the concept until the story was about Gordon Freeman and the Black Mesa Research Facility. Gabe Newell (Ed note: one of the creators) wanted the company to really focus on providing a more story-based exploration, rather than straight action."

Their company, Valve, would hire novelist Marc Laidlaw to shape the story into what it would ultimately be. The big first-person shooters of the day were usually flimsy on plot and character development. John Carmack famously said, "Story in a game is like story in a porn movie. It's expected to be there, but it's not important." For the same of game design, this is a pretty common opinion. The systems are the most important part when looking at the game through the lens of the actual player's experience. However, that does not mean that those same gameplay systems cannot be used in service to a story. And if the story is going to be there, why not try to make it a good one? Laidlaw put it like this: "In a lot of shooters, for all you know, you could be a weapon walking around a level. It's clear in *Half-Life* that's not the case." Obviously *Half-Life* was early in the story driven type of games, and it was a "game changer" for them and the gaming industry.

Ironically Marc Laidlaw signed books for us back in the 1990's. His novels "The Orchid Eater" and "The 37th Mandala" sold quite well at our Overlook Connection

bookstore. I had no idea of his video game connection to *The Mist* with Half-Life until researching for this piece. It's a small world! I hope you're doing well, Marc.

Entering... *The Mist*

by *Dave Hinchberger*

In early 2007 I had heard that Stephen King's *The Mist* was going to be a movie! Frank Darabont would be filming in the spring. The director and screenwriter who'd brought us previous collaborations with Stephen King

of *The Shawshank Redemption* and *The Green Mile*. I checked in with Frank Darabont and he said this was indeed happening. They would be filming in Shreveport, Louisiana. Being that Shreveport is in the South this was about a 9-hour drive to visit the set and possibly get an interview with Frank. Frank had been a customer for years. In fact, he rang one evening to order the leatherbound version of *The Complete and Uncut Stand* limited edition from us, an important release from Stephen King. At this point he also had the gorgeous period drama *The Majestic* under his director's belt. With many accolades and nominations for all of them, the world over. Here was a man who had brought Stephen King stories to the screen that made such an impact on me and millions more. And now he was going to be filming one of my all-time favorite Stephen King stories... The Mist!

When I inquired about the filming Frank said "come on down!" Ironically this was also around the same time I was to get married to my lovely LeeAnn in June, in just seven weeks. I was pondering going down to *The Mist* set for a few days. Now you may think that this

is a no-brainer, get down to the bus station and get to Shreveport quick, right? Of course, right. I wanted to go but I also had a wedding coming up and I was running a bookstore and a publishing concern. So, I had a lot of irons in the fire and a major personal event in my life that was about to take place.

Yep, I had to go. I would regret the opportunity for the rest of my days if I didn't take a few of them to go down and see what *"Mist* magic" Frank and his team had conjured up for not only one of my favorite King stories, but for Constant Readers everywhere.

I had to be a witness.

Ironically one of my best friends, Kevin, his sister Alix Madigan was also in Shreveport and in the process of producing a new Renny Harlin film with Samuel Jackson, titled *The Cleaner*.

I said, "well, let's go buddy," it's obvious this was meant to happen and we headed out to Louisiana, to... *The Mist*.

After a grueling day taking turns driving we finally arrived at our hotel, the El Dorado, in downtown Shreveport. We went ahead and checked in, dropped our bags in the room, and headed over to the studio... by literally just crossing the street. Our hotel faced the studio. The Shreveport multi-storied convention center was right across the street. After hurricane Katrina threw New Orleans around and made a mess the movie business moved up north to Shreveport. We went around the side and met Frank's assistant to bring us in the building which had now been transformed into

something unique. Little did I realize that I was about to walk into a magic moment for me as I stepped inside, into another world.

Convention centers are just huge ballrooms that could be used as one facility or segmented into several rooms. When we walked in it was obvious we weren't in Louisiana anymore. I felt like we were on a studio lot back at Warner brothers in California. It's the craftsmen who build it that make it their new home and they did so here. As we walked in, discussing the filming, how it was progressing, etc. we came upon this huge clear plastic wall. On the other side of it were these… white clouds, is the best way I can describe it… a mist. Now, I must tell you I wasn't expecting a real mist. I had a thought that the mist effects would be CGI put in after filming. I asked our escort as we were starting to go through the plastic wall about what the mist was made of? She said "there is a list posted up over here of all the contents of what is creating the mist. I can't tell you exactly what it is right now but you're welcome to look. I do know that coconut is involved." Interesting.

As we entered my mind took over, "You are about to enter another dimension…next stop…*The Mist*." Good ol' Rod Serling interior

monologue, always within synaptic reach.

We went through the opening in the plastic that folded back together once we got through now enveloped in the mist, and lo and behold we walked onto something I wasn't expecting… a parking lot. I mean an honest to goodness, real, parking lot with lines for the cars to park, with vehicles parked there. I was also too caught up in the fact that I was walking into my favorite story. A mist surrounded this huge parking lot, and at the edge of that parking lot? A massive grocery store… A grocery store inside this building! I was gobsmacked. If you've seen the film then you know what the grocery store looks like from the outside there was the title of the store, the huge glass panes across the front, the electric entryway doors, sacks of dog food could be seen stacked up on the other side of the window panes, with bags of fertilizer out front.

As we're walking through the mist getting ready to enter the grocery store (I did say this is a grocery store building inside a larger building right? did I already mention that? okay I just want to make sure… I'm still a little bit in shock at what I'm seeing) there's red stains of blood and viscera slathered in a straight line on the parking lot close to the front door of the store. Little did I realize that this was what was left of actor Bryan Libby's part as the biker there on the ground. The actor that was in Frank's first film, a Stephen King story, "The Woman in the Room," and every Darabont film thereafter.

The fiction was becoming movie fact right in front of me.

The official sign outside Frank Darabont's office for *The Mist*

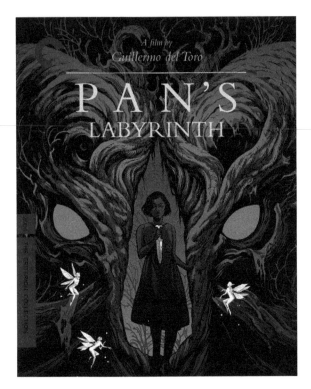

We hesitate outside the grocery store for a moment as they film within. Our escort gets the go ahead and we walk through the grocery store doors. I half-expected the electric rubber mats that we walked on to automatically open the doors as any grocery store would but no we had to push our way through. At this point in the film, the power was out and it was dark inside. As we entered there was the row of cashier stands for folks to check out with their shopping. People were milling about but obviously getting ready for the next shot Which curiously would be a poignant moment in the film when I viewed it in the theater later that year. To the right of us was the wine shop area and standing in front of it was actress Marcia Gay Harden.

Frank Darabont was sitting there in front of a couple of monitors next to one of the cashiers stands like he was going to be checking out soon. The only thing he was checking out was the monitors in front of him, obviously engaged. They were getting the shots set up so we just walked around and stood behind him and his team as they got ready to film this shot.

Frank said "action!" and filming began. This was the scene where Marcia Gay Harden has suddenly been approached by one of the flying bugs who have entered the grocery store. This mutant bug has landed on her chest and is slowly crawling up the front of her torso towards her head.

Now this is what we saw in the film when it was released that November in 2007. What Kevin and I saw was one of the crew holding a pole and at the end of it was a large elongated silver cylindrical looking object. This was filling in for the CGI that would come later created by Cafe FX, an outfit that Frank had discovered after seeing Guillermo del Toro's *Pan's Labyrinth*, and all the magic they created with the creatures in that film.

Marcia Gay Harden had finished filming her scene. The mutant creature bug, after crawling all the way up to her face decided she wasn't of interest, flew off her, hesitated, and then fluttered away. In her mind, God had spared her, thinking she obviously had been chosen to lead the frightened within the grocery store. Her moment of self-instilled greatness is at hand.

After Frank yelled "cut" he turned around to all of us, crew, make-up artists, removed his brown cigarette and said "religion will take you down, it will take you down, and it will fuck you up"

Kevin turned around to me and said "there's the line for your piece right there!"

It was interesting standing outside the Shreveport convention center after spending the first day on *The Mist*. Here we are out on

the street sidewalk in front of us, but within the building behind me was a whole grocery store built inside, surrounded in mist. Surreal as it was sunny and nice here in the real world.

So, let's talk about this grocery store. I had some time to walk around and look at everything. Most of the food on the shelves were real; bread, packaged pastries, chips, canned food, it was a real grocery store (Constantine Nasr's article goes into more detail about this "real" food). I went to the freezer section and obviously there were lights on in the freezers but there was no cold emanating out of them. Any meats that were packaged were plastic but they looked real enough. Frank's assistant informed me that they had six truck-loads of food brought in to fill up the store. She said there was so much food left over that they donated it to local food banks, helping the local community.

They stopped filming to change out the camera film. Frank said, "Dave, come with me." I had about fifteen minutes with Frank and let me tell you those were fifteen precious minutes because there wasn't a lot of downtime during their tight schedule. I mentioned to Frank about the extra food being donated to the local community and I thought how wonderful that was. He asked me "now what did they

do with the food?" I reiterated what I'd been told but after that I realized that this was a feature of the process that the director didn't have to concern himself with. He was there to bring this story to the screen. He was certainly involved with many aspects of how the sets looked, etc. but he didn't need to know about the minutia of how certain things were taking shape. There was a whole crew to take care of those details.

There are many moving parts on a film set most of it beginning months and even years previous with the writing of the script, and the production values of how the film was going to be produced. For example, the drawings that were created by Bernie Wrightson and other artists to design the creatures that would appear. The folks who had to create this store, this amazing grocery store, that stood on its own within this building. That took a couple of months to build alone. Granted this was also the main set for the whole film but they took care in the details. Down to the grocery store book display that spins around they had about 20 or 30 Stephen King paperbacks.

As this was our first day on the set was also the day that we had traveled so after a few hours I got my buddy Kevin and we went out and had a nice steak dinner and a couple of shots at the bar. It had been a long day but well worth coming out to see the wizardry of it all.

The next morning Kevin and I headed out and took the elevator to the lobby. We must have hit every floor on the way down, with folks coming and going. The last floor stop,

Thomas Jane, Dave Hinchberger, & Frank Darabont on the set of *The Mist*

before the lobby, we had one guest. His eyes looked up from his Blackberry phone but kept his head down. He sauntered in and stood between us. I thought he looked familiar but… well, I'll come back to this moment later. We grabbed some breakfast and headed over… or should I say crossed the street… to get to *The Mist* set. As we were walking through the side parking lot before entering the building there is a long line of actor's trailers. These were the trailers used for the day-to-day to get dressed out or just hang until it was time for them to be on the set again.

Once again we entered *The Mist* and crossed through the parking lot... you remember, the parking lot, the one with cars, sitting in front of the grocery store in the film.

As we came up to the side of the store, where you could also enter, you could see that what would normally be a cement brick wall of a self-standing store was in fact a wood structure with nails sticking through it. You literally couldn't lean up against it anywhere or you'd get punctured. All part of the façade that you never see in finished films.

As we came up to the front of the store I noticed through the big plate glass there wasn't anyone within so there wasn't any filming going on in that part of the store. Kevin and I slowly opened the door making sure we didn't make any sound. On a film set one thing you learn is if there's filming going on stand still don't make any noise not only is someone filming nearby but you don't want to be a distraction for those that are working. We entered but there was filming going on in the aisles and in the back of the store near the freezer section again.

We watched Thomas Jane prepare for a scene. He geared himself up by stamping the floor with his foot and breathing heavily through his mouth and nose, his whole face if you will. Preparing himself, gearing up for an intense scene. We were now in the front of the store before he talks to Jeffrey DuMunn (as Dan Miller) and the rest of the fellows preparing to go to the pharmacy for supplies.

I hung out in the butcher shop for a while as no scene was being filmed in there to type up notes. I also had a chance to visit with movie photographer Ralph Nelson about his career of taking photos for film. At that point in 2007 he said he'd been working about thirty years in the business, full time. His photography is seen on posters, books, records, you name it, you've probably seen a bevy of Ralph Nelson photographs over the years. He's worked on several of the *Star Wars* films, All three *Back to the Futures*, *The Green Mile*, *The Majestic*, now, *The Mist*.

I asked if there were a lot of opportunities for photographers to work on film as a still photographer such as himself. He said at the time there were only about five full-time photographers for film and about thirty part-time. A lot may have changed since then as that was 15 years ago as I write this and it seems like there's more filming going on now more than ever. I realized that I was talking not only a person who was a film historian recording all these moments for decades, but he was also a part of the landscape and I was honored to have met him. The photo you see of me, Frank, and Thomas Jane was taken by

The Wall of Actors right outside Frank Darabont's *Mist* office.

Stephen King's
THE MIST

From the Novella by
Stephen King

Screenplay by
Frank Darabont

Goldenrod - Mar. 5, 2007
Green - Feb. 19, 2007

The Mist script, signed by Ralph Neslon, Ron Clinton Smith, Jeffrey DeMunn, Greg Nicotero, Thomas Jane, and Frank Darabont.

Ralph Nelson with my camera. Constantine Nasr was standing nearby and said "Dave, you have a Ralph Nelson original!"

I had seen Ralph once before on another film set: in Tennessee on *The Green Mile*. I was there for a couple of days for that filming and we were literally out in the middle of nowhere off a dirt road filming the scene with Tom Hanks (as Paul Edgecomb) interviews Gary Sinise (as Burt Hammersmith) on the back porch of his house. As I was a guest of Frank Darabont I respected the fact that this was a film set and I was a guest. Being a guest, you don't pull out a camera during a filming scene or at other inappropriate moments. This is a professional space and everyone should certainly be aware of that. I did have my camera and I did take a few photos unobtrusively. It wasn't during filming but actually in between when they had to change things around. At some point while I was taking some photos of this immaculately groomed yard with a dog house within it (which didn't end up in *The Green Mile*). I turned around and I could see across the way this fellow with curly hair and a large camera

Ron Clinton Smith, Dave Hinchberger, Jeffrey DeMunn

While Ralph and I were visiting in the butcher shop I told him about this moment that I had seen him once before and in what context. He said he didn't remember that, but then again why would he? But I never forgot it.

We discovered where the extras were all hanging out until they were called up for a scene, in the grocery store. Kevin and I spent lunch with them one day as they served up a buffet for the group. We sat around eating and talking about the local scene of Shreveport with the filming industry booming in their community. They were some nice folks, even if they were marked up with blood smears, and scars from bug battles in The Mist. After lunch we all got together and grabbed a quick photo. A moment on *The Mist*.

Dave and Kevin Madigan with the Extras!

hanging down from around his neck. He was pointing towards my area and as it didn't seem there was anybody else around me I could only imagine he was talking about me, taking pictures. It was then I assumed that this was the official photographer and I'd better keep an even lower profile being a guest on the set.

The man with all the curly hair? That was Ralph Nelson.

The afternoon of the second day, I was wondering around the complex looking in at all the departments that were set up, getting a real idea what was here. Frank Darabont's office, as well as the production office, was on the second floor. As I came upon Frank's office a fellow was on the floor, on his knees, his back to me and looking at a huge poster of the sci-fi film, *Them!* As he turned around to look up, it was Greg Nicotero! This was his birthday gift from Frank from a surprise birthday party the night before. Greg's wife had also flown in for the occasion. I just remember the *Them!* poster was quite large. He said

Warner Bros. 1954

<table>
<tr><td>Weather
High: 70 Low: 49
Details: 2A</td><td>Celebrating Heritage
Lorem ipsum dolor sit amet, consectetuer adipiscing elit, sed diam nonummy nibh eusmod tincidunt ut laoreet dolore magna aliquam erat volputate.
Living • Page 6B</td><td>Your source for local jobs
visit us on the web at
www.castlerocktimes.com
WEDNESDAY, AUGUST 9, 200X</td></tr>
</table>

The Castle Rock Times

Castle Rock High heads to Top 20
SPORTS, 1C

Cat Tales
Local novelist finds inspiration in furry friends
LIVING, 6B

Election gets little attention

Mcorper suscipit lobortis nisl ut aliquip ex ea commodo consequat. Duis autem vel eum iriure dolor in hendreblandit praesent

POLITICS, 1D

The Castle Rock Times

To subscribe:
xxx-xxx-NEWS

Electric storm largest on record
Thousands in the dark as power outages grip the region

By Lorem Ipsum
Staff Writer

Lorem ipsum dolor sit amet, consectetuer adipiscing elit, sed diam nonummy nibh eusmod tincidunt ut laoreet dolore magna aliquam erat volputate. Ut wisi enim ad minim veniam, quis nostrud exerci tation ullamcorper suscipit lobortis nisl ut aliquip ex ea commodo consequat.

Castle Rock resident Charlie Cobb sent in this photo of the storm as it lit up the sky outside his home on King Road.

Rabid Saint Bernard traps woman and child in Pinto

By Consectetuer Adipiscing
Staff Writer

Lorem ipsum dolor sit amet, consectetuer adipiscing elit, sed diam nonummy nibh eusmod tincidunt ut laoreet dolore magna aliquam erat volputate.

A sigh of relief: "We're just glad it's over," said Trenton of the ordeal.

Sheriff seeks help from psychic in ongoing murder investigation

By Baoreet Dolore
Staff Writer

Lorem ipsum dolor sit amet, consectetuer adipiscing elit, sed diam nonummy nibh eusmod tincidunt ut laoreet dolore magna aliquam erat volputate.

Dead, not only as part of the special effects and make-up team of KNB EFX Group, but he's also written and directed episodes for this series. Before the explosion of TWD, he and KNB EFX were involved in so many films, and in the land of Stephen King films *Misery*, *Desperation*, *The Green Mile*, and where it all started for Greg and KNB, *Creepshow 2*.

I found myself in what could only be described as the "creature room" because coming through the door, on my left, were creatures from *The Mist*, with large heads, and gaping mouths full of protruding teeth, all piled together in a mound. There were also elongated tentacle pieces strewn about. All of it dark and pink and purple, and realistically menacing. Over in the corner sitting in front of a mirror was one of the Arrowhead Project military actors. He was looking… well… not good. He was all burnt up! Burnt up with latex burned skin pieces being applied that is. Obviously getting ready for his big burn scene. Greg and I were looking at the Drew Struzen book I brought along, just a refresher and I knew he was doing work for this film. I asked Greg if he'd pose with one of his mutant bug pals and we took a couple of shots as he mugged (bugged it!) it up (no KNB EFX fellow was harmed during these photos… but hamming it up sure!).

"Dave, have you ever seen a poster this size?" "I have" I said, "but you'd have to buy a new house to just hang these up, they're so big."

Greg Nicotero is well known these days with the success of his involvement in *The Walking*

I learned that they had just filmed the storage door scene with Chris Owens (bag boy) being pulled under the door the day before. It was now being torn down and construction was onto the next project for another scene. Yes, they built a room, filmed it, and then created another room in its spot. For *The Mist* there aren't a lot of rooms, but most of them were created and filmed on the same spot. Boggles the mind how much effort is put into these productions (Did I ever tell you about the time they built a backup bathroom for Tom Hanks pissing scene? It was in a real barn out in the middle of nowhere Tennessee for *The Green Mile* just as a backup if the current filming went awry due to weather? Another time I'll spill the beans).

I came across the Drayton's mailbox sitting on a workbench, on its side. The paintings (actual Drew Struzen paintings) from David Drayton's studio were propped up in a wide-open room. I asked someone on the set how long the actual shoot was and they said thirty-three days. They eventually went over a few days, but it was very close. There were three studios: A, B, and C. The largest of course held the Food House grocery store, which was a fixed presence during the whole shoot (and let us not forget the parking lot!). The other studio spaces were either building new sets, or tearing them down for scenes coming up.

I believe the second largest set was for the pharmacy. It was impressive. Approaching the front of the store, again this is "inside" a studio, with large paned glass for the store front, glass doors, it was all too real (little did I know… read on). Upon entering the pharmacy, it was truly amazing how many details they gave this store. It featured a lunch counter with lots of short, round, cushioned spinning stools. Sitting / laying on one of these stools was a customer who met his fate by the hand of some deadly creature, the body was all emaciated and blue. Behind the counter was an old Coke dispenser, milk-shake maker, Bordon ads for milk on the side of a small fridge, sink, lots of glasses. On the wall above the back counter, it featured one of those felt menu boards that had removable letters showing what they offered, drinks, sandwiches, milk shakes, etc. This was something created out of time. An old soda

shop in the pharmacy look, places I grew up with. Hell, it even had formed dining benches I remember from the 70's, that could seat about 15-20 folks.

While I was looking around the full greeting card stands, the Kodak film dispenser – full of film boxes, a rack of sunglasses. Then there was the pharmacy window, with pharmacist (in his official white smock mind you) leaning dead against it. Shelves behind him full of prescription bottles, lots of official papers taped and spread about. A true drugstore. There were folks dead, and hanging, from the ceiling. One encased in what appeared like thick spider webs, the other not webbed yet, but I'm sure he'd be enveloped soon. There were so many shelves within this store, not like today's modern metal shelves (although there were a couple), but wooden shelves you might find in much older homes. It had an older look to the whole place. Well, there was a reason.

While I was touring the King Pharmacy set one of the films crew members came wandering in and we began chatting. I mentioned I was amazed at how good this pharmacy looked, especially in its obviously aged state. He said there was a reason why it looked like it did: it was in fact a real pharmacy. What? I was confused. I said "What do you mean, a real pharmacy?" He said "this is a real pharmacy that the advance scout team found somewhere in Texas. It had been permanently closed when the pharmacist passed away. His widow, who still owned the pharmacy, just locked it up and left it as you see it here." Again, I was confused because this didn't seem to make sense to me. I said "you mean they moved this real pharmacy? Here, to the set of The Mist? From Texas?" "Yes" he said "the whole lot. The lunch counter, the tables, greeting card stands, everything here is from that pharmacy. We just had to build the shell to put the pharmacy in." I asked "so did you purchase this from the widow or…?" He said they had leased it. When the filming was done they would take everything back and re-insert it in the original building the way they found it. Not only did they not have to build a pharmacy, they had a real honest-to-God built in set waiting for them. One that was decades old. I was blown away at the thought of all this. The actual history of it and the fact that it was now part of Stephen King / Frank Darabont history appearing in The Mist. The crew member took me to the counter at the end where there was a photograph on a flyer of the actual pharmacist taped there. It appears to be a flyer identifying his involvement in a local church. The A. Miles pharmacist was now about to be a part of Stephen King history. I'm one of those fellows who would have liked to visited the actual pharmacy after it had been placed back in Texas. That was sixteen years ago, so I can only imagine that is all gone now. As you can see in the photo the King Pharmacy hadn't been painted on the front glass yet and only discovered its name when we all saw The Mist in the theater.

You did see it in the theater, right?

Seeing a few days of The Mist filming in this microcosm set in Shreveport Convention center (then by Stage Works of Louisiana) was probably one of the most unique set experiences I'd been to. Practically everything was right there. Except for outside scenes of the Drayton home and the Food House (Tom's Market, with a façade built of King's Pharmacy next door) almost everything was filmed within this building. An incredible task by Frank Darabont's team.

And now… for the rest of the story… Remember I discussed earlier about a fella that looked familiar as he entered our elevator on our way to The Mist set? Well, the elevator doors opened, and as I said he had his head down but eyes looking up to see who was inside. I thought it was kind of odd, but then he raised his head, smiled, and said "good morning fellas!"

It was Michael Clarke Duncan. I couldn't believe it. What are the odds we're going across the street to the filming of a new Frank Darabont movie… and here's one of the stars from the last Stephen King / Darabont production, The Green Mile. I looked at him and said nonchalantly, "Are you here to see Frank?" I was trying to keep it interesting. He looked at me quizzically, as he should have, and then his face brightened up and said, "No, in town for other business." I said "I just want to say how much I enjoyed your work in The Green Mile." He stuck out his hand and we shook and he said "Thank you, I appreciate that." With that the doors opened and he said "have a great day" and waved at us as he left. I must tell you I was a bit in awe of the man, and was so surprised when he entered I wasn't sure what to say. One thing's for sure, if you believe in portents, then it doesn't get any better than Stephen King's John Coffey walking into your day for a few minutes… on the way to The Mist.

Cheers!

On the set of *The Mist*

by Bev Vincent

In March 2007, I had the opportunity to visit the set of The Mist, *which was filming in Shreveport, La. During an afternoon break, the publicist took Chris Hewitt from* Empire *magazine and me out to the "circus" where the actors' trailers were set up so we could get some interviews. First, we encountered Marcia Gay Harden (Mrs. Carmody) playing with her children. After that, Toby Jones (Ollie Weeks) invited us into his trailer for a chat. Finally, Thomas Jane (David Drayton) appeared at his trailer for his daily cigar and invited us in out of the sun.*

Marcia Gay Harden

HARDEN: I'm loving the character. When we began planning her things began to fall into place. You should ask hair and makeup and costume to show you the five different looks I presented to them. They came to my house late at night in L.A. They got off at ten and left at one in the morning, and there were these five different looks. There was the nun, the preacher's daughter, Tammy Faye Baker, the town snoop and the hippie. That was the five characters, and [Frank] picked the nun with the thick eyebrows, but then we talked about it and I thought maybe the preacher's daughter. The language is so religious…almost poetic, which makes it difficult to seem natural. The puling, the earth's lips vomiting forth . . . there was one we didn't get to yesterday, "slithering snakes." Very, very declamatory and dialog that typically one would turn off to. I wanted you to be able to listen to her and even wonder if she's not right…because I think she is, it is the end of the world…monsters…

Q: That's actually an interesting take because Mrs. Carmody, for people who've read King, is like a negative stereotype, but it's true, it's actually true…this is the end of times

HARDEN: It is, as far as you or I would experience. If someone said there's monsters and scorpions and man-eating bugs and a mist and everybody is fighting and no one is surviving, I would say it's the end of the world, it's apocalyptic and yet people are far more comfortable attributing it to, or allowing it to be science or the military . . . and the world will return to normal. I don't know how the movie ends—it's not in our scripts.

Q: Oh yeah?

HARDEN: Yeah, but I did read the book and even in King's book they end up in a diner along some highway, still surrounded by mist, and they could only be thinking "sequel." I was sorta half kidding—couldn't they just shoot me in the leg or something so I can come back, but I don't know if he's going to do that.

But still we picked the preacher's daughter and so she began with—the prop people gave me this scarf and I kinda put it up on my head, and then props just happened to put white gloves in my purse but then I'm wearing those. So she really came in lovely and perfect and very buttoned down and it seems like

the character demises until pretty much what you saw yesterday. The hair is down, and she's actually a much more sensual person in her power and in her preaching than she was at the beginning.

Yesterday was all improv, which was interesting. In that moment we decided to go on and suddenly it came down and together and there were tears, and I've seen that [with televangelists] on TV. It's also embarrassing because there were moments when I would lose the thread. I did buy a book that's called

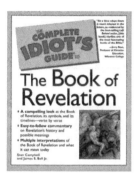

The Idiot's Guide to Revelations and I was reading that during the first part of it so that when he would let me go on I would know what to say and there is a lot of dialog about the *Seventh Seal* and the *Whore of Babylon* that's quite interesting.

The extras in this film, the people in the store are like a Greek chorus, and if they're not activated—they're really a third partner. They're there and they're the mob mentality. The thing that was interesting to me about it was *The Lord of the Flies* aspect. This is society in an extremely tough situation where it is a world unknown outside your door. Do you hold together? Do you pull apart? What part of people's personalities pull apart? Where do people crack? And people do crack. It's like all the stories about post-traumatic stress disorder and they crack. Some are killing their wives; some are doing bizarre things and then there was the recent case where a guy from Pennsylvania had that horrible incident. He cracked due to an incident that happened years and years before. Something in him just went off. Normal people, which is what Frank and I were interested in, they might be minutely peculiar but you wouldn't attribute to them the potential for such insanity that they'd wreak on society.

In her case—I have a whole backstory for her—in her case she certainly does crack, but part of what makes her crack is power. She was kind of written to be sort of a hefty, overweight

woman, not an attractive woman in any way, but we felt that you'd walk in the door and you'd go: she's bad, and so you're setting up as a script that is a creature feature and it does have good and evil—as is necessary in almost any drama—but so obvious. So we've given her these moments and episodes: Please God, let me speak through you, let me be your ambassador in prayer, Let me be the voice for you. That was what brought that heightened moment down was when I said, I want to help you—I don't want to hurt you. The personal is always what makes things, the idea or your destination or the personal journey, and that's what we've been building. I'm—we're the raw material, and [Frank] will cook it. I hope some of that stays and doesn't end up on the editing room floor, but you never know.

[The DVD extra scenes option] doesn't matter. It's nice that you can rent the DVD and see the great scene that you worked so hard on and you put yourself out there and you were great [only to have it cut], but it doesn't matter. What's in the movie—for me anyway, the play is important, the story is the thing. And the more responsibility I have for telling the story, the better. You know, I don't even mind if they cut scenes I'm in. You can cut that scene, you don't need it, don't need it, don't need it, but there's other times where I think, "Ah, you cut the people story to make it a plot."

Q: We were standing a long way away from you, back at the monitors, and even the people behind us were going "Hallelujah."

HARDEN: I looked out and I saw the little girl was crying and then there was a big smile on her face—it was really wonderful to do. [Frank] has encouraged clapping and acclamation all the way through. And that's why I think in these moments, if there is applause, we're all in it together, we're telling the story together and it's truly invigorating. Everybody was so on board, and by the way it happened in five minutes.

I tend to kinda form a bond on every film, and the first people you always form a bond with are the makeup people. We chose the look, we came in and we met with the costume-wardrobe people, but then I brought my hair, my extensions, for the hair people here, and they were like, okay, okay. But when I told Alan the concept—he's the makeup artist—that I wanted these really thin eyebrows that we could even cover over with a little makeup that we could draw a little line on, he was horrified. "No, you don't want to do that." But then we did it and everything just came together. Everyone was excited about the creative process. Even like I said, the props will bring me a candy bar and ask what is she going to want now. Frank and I walked through the set and I said, where is *my* area? And he said you're probably going to be over here in the produce aisle. I want a chair unlike *anybody* else's chair. And he said we've got all these lawn chairs and I was like anybody can have a lawn chair. I want a chair. I want a throne. And then they found this throne for me and they built a little platform and they equipped the thing. And I said I bet I have a shopping cart, scoop things into it and I was the first one to get a rice bag for my pillow and the first one

to get my sleeping bag and I have curtains for my privacy and no one else has curtains and there's all these things. So she went from being a fat ugly lady in a pant suit to really being a diva, which I don't know if art imitates life or the other way around, but that's what happened.

You know I never understand the moment that things [getting cast for a part] come down or how it happened. I think he knew I was interested and then we pursued each other to make sure we were on the same page, because I've never done a Stephen King movie. Frank's reputation is of someone who brings humanity to a script that could be just a horror film. I love all the bugs and stuff and I love doing horror, but what is human story? The mob mentality. They don't have power over the mob. Many wars are waged in the name of God. Many atrocities occur in the name of God. So that's really the underbelly.

I did ask him if he would not really kill me off so I could come back. I love working with Frank. He's given me the kind of freedom that you witnessed yesterday, it was wonderful and he actually came up to me at the end and said, "You're fearless." I'm not sure if he meant "shameless." I hope he meant "you're fearless" and not "you're shameless." But he gives the freedom and he's been so intrigued with allowing the creative process.

Toby Jones

Q: I'm interested to see that you're not keeping your American accent between takes
JONES: I don't want to wear it too heavily. I just let it drift in and out otherwise it'll get too heavy. I often think that actors…[in American accent] 'see how good my American accent is.' You never really see good American accents. It's like, "Isn't that the best CGI? Isn't that the greatest CGI?" The best CGI that you've ever noticed.

Playing Truman Capote, it was impossible to not stay in his voice the whole time. Because it was a totally different mouth shape. I'd do about an hour and a half to get my jaw in the

right place to do it at the beginning of the day, so that to go back into this lazy way of talking—I'd have be having to do that all the time.
Q: Do you know how you got the job? Was it Frank?
JONES: I think he saw *The Painted Veil*, actually, and he really liked that. It's one of those things as an English actor you're not quite sure how it did happen because of what happens in L.A. You're aware of your representatives in L.A. having talks with agents. You actually hear about it quite late on. I was one of the last people to come on board, which created huge problems with the visa. It's such an issue, the

visa. You need much more notice now than you used to need because of 9/11. It was touch and go right to the last minute.

Q: They have to prove that you can do the job better than any American actor:

JONES: You have to prove to be unique...but once you've done a couple of jobs in the states, I think it's easier. You have to have various testimonials saying, oh, yeah, the guy is unique.

Q: So your involvement with the project came about because of Frank. Had you read the novella?

JONES: I hadn't read the novella. I was very aware of Frank, obviously and *The Shawshank Redemption*, which is just kind of standard viewing for everyone, it's what people watch. In fact, you'd have a harder time not watching it here in the states. It's kind on the TV all the time. It's incredible. It's part of the visual wallpaper of people's lives. It's in my favorite top ten. It's a great, great film.

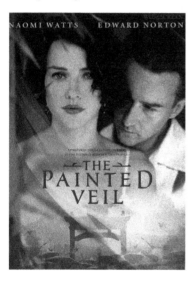

Q: So Frank approached you about it.

JONES: Frank said I'm sending you a script, I hope you enjoy it. And I can't say that Stephen King is someone I've read loads of; I haven't. I am aware of his stuff on film. To me it's a great character, it's a fantastic character to play. The unlikely hero. It's a fun thing to play, and also I've never done what you might call a genre picture before. It requires a special thing, really, in a way because you're operating in the area of action over character, so any character that happens to emerge is—to a certain extent that's true of all films, but in a sense the action

is the thing that people are watching. Anything they learn about character happens because of the way you respond to extraordinary circumstances. Which you could say of normal films, it' just that I think that sometimes in European films, or in more independent films, the story will be about the characters. The story will be about understanding the character above and beyond the narrative. So here I am, in Shreveport—I'm just trying to understand the fact that I don't need to worry about a lot of things that you'd need to worry about normally, I think. Well, you do need to worry about them, but there won't be so much concentration on them as they usually do. In some way, the audience in one of these pictures are constantly in the present. They're not too worried about what happened ten minutes ago, fifteen minutes ago. The momentum of the thing is moving forward, and as an actor you're concerned in a sense with trying to create a certain consistency, but really I suspect that a story like this will only matter to the actors. I think the audience will be only interested in the future.

Q: Coming into the project late, did it hamper your preparation in any way?

JONES: I think in a way—the way he writes, Frank, it's very direct stuff. There's no piles of research, to do, you know. I'm doing this [*The Old Curiosity Shoppe*] next and there's loads and loads of stuff to do for that. Absolutely loads of stuff to do for that. That's a reading list, or Truman Capote is a big reading list and a big video list that for your own peace of mind you have to have done. But here you really have to bring yourself. You have to show up and do what the action requires you to do.

Q: Is it fun for you to do a special effects film like this?

JONES: Filming is always fun when it's moving forward and here, because there's not loads and loads of time—I mean he was telling me he got *The Green Mile* for like four months and here we are making a special effects movie in six or seven weeks. I was going, you know, this will be interesting to see how this is going to work. I've been involved in special effects movies before, but they normally luxuriate in months of prep and puppetry. But one of the huge pleasures in a way—I love filming anyway because you're working with people and a crew that are usually very, very good and very, very fast, but here you're working with puppeteers and CGI people who are able to do their stuff at such speed it doesn't really ruin the momentum of the take. Often as an actor you just get bogged down in . . . and there must be some weird mental name for this . . . if I'm doing a play and we rehearse a scene and we'll run a scene and I'll have done it once and I'll be able to remember all of this stuff, all of this physical stuff I was able to do after I've practiced it once, I remember a whole complicated series of physical activity and for whatever reason I'll be able to remember it. Here, you'll be studying "if you could just place it there...not there" [uses a TV remote to demonstrate two positions a few inches apart] like that and I'll begin to get a kind of amnesia as to whether it was there or there and I think it's because when you're doing special effects stuff I think it can have that kind of—you begin to become sort of blind to anything but these fractions of seconds.

Q: The minutia overwhelms the big picture.

JONES: Yeah, yeah... I just get zapped, I think. He won't tell me how I've died. I think I won't find out until I've seen the picture. But I have an idea that I'll play it kind of very, very optimistic—the moment where I make a break for the car (beams optimistically and beckons)

"Come on, come on" (smile transforms into a look of abject horror).

Q: Are you familiar with the genesis of your character's name?

JONES: No. Do you know?

Q: It's from Ed McBain, the crime writer. One of his regular characters was Ollie Weeks.

JONES: It seems [King] is really into this cross-referencing, is that right? So there's loads for people to look at.

Q: The painting that Thomas Jane's character is working on is a *Dark Tower* movie poster. And the "serving Castle Rock" sign – that's King's mythical town.

JONES: Part of the pleasure for the audience is this cross-referencing, is that right? And Frank will be steeped in that, will he?

Q: His first movie was an adaptation of *The Woman in the Room*, and he's got the rights to *The Long Walk*.

JONES: So he's Mr. Stephen King on screen right now. I've never really been clear on this—the whole idea of genre, what it's supposed to help you with . . . is it supposed to help you with how you sit in your seat in the cinema in the sense that, ah, I know what I'm going to get. To me what's always interesting about a film is how the genre, the edges of the genre, how they are kind of bent. If the film was literally like constant consternation, it would be almost impossible. It's not a form of acting I'm aware of.

Thomas Jane

(Thomas Jane emerges from his trailer and offers a cigar to one of the crewmembers. They go through the ritual of chewing off the ends and lighting them.

JANE: Where do you want to go?

Q: Wherever you want to hang out is fine.

JANE: (grabs my copy of the script and flips through it) It's got no ending.

Q: The movie that never ends.

JANE: That's right. We'll be here forever.

Q: Does yours have an ending?

JANE: Yeah. So far. You know how hard it is to keep a secret with the internet these days,

man. That just sucks. You know, you try to give people a surprise but somebody out there just loves to be the guy to blow the surprise. They love that, you know. I just want to knock that kid out, I tell you. Some kid comes to school and they're all "I'll tell you the end of the movie" or whatever.

Q: This is your second King adaptation.

JANE: *Dreamcatcher*, yeah. Some people liked that.

Q: Are you a fan?

JANE: A Stephen King fan? Oh yeah. Oh yeah. A fan since I was a little kid, yeah. I've read pretty much everything that he's written. I haven't read *The Dark Tower* series, you know.

Too much of a undertaking, you know. Yeah, I've read . . . I'm a big horror fan. I love horror films and books and comic books, all that shit. It's fun stuff.

Q: So you've known about *The Mist* for a while. It's been on your radar.

JANE: No, Darabont sent me the script last year. No, I didn't even know he had it lying around, but apparently he's had it around for a while. Did you have a chance to talk to Frank?

Q: Yeah.

JANE: Maybe 12 years.

Q: 94, or something like that.

JANE: Oh yeah, is that right?

Q: He said it was almost the first thing he made (Jane turns around and walks away, going into the trailer without saying anything.)

JANE (from inside trailer): It's a little cooler in here, you guys.

Q: Yeah, he almost made this one before *Shawshank*.

JANE: Oh really? This is the mockup for my comic book *[Bad Planet]*. I wrote it. This is #2. Bernie Wrightson did the cover. They just did a mock up for us because we're going to put it in the movie. The scene where he's going into the pharmacy to get supplies and there'll be a rack of comic books and I'll grab some and stuff them in my back pocket and this is going to be on the rack, so I'm really excited about that. We're publishing—I have a company called Raw Studios and we're publishing two books right now. One's called *Bad Planet* and the other one's called *Alien Pig Farm 3000*. Rednecks versus aliens. I'm having a blast.

Q: There's a great subculture of redneck horror right now. That'll go down really well.

JANE: So this I wrote with Steve Niles, who wrote *30 Days of Night*, so I'm really excited about that. Comes out in June, I think. Right before ComicCon.

Q: Are you going to ComicCon as well?

JANE: Yeah, we've got a booth. I've got a bunch of shit to do down there. I've gotta promote *Mutant Chronicles*. So you know my buddy Jonathan Schaech. Is he still in town?

Q: He starts filming the remake of Prom Night on Monday. He just found out two days ago. He's gotta shave his head.

JANE: They're remaking *Prom Night*. Why the fuck would they want to do that? Why in the name of the good, good Lord would they want to do that?

Q: A new crop of teenagers to show naked.

JANE: Maybe they have a new take on it.

Q: So, when Darabont told you about *The Mist*, that was when you first heard about it?

JANE: Yeah. Of course I'd read *Skeleton Crew*.

Q: You're getting close to the end of filming.

JANE: Yeah, we're getting close.

Q: It's been a pretty intense shoot.

JANE: It really has. Every day.

Q: I think Frank Darabont was asleep on the loading dock when we left yesterday afternoon. A five-minute breather.

JANE: We're working hard, man. It's a pretty tight schedule so they've been working our a… they've been working us really hard. In order to get everything we need, it's just nonstop, you know. Every moment counts. We'll go a few days over just because the schedule was way too ambitious for us to get everything we need. But the good news is, we're not leaving anything behind. Most movies with tight schedules you're always missing stuff and you don't have time to do certain shots and all that. Not so here. The way they've designed the shoot, we're never waiting around more than ten minutes for them to flip the lights around. Very fast. That's why we're able to get what we're getting because we're never waiting around for an hour for them to light the fucking thing and then one or two takes and we gotta move on because there's no time. All the time's eaten up with the fucking lighting. Boy, I tell you man, we're lucky. You can do that

but you gotta have a lot of money and a lot of time to do that. To do it right. I'm going to direct a movie this year or next year and I'm going to do something similar. Light it and go. Don't fuck around.

Q: Was it the role or was it the way that Frank wanted to shoot the thing?

JANE: Was it the role? Yeah. Absolutely. Frank called me and said I want to send you a script. I'm not going to tell you anything about it. I want you to read it and he sent it over and it's one of the best scripts I've ever read. I'm not just saying that. Frank, if he's anything, he is one hell of a fucking writer. So that was a pleasure. That happens maybe once or twice in a career—this guy says, hey, I want to send you something and he sends it over and it's one of the best things you've ever read. The part is fantastic and it happens to mix the two things that I love the most, which is genre movies, the horror/sci-fi type stuff, with action, there's really good action, so that's a rare combination right there. I feel like, I feel like I stumbled into something—I was invited into something— very special. So I really gave it my all. I've worked really fucking hard on this film. I had an offer to do another movie in between the one I just finished and I turned it down because I wanted to dedicate the time that I knew I would need to prepare for this one. Most of the time you can walk through a genre film, you know? There's not a lot of prep that you need. You just scream. Look scared. This really requires some acting to pull it off. We have great actors, everybody's great.

Q: We talked to Marcia Gay Harden earlier, and it was interesting, her take on her character. In the novella, Mrs. Carmody is completely negative but her spin on it is: her character is absolutely right. It is the end of times. It is the end of the world. That's the first time I've heard anybody make that observation about the character, but on the surface of it, it has some obvious truth.

JANE: Oh, yeah. In a weird way, she is. That's the scary side. She's great. When you play a bad guy, which she kinda is, or turns out to be in the movie, you gotta believe where you're coming from. She certainly does.

Q: What's your take on David? What sort of character is he?

JANE: I can never answer those kinds of questions. I just don't know where to begin. He's just a guy, I guess. I say that about everybody I play. He's just a guy.

Q: In the film he is a painter of movie posters. The movie poster they've got set up in your studio is of *The Dark Tower*. Another nice detail for the King fans.

JANE: Oh, they'll love it. Yeah. Somebody just got the film rights to that.

Q: JJ Abrams.

JANE: Yeah. They say it's gonna be a film and not a TV series. That'll be good. Have you seen *The Host* yet? Another thing about Shreveport—you can't find a fucking movie in town. I was dying to see *The Host* and by the time I get back to L.A. I know it's gonna be gone. It really sucks. It came out like two weeks ago. You know movies today. If it lasts two weeks it's doing good.

Q: You've got this and *The Mutant Chronicles*. Anything else in the future?

JANE: *Killshot*, Elmore Leonard. We just did reshoots on that with Diane Lane and Mickey Rourke and myself up in Toronto. That movie's looking good. We changed some shit around. I think it's going to turn out really well. I have high hopes for that. The acting is going to be dynamite. The story's good. I think we're good there.

Punisher II, if we can get a fucking director and a script that makes half a fucking sense. The problem is everybody turns in a draft . . . everybody's watched every bad action movie from the 80s. All the fucking scripts come in like a bad Steven Segal film, you know? People just don't get it. I want Taxi Driver. I want a fucking dirty, mean, bloody New York story. I want a cop story. I want cops and robbers. Good guys and bad guys. I want *Serpico*. I want fucking *Dog Day Afternoon*. I want *Taxi Driver*. I don't want *Under Siege*.

Q: Have you thought about giving it a shot yourself?

JANE: I'd give them all the notes and stuff. We need a writer. I need a guy who can really take it home. I'm not that. I give them notes. I'm not a guy that's going to be able to deliver a finished, professional script, you know? I gave them a lot of good notes though. Hopefully we'll get something decent. I'm not going to do it if it turns out to be a piece of garbage. If Dolf Lungren's not busy.

Q: The last one was pointing in the right direction.

JANE: Yeah, yeah. It's not rocket science. Fucking deliver a good story.

Q: The guys from KNB are doing some pretty impressive stuff.

JANE: KNB is awesome. They're my heroes. Aren't they fantastic?

Q: It's a good role in that it gives you the chance to be an action hero, but David also has his concern for Billy going all the way through the movie, guilt that he's left his wife behind. It's a tough part.

JANE: Yeah, you know, he's a father. He's an artist, he's a father. Artists are a little bit reclusive so he's not like a guy who's automatically going to jump out and run to save people. He's not an action hero kinda guy.

Q: Do you prefer the monster stuff in this movie to the dialog?

JANE: Nah, I love a movie where I can act. This is a mockup poster [for *Dark Country*]. Right now Dimension and Sony are interested and we're budgeting it out. We'll go with whoever gives me the most money.

Q: Based on original material?

JANE: Yeah. Guy named Tab Murphy came up the story. He wrote *Tarzan* and *Atlantis* for Disney. Got tired of writing talking animals. Came up with a great story. I want to shoot it in 3D.

Q: Interesting project to be your directorial debut, isn't it?

JANE: Yeah, it's a bit of a challenge. People are,

like, are you nuts? Just direct a fucking movie.

Q: Why did you wait so long to direct your first movie?

JANE: It's not that I've waited. I've wanted to direct, but I wanted to find the right project. I want to do something small. This movie has four characters. I wanted to do something that was small enough that I could contain it and do all the things I wanted to do and cut my teeth learning how to direct. There's a lot of criteria to pick the right project. I think a lot of people dive in to directing, they get in over their heads, they bite off more than they can chew and they get swallowed up and they never fucking direct again. They get chewed up by the studio, they get chewed up by the critics, they do something that was in over their head. Or a writer will write something and guys will give him money to direct it and figure he wrote it, he must know how to tell a story and that's not true at all. I've had the chance to work with some great directors and learn from them.

As much as I'm acting in this thing and having the time of my life, I think it's the best work I've ever done in this film, but it's because I'm working with a great director and I have great material to work with. The script is a great piece of work, a very solid piece of work. And it's in the hands of someone so capable of bringing it to life. I'm having a great time on the acting side, but I'm also learning a fucking hell of a lot from the guy. I've learned from other directors I've worked with, too.

Q: What does Frank bring to the table that's different from other directors?

JANE: He has a great eye. You know what it is? It's pace and it's tone. He knows how to set a tone that's believable. And he has great taste.

Frank Darabont directs a scene with Toby Jones and Jeffrey De Munn

He has an ear for the truth, he knows what's real, and he also lets everybody do their job. He hires really good people, he lets them do their job. He doesn't get in their way. He expects you to bring it and everyone feels that and they do it. Some directors try to get too controlling and they try to micromanage everything and then everybody starts doubting themselves and their work falls apart. He brings out the best in people by allowing them to do what they do and trusting their opinions. He listens, takes advice from everybody and anybody. He's got a clear sense of the story that he wants to tell, so you can ask him a question—hey do you think we should?—and he'll have a very clear answer. No, and this is why—or that's a good idea, and this is why. He knows the story that he wants to tell in each moment of the film. He makes it a joy to work for him. You want to do your best. You feel that everybody wants to do their best.

Q: That was an observation Rich Chizmar had yesterday. Everyone here is so focused. People weren't sitting around gossiping or chattering. Everybody had a job to do and they were all doing it.

JANE: Frank set that tone the first week of shooting. The first week everybody's getting to know each other. The second week everybody knows each other so they're joking, and they're having fun and they're killing time and one morning he came in and he goes "All right. Chit chat's over." You respect the guy. He's not a dick but when he has something to say, he says it very firmly and that's the way it's going to be.

He's like, "We need to focus, I need to focus, so no fucking chitchat any more. Take it outside." It's very cool, so that's why you see everyone's like that. It took about three days of him reminding everybody. "Knock off the chitchat. Cut it out." Now you see very little of that going on, and when it does it's softer. He sets that tone on purpose. It didn't just happen, you know. Because as a group, everyone just wants to get along and get through it, but he focuses everyone. And then everyone sees the work that's being done and then that makes them want to be focused. It's very interesting how a good director works his crew and gets the right attitude and keeps people focused and then because people start doing better work then they want to be focused and then you find other people telling people to shut up and everybody kind of gets into it. It's great to watch that. Great to see that.

Q: You're shooting mainly chronologically

JANE: It helps a lot for this movie. It's a cumulative experience. The disaster that everyone's going through. Another great thing about this movie is that it's an experience that you could replace the monsters with terrorists or poison gas or a burning building or an earthquake. You could replace the monsters with a war—it could be the Nazis—and you'd have very much the same kind of film. That makes it relatable in a human, very real way. I think the best horror movies allow us to believe in the horror. Take *The Exorcist*. They allow us to believe in what we're seeing. I think that is done very effectively in this movie. Because human beings are reacting in a very truthful manner to the given circumstances. In this case it's monsters from another dimension. It could just as well be the Nazis, you know who in their own way were monsters from another dimension. It's nice to have a cumulative experience where we get to experience our characters kind of walking through the different stages of human society breaking down, going through all this stuff, and we get to go through it chronologically.

The Mist Limited Edition Lithograph Only 500 Signed Copies
17" x 11" Signed / Numbered by artist **Glenn Chadbourne**

Skeleton Crew: Unpublished Stephen King Anniversary Cover Lithograph Only 500 Signed
Copies 17" x 11" Signed / Numbered by artist **Pete Von Sholly**

Available at **StephenKingCatalog.com**

Expiation, Locked & Loaded: *Mist* by a Mile

by **Stephen R. Bissette**

Stephen R. Bissette asserts why Frank Darabont's adaptation of The Mist *was, and remains, precisely what it was, and is, and should be: the horror movie America deserved & deserves, now more than ever*

> **"** Well, we gave it a good shot—nobody can say we didn't. **"**
>
> – **Dan Miller** (Jeffrey DeMunn)

"Expiation" was a term likely unfamiliar to many readers and viewers of both Stephen King's novella and Frank Darabont's film. While there's much theological banter over the precise meaning of the term—and how it differs from propitiation,[1] a similar word which King chose not to run with—the expiation the fanatical, opportunistic Mrs. Carmody (Marcia Gay Harden) craves and raves about and rallies her makeshift congregation around in Frank Darabont's *The Mist* requires a sacrificial lamb: the film's young son, Billy Drayton (Nathan Gamble).

Mrs. Carmody hasn't quite taken over the U.S. House of Representatives or Senate as yet, but give her—and hers—time. We get closer every election cycle. Until then, we don't need to wonder what form blood expiation *might* take, or what Billy's fate *might* be: the worst already happens, and happens, and happens without end, amen. Blood sacrifices to "almighty" powers are willingly offered up daily in America, and I'm not referring to what's unseen or imagined in the mist, or in *The Mist*.

Frank Darabont exacted a promise from Dimension Pictures producer Bob Weinstein that Darabont's scripted conclusion would not be altered, and Dimension honored that commitment, despite its considerable cost in audience outrage, critical brickbats, and lost box-office potential. It was a very conscious,

calculated decision on Darabont's part, and King approved. *Entertainment Weekly* critic Owen Gleiberman wrote in 1994, "You need a certain craftsmanship to traffic in twin brands of manipulation—the exploitative and the sentimental—and there's no denying that Frank Darabont, who wrote and directed *The Shawshank Redemption*… knows just what he's doing… and Darabont is an accomplished button pusher…you always know exactly who to root for and against." ("Movies: It's About Time," *EW*, September 23, 1994, pg. 44). And oh, what buttons Darabont pushes in *The Mist*, to the very last shot.

Let's face it, Darabont was spot on. Most King fans still state their preference for King's open ending (as in Alfred Hitchcock's 1963 *The Birds*[2]), but love it or loathe it, *The Mist* movie nailed a

Frank Darabont at the other end of the clothesline, on the set of *The Mist*.

The Mist advance movie poster. Signed by Frank Darabont, Laurie Holden, Thomas Jane, Marcia Gay Harden, Jeffrey DeMunn, Drew Struzan, et el.

hard truth of our culture, country, and century thus far.

Fearing the worst, America and Americans allow the slaughter of our children and grandchildren every single day to slake an insatiable all-consuming fear. Fear, fealty, property, and profit, not prophets, fuel the blood-spilling, rationalized by an interminable irrational fealty to the Unholy Trinity: the sacred Second Amendment, the NRA, and the divine profits due legally-sheltered firearms manufacturers. These daily sacrifices do not ease or address our fears: they *are* the ravenous monsters of *The Mist*, what we *should* face and fear. "The Beast will leave us alone tonight," Carmody quietly says after an orchestrated, sadistic sacrifice to the monsters of the mist—before deciding Billy should be next. That Billy's sacrifice is exacted not by the zealot Carmody, but by *Billy's own father* (Thomas Jane), in a marrow-shrinking moment of all-consuming dread and despair—an act of "mercy"—is what nobody wants or wanted to hear, much less see. Nevertheless, it's the cold, still, shattering, earnest, agonizing heart of the

film. "Promise you won't let the monsters get me," Billy says to his father, "ever, no matter what." With the pull of a trigger, succumbing to fear, the promise is kept and broken—and make no mistake, fear *is* the monster.

In life, as in the film, we don't see every Billy's death, so like the fear driving this mad addiction to firearms, the children sacrificed daily remain invisible, offscreen, acknowledged but not really felt, real but not real, so the sacrifices never end.

To fight, to feed, the fear, *the sacrifices must never end*. Eternal expiation—to what end? "They're dead—*for what?*"

Nothing, but nothing, countered the father's grim decision that made Billy's fate the horrific inevitability Darabont knew it was. Worst yet, nothing has changed since 2007.

Terrified at what *might be out there*, Billy's father's decision is repeated in reality, every second of every minute of every day, in 21st century America.

Thus, Darabont's *The Mist* remains the most truthful, terrible, essential post-Millennial-shift monster movie of 'em all.

Mist Opportunities: The Long Story of a Short Novel

by *Kevin Quigley*

"Now, artistically speaking, there's nothing at all wrong with the novella. Of course, there's nothing wrong with circus freaks, either, except that you rarely see them outside of the circus."
– Stephen King, "Afterword," Different Seasons

What makes a book a book? Seems like a fairly straightforward question. Pages. A cover. Some written material inside. A stitched binding if you're fancy, glue if you're basic. Without getting into technological nuance (yes, audiobooks are books; yes, ebooks are books), that's the standard definition. Everyone knows what a book is.

Ah, but what about a *novel*? What makes a *novel*?

In his "Afterword" to *Different Seasons*, one of King's earliest and best examinations of his own writing process (and, incidentally, the world of publishing in the early 1980s), King lays the concept out. There's no hard and fast rule of what makes a novel, but once you approach 40,000 words, you're edging into novel territory, with an italicized title and all the pomp that comes with that. 20,000 words and under is short story territory, the title wrapped in quote marks to denominate its lesser status. Somewhere in between – also titled with quote marks, although in this case those quotes feel a little ironic – lies the realm of the novella. It's that realm I want to talk about here.

Stephen King published "The Mist," a new story commissioned specifically for the 1980 anthology *Dark Forces*, edited by King's then-editor, Kirby McCauley. A *tour de force*, "The Mist" presented a thrilling and claustrophobic science fiction/fantasy/ horror story that leaned toward Lovecraft and terminated with one of King's more ambiguous endings. It was fiction King hauled out of himself after a sweaty bout of writer's block … and it was long. Long enough for the cover of *Dark Forces* to declare that it was a "new short novel by Stephen King." I guess the term *novella* wasn't quite in the King vernacular yet.

Although … *was* it a novella? "The Mist" tops out somewhere between 40,000 and 50,000 words; by King's own estimation, that makes "The Mist," well, *The Mist* – italicized instead of wrapped in quotations in the hierarchy of fiction. Ah, but here's where the vagaries of style get muddy: because it's a part of a collection, even a short novel gets the quotes treatment. For now.

Let's take a quick stop at 1982's *Different Seasons*, King's first foray into the four-novella collection, comprised of "Rita Hayworth and Shawshank Redemption," "Apt Pupil," "The Body," and "The Breathing Method." Even now, it's considered a high-water mark in the canon of King's writing. I keep going back to that "Afterword," though, the one that very clearly defined the parameters of a short story, a novella, and a novel. Most of the *Different Seasons* work fits the criterion of a novella … although, interestingly, "Apt Pupil" is longer than *Carrie* was, and *that* was a novel. It makes sense that the four stories fit into a single volume, especially one set at a remove from King's other horror-driven writing at the time. The tales, all distinct in their subject matter and tone, still felt of a piece with one another, in part because of the framing gimmick – supported by the internal subtitles ("Hope Springs Eternal," "Summer of Corruption," "Fall from Innocence," "A Winter's Tale") and line illustrations – of each story representing a specific season.

Speaking of seasons, let's take a side trip into

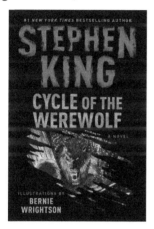

Cycle of the Werewolf, a book that originally started off as an idea for a calendar. Publisher Chris Zavisa of Land of Enchantment Press had tentatively propositioned King with the idea in 1979: King would write twelve little vignettes and Bernie Wrightson would do some illustrations and people could hang it on their walls and read a new King story over the course of the year. King had agreed, but by 1983, the project had mutated into something else: a short novel, with vignette-chapters corresponding to the months of the year. It made sense in a career of a man not known for his brevity: if you want a novel, plan a novella; if you want a novella, propose a calendar. Cycle, accompanied by full-color and black-and-white illustrations by famed artist Bernie Wrightson, was originally published as a limited edition, then came to the mass market in May of 1985. Its word count is that of a novella – heck, maybe even a long short story – but it was packaged and sold as a proper book. More than anything King would publish in the 1980s, Cycle of the Werewolf would prefigure a trend that King would adopt in the aughts and 2010s … and that would have an impact on the

future of "The Mist."

King's concept of cohesive short collections continued in 1985's Skeleton Crew, a powerful anthology of tales that kicks off with the story in question. "The Mist" makes its official debut in a book by Stephen King, and serves as an introduction to a work whose stories feel deliberately written, chosen and sequenced to achieve the emotional and thematic heft of a novel, despite the

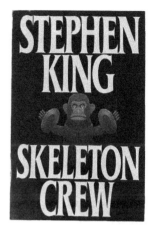

wildly varying subject matter. Here again, "The Mist" is treated as one cog in a larger machine, the gear that sets the mechanism of Skeleton Crew turning, just as it had done as the start-off story in Dark Forces. But the fact that it works so well in Skeleton Crew doesn't shake off the question of whether it could work on its own. Is it a novella or a short novel?

Things get even more complicated when you consider the strange case of The Bachman Books. The short history is that Stephen King had published five short novels between 1977 and 1984 under the name Richard Bachman. The subterfuge culminated in Thinner, the book that broke his cover and forced King out of the Bachman closet. The first four of those novels – Rage, The Long Walk, Roadwork and The Running Man had all gone out of print; in order to satiate the mass desire for these lost works, publisher New American Library

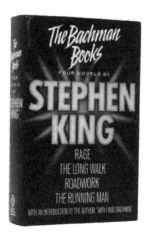

bundled them into an omnibus edition titled The Bachman Books. Clearly, these books were considered novels when they were first published (here is where we note that the early book Rage is shorter than both "Apt Pupil" and "The Body"), but collecting them into this anthology made them feel like another *Different Seasons*-type novella collection, a bridge between that book and the upcoming *Four Past Midnight*.

And what of *Four Past Midnight*? Coming right on the heels of 1990's re-release of the massive unexpurgated version of *The Stand*, this hefty volume was a lot longer than *Different Seasons*. It was longer than most King *novels*, beating

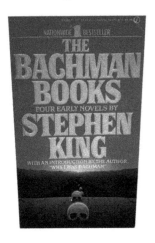

out tomes like 1987's *The Tommyknockers* and later books *Needful Things*, *Insomnia* and *Duma Key*. By 1990, after titles like *It*, *The Drawing of the Three*, and *The Talisman*, we were used to – even expecting – Stephen King to overwhelm us with these gargantuan releases. But both "The Langoliers" and "The Library Policeman" were longer than *The Long Walk*, *Carrie* and *The Running Man*, with "Secret Window, Secret Garden" not far behind. If *The Bachman Books* was a collection of novels masquerading as stories, *Four Past Midnight* was a collection of stories that could have been novels.

Then, surprisingly, a new trend starts to emerge in 1992 with the publication of *Dolores Claiborne*, a novel shorter than "The

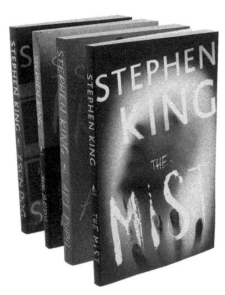

Langoliers." Originally, King intended *Dolores Claiborne* to be published in a larger volume titled *In the Path of the Eclipse*, along with paired novel *Gerald's Game*. By breaking these titles into separate works, perhaps King realized the worth and power of letting these shorter tales stand on their own as separate entities. Novels? Maybe. Books? Absolutely.

In 1999, as Stephen King was hot off the success of a new, robust novel (*Bag of Bones*) with a new publisher determined to bring the novelist to a wider market, a slender surprise novel popped up in stores. Of this thin new book, King said, "If books were babies, I'd call *The Girl Who Loved Tom Gordon* the result of an unplanned pregnancy." It's a little easier to call *Tom Gordon* a novel than, say, *Cycle of the Werewolf*; it's longer than *Carrie*, longer than *Rage*. The status of *Tom Gordon* and *Dolores Claiborne* aren't really in question; it's the stuff we're calling novellas in relation to these books that is most interesting. All but one of the *Four Past Midnight* novellas are longer than *Tom Gordon*, as is "Apt Pupil." What is a novel? What is a book?

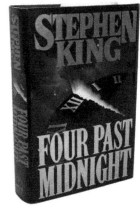

The question gets even more deliciously complicated when King released the first of his short Hard Case Crime novels in 2005. *The Colorado Kid* was originally published in mass-market paperback only, by a publisher specializing in re-publishing classic pulp and *noir* crime fiction, as well as brand-new work in the same genre. King's latter two books from the publisher – *Joyland* and *Later* – would be relatively slim books, but *The Colorado Kid* was downright *skinny*. Shorter than anything in *Four Past Midnight* and most of the tales in *Different Seasons* (save "The Breathing Method"). By King's definition, *The Colorado Kid* is absolutely a novella ... but whether due to its publication as a book or to the nature of the story itself – open-ended, like *Cell* or *Pet Sematary* or *The Long Walk*, connecting it to a larger, deeper, richer story than is perhaps on the page – it

has never quite felt like a novella. Then again, neither do the classic crime novels *The Postman Always Rings Twice* and *Double Indemnity*, by James M. Cain – both around the same length, both full stories with lasting impacts. Maybe it has less to do with word count and more to do with vibes.

And here, finally, we come to *The Mist*. Yes, italicized.

In 2007, filmmaker Frank Darabont, writer/director of King adaptations *The Shawshank Redemption* and *The Green Mile*, finally tried his hand at a making a film that wasn't a Stephen King period prison piece. *The Mist* had an all-star cast, an unnerving twist ending … and a mass-market tie-in paperback. At long last, King's "short novel" was finally being treated like an actual novel. And it was popular, too, hitting the Top 10 list on the *New York Times* bestseller list. Consider that: as a novella, "The Mist" had originally been published in an anthology, and later as part of *Skeleton Crew*, which for a time was the most popular book in the country. Now, twenty-two years later, it was presented as its own novel, and again becomes one of the most popular books in the country. There *is* something in *The Mist*.

Maybe it's a coincidence, but the release of *The Mist* as its own book seemed to kick off a few trends in King's publishing. In 2009, with the arrival of one of King's most bizarre publications to date, *Stephen King Goes to the Movies*. A collection of shorter work that had been adapted to film, the tales feel chosen at random, combining King short stories "1408" (originally from *Everything's Eventual*), "Children of the Corn" (*Night Shift*), and "The Mangler" (also *Night Shift*), as well as novellas "Rita Hayworth and Shawshank Redemption" (*Different Seasons*) and "Low Men in Yellow Coats," here strangely retitled "Hearts in Atlantis" with "Low Men in Yellow Coats" as a

subtitle, even though a different novella named "Hearts in Atlantis" also came from the collection *Hearts in Atlantis*, yet the film *Hearts in Atlantis* was based on the novella "Low Men in Yellow Coats." I told you it was bizarre.

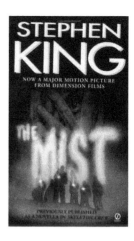

A year later, a slim book called *Blockade Billy* arrived in bookstores, followed later by *Gwendy's Button Box* (written with Richard Chizmar) in 2017 and *Elevation* in 2018, all three solidly novella length, and at least one – "Blockade Billy" – was eventually folded into a longer collection of stories, *The Bazaar of Bad Dreams*. Mostly, though, the trend went the other way. Not long after *Elevation* went to #1 as a hardcover, older King novellas began doing what only *The Mist* had done before: shaking off the shackles of the collections to which they had been changed, and emerging as their own self-contained work. King's publisher Scribner published *The Body*, *The Sun Dog*, and *Apt Pupil* as their own books in 2018, with *The Langoliers*, *Rita Hayworth and Shawshank Redemption*, and *1922* (from *Full Dark, No Stars*) later. Amusingly, 2021's box set, *Stephen King Short Fiction* attempted both what King's novella collections and *Stephen King Goes to the Movies* had done to varying degrees of success: combining some of these long tales into one package. The collection included four slender books: *Apt Pupil*, *The Sun Dog*, *The Body* … and *The Mist*.

It's been a strange journey for this unusually resilient long tale by Stephen King. It arrived in the world in 1980, years before the first Stephen King novella collection hit the market. It has asked, at times, to be considered a short novel, a long short story, a novella, a book and a volume in a larger collection of unrelated tales. Is there an interesting future for this terrific tale? As proven by the book in which this essay appears in proves, I have reason to hope.

Pete Von Sholly:
The Man of Many Hats

by *Andrew J. Rausch*

As a child, two of Pete Von Sholly's primary interests—monsters and drawing—collided. The young artist began sketching creepy crawlies and the things that went bump in the night that he saw in his beloved Famous Monsters of Filmland *and in the black-and-white creature features. Most children eventually put away their childhood loves and preoccupations, but not Von Sholly. Instead, he embraced these things just a little tighter and found a way to make a career doing what he loved.*

Von Sholly eventually became a storyboard artist and has worked on more than 100 feature films, including entries in the Friday the 13th, Nightmare on Elm Street, Child's Play, *and* Hellraiser *series. He has also worked on three Frank Darabont-helmed Stephen King adaptations (*The Shawshank Redemption, The Green Mile, *and* The Mist*).*

Von Sholly has also published a number of graphic novels and books containing his art, and he's created the artwork for illustrated editions of novels by such legendary writers as H.P. Lovecraft, Joe R. Lansdale, Ramsey Campbell, and, of course, Stephen King.

He was kind enough to sit down with me for a few minutes to discuss his King-related work.

ANDREW J. RAUSCH: How did you get into creating film storyboards? That's an interesting niche.

PETE VON SHOLLY: When I was young, I wanted to be a comic book creator. I wanted to be Stan Lee and Jack Kirby rolled into one guy! I never heard of storyboards until I moved from upstate New York to Los Angeles and discovered the animation business. A place where one could make a good living as an artist, with health benefits and such. When I saw the storyboards I thought, "These kind of look like comics. Maybe I could learn to do this." So I sought work and help to get experience and learn everything I could about

drawing for film. Film has special rules that don't apply to comics at all, and there are other big differences like using real cameras that had to *fit* somewhere. But decent, clear staging and drawing and putting emotion and drama into your storytelling and characters are quite similar to print work. So I started in animation at Filmation and Marvel and freelanced for Ruby Spears, Hanna Barbera, and others, and then I managed to make the leap into live action. I have bounced back and forth between them over the years. Feature animation is a whole other thing, too.

AJR: You've worked with Frank Darabont on several projects. How did you meet Frank?

PVS: I met Frank at Chuck Russell's house when they were writing partners on *Nightmare on Elm Street 3: Dream Warriors*. I liked them both very much and worked a lot with both of them. Pretty good stuff for a novice storyboard guy! Frank and I bonded right away over our love of monster movies and the new phenomenon of garage kits, mostly from Japan (Billiken and Kaiyodo) and people here like Jeff Yagher who were making their own.

Susan Malerstein-Watkins, the script supervisor, with Frank Darabont on the set of *The Green Mile.*

AJR: Were you a fan of Stephen King's work prior to working on the art for Darabont's films?

PVS: I was, in fact, a Stephen King fan for many years. I always liked his books better than any of the adaptations until Frank came along. It was very exciting to be part of a King project. *The Shawshank Redemption* was the first one for me, and it's a great movie with a great story underneath, which helps.

AJR: What was your favorite King book or story prior to that?

PVS: I liked *The Shining* and *The Stand*. I also liked several of the short stories like "The Raft," "The Boogeyman," and "The Jaunt." I especially liked the idea of that club where stories are told and books exist that were never written. I think King's childhood was much like mine in terms of what movies we saw and enjoyed. For instance, I see "The Raft" as "*The Blob* in a lake" and "The Jaunt" as a twist on *The Fly*, but without the gene mix, of course. King seemed like he was doing his own take on a lot of genre faves and then taking them into new territories, which I enjoyed.

AJR: As you mentioned, Darabont's King adaptations are the best ones, or at least some of the best. What do you think it is about Darabont's films that make them so much more effective that the others?

PVS: I think Frank picks good stories and he "gets" them. He keeps the feel and the intent of them better than most filmmakers, although I really love [George Romero's] *Creepshow!* The only place I didn't really like what Frank did was *The Mist*—specifically the ending.

AJR: Was that ending in the original storyboards, or was that a decision that was made later?

PVS: We didn't storyboard the end sequence. That may have been done by someone else. We just did three major scenes that took place in the supermarket and in the pharmacy. I know Frank had to fight for his ending. I believe the studio was like, "Are you sure about this?" But they respected him and his choice in the end. King's story ended with everything up in the misty air. By the way, I think *The Mist* may owe something to *The Crawling Eye*, but I may be off base. Frank's ending was like the mist was clearing up and the army was mopping up, so the killings were unnecessary, and that was the gut punch he achieved. I didn't like it, but of course it wasn't up to me.

AJR: You showed me a short comic you wrote based on *The Mist* in which you wrote you're own alternate ending. I really liked that. What's the story behind your creating that?

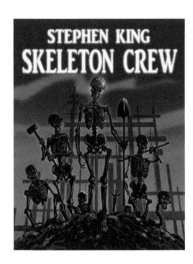

PVS: I didn't like the ending of *The Mist* in King's story, and I didn't like Frank's version of it either. That said, I think if I'm going to criticize something, I should put my money where my mouth is and suggest something better, or at least try. So I did my own version and called it *The Missed* and suggested another ending— not one that answers all the questions, but one that takes us to another level. How well it works depends on you, I guess. I think it was "don't just gripe, bring something to the table," you know?

AJR: What is your process when you work with Darabont?

PVS: Frank and I worked very closely and took the sequences one at a time, usually with a focus on special effects and stunts—things that need "boarding" the most, generally speaking. *The Shawshank Redemption* did not need a whole lot of boards compared to *The Green Mile* and *The Mist*, but we all went to Ohio to the location, and that was rare fun. It was very collaborative with Frank. He was receptive to ideas, and that made it more fun for me than just being told "draw this, draw that," which is how it is sometimes. Things didn't always make it to the big screen the way we boarded them for many reasons, but a lot did, and it was a great treat to watch your drawings come to life on screen—sometimes very close to what we envisioned.

AJR: Which of the Darabont projects did you enjoy working on the most?

PVS: I enjoyed *The Shawshank Redemption* because we went to Ohio, as I said, and I visited the sets and watched them recreate the whole huge cell block in a warehouse. I enjoyed *The Green Mile* because they shot it here [in Los Angeles], and I visited the set and watched them shoot some of it. But the main thing about all of them was just the fun of working with Frank, who is a considerate, generous and brilliant guy.

AJR: You also did the artwork for the PS Publishing edition of King's *Skeleton Crew*. What can you tell me about your work on that project?

PVS: Pete Crowther at PS asked me to do it. I had to create one illustration for each story, some of which were challenging. It was kind of tough because my art tends toward the dreaded "C" word...*cartoony!* I'm not an illustrator, per se. I did my best, but I think some King readers would have preferred a more realistic approach. Some of the art I feel good about, and some...it's okay, but I was out of my comfort zone here and there.

AJR: In closing, do you have anything you'd like to say to the Stephen King Constant Readers out there?

PVS: I'd like to say that it's always been a privilege to have worked with Frank Darabont and a privilege to have been asked to add my pictorial two cents to the vast array of amazing work inspired by the writings of Stephen King. I hope to do more. It's also a prvilege to be part of this unique publication. So thank you for asking!

Check out: **vonshollywood.net**

Stephen King Standee
Front   Back

Dick and Jane of the DEAD

Graveyard Die-O-Rama

and the UGH! Annuals

Available at **vonshollywood.net**

THE MIST, AS YOU MAY KNOW, IS THE TITLE OF A GREAT STEPEHEN KING STORY THAT WAS ADAPTED AS A FEATURE FILM AND EVEN A STREAMING SERIES. KING'S STORY IS LOADED WITH SUSPENSE, DRAMA AND, OF COURSE, HORROR! BUT I COULDN'T HELP WONDER IF THERE MIGHT NOT BE A LITTLE MORE TO EXPLORE WITHIN THE FANTASTIC SETUP OF A MYSTERIOUS, CREEPING, MONSTER- FILLED, ALL-ENCOMPASSING FOG THAT APPEARS FROM NOWHERE AND SLOWLY BLANKETS OUR ENTIRE WORLD. THE OPPORTUNITIES ARE SO MANY, INCLUDING THE TAKEN AND ALSO...

THE MISSED!

HER NAME, WHEN SHE HAD ONE, WHEN THERE WAS ANYBODY TO KNOW IT, WAS JAYNIA. SHE WAS STUDYING BIOLOGY IN HIGH SCHOOL WHEN THE GREAT JOLT CAME.

THE JOLT SHOOK THE EARTH AND PRECEDED THE COMING OF THE THICK CURLING FOG THAT COVERED IT!

IT WAS SUPPOSED TO HAVE TO DO WITH SOME KIND OF GOVERMENT DELVING INTO "ALTERNATE REALITIES". AT FIRST, PEOPLE TRIED TO BE CALM, TO PRETEND IT WAS JUST SOMETHING WE'D FIGURE OUT, SOMETHING WE'D FIX OR SOMETHING THAT WOULD JUST GO AWAY IN TIME...

BUT THE FOGGY SHROUD DIDN'T GO AWAY. AND NOBODY DID FIGURE OUT WHERE IT CAME FROM OR WHAT IT WAS OR HOW FAR IT WENT. AND OF COURSE THERE WERE ALL THOSE MONSTROUS THINGS THAT CAME WITH IT AND WERE CONCEALED IN ITS MILKY DEPTHS. CONCEALED UNTIL THEY DECIDED THEY WANTED TO FEED. OVER TIME PEOPLE BECAME HARD TO FIND. THE MONSTERS WERE NOT.

THEY SAY THAT PEOPLE UNDER INTENSE STRESS CAN SOMETIMES FIND INTENSE INNER RESOURCES TO MATCH IT.

MIST AND MONSTERS OR NO, JAYNIA HAD TO *SURVIVE* AND SLOWLY BEGAN TO OBSERVE THE *BIOLOGY* OF HER STRANGE NEW WORLD

NOT *ALL* THE "NEW" CREATURES WERE PREDATORS.

AND ONCE YOU GOT *USED* TO THEM...

...THERE WERE THINGS ONE COULD *EAT* TO SUSTAIN LIFE.

JAYNIA WANDERED THE WORLD, SEEING INCREDIBLE NEW THINGS DAILY.

EVIDENTLY THE CREATURES OF THE FOG COULD SEE THROUGH IT QUITE WELL. SOME ZOOMED PAST HER IN BOUNDING HERDS!

BUT THE *REAL* BURNING QUESTIONS REMAINED. HOW *MUCH* OF THE WORLD DID THIS MIST COVER? WHERE DID IT *END* AND WERE THERE *PEOPLE* ALIVE THERE?

WHERE MIGHT THINGS BE *NORMAL?*

THE IMPOSSIBLY LARGE *GIANTS* WERE USUALLY SEEN ONLY AT GREAT DISTANCES AND JAYNIA COULD NEVER BE SURE THEY IF THEY WERE *LIVING THINGS* OR SOME KIND OF GEOLOGIC FORMATIONS. UNTIL ONE CHANCED TO AMBLE *PAST*. IT WAS LIKE BEING AN *ANT* IN A GARDEN AS AN *ELEPHANT* STROLLED BY!

NOTHING THAT *BIG* WAS SUPPOSED TO BE ABLE TO *LIVE* ON THE SURFACE OF THE EARTH,

IT WAS A *BIOLOGICAL* IMPOSSIBILTY.

BUT THEN, WHERE *WAS* SHE EXACTLY? COLD *DREAD* CREPT INTO HER HEART AT THE THOUGHT.

IN AN ABANDONED DEPARTMENT STORE SHE FOUND AN INTACT BATTERY-POWERED *DRONE*. COULD IT POSSIBLY FLY *ABOVE* THE SHROUD AND REVEAL... WHAT?

THE DRONE WAS ABLE TO FLY THROUGH THE MIST WITH EASE.

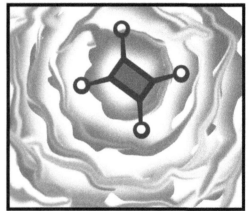

BREAKING THROUGH THE SOUPY ATMOSPHERIC MIASAMA, THE DRONE LOSES ITS *GRAVITATIONAL* CONNECTION WITH THE GROUND AND DRIFTS FREE IN AN UNKNOWN *VOID* POPULATED BY UNKNOWN STARS AND PLANETS!

MY GOD... WHAT... WHAT...

AS SHE REELED FROM THE SIGHT OF AN *ALIEN* UNIVERSE, SHE WAS DISTRACTED BY THE SOUND OF *GUNSHOTS* EMANATING FROM A PARKED SUV AND RAN TO INVESTIGATE.

IN THE CAR WERE TWO *CORPSES*, A MAN AND A BOY, WITH FRESH *BULLET WOUNDS!* WHAT HAPPENED HERE AND *WHY*?

THE UNFAMILIAR SOUND OF HOWLING *WIND* DREW HER ATTENTION AWAY FROM THE TRAGIC SCENE...

THE NORMALLY *MUTED* ATMOSPHERE WAS *TORN* AND *THIN* HERE AND AS SHE APPROACHED THE *EDGE*, SHE UNDERSTOOD THE GREAT *JOLT* AND WHAT IT MEANT.

THERE WERE THINGS MOVING ABOUT, TOWERING OVER THE GIANTS. IF SHE WAS AN ANT, THOSE ELEPHANTS WERE CATS AND DOGS TO THEM.. THERE WAS NO NORMAL EARTH TO FIND. THE OLD EARTH, THE PART NOT *SHIFTED*, WAS *ELSEWHERE* IN THE COSMOS NOW. THE REST OF IT WAS HERE, FOREVER ENSHROUDED BY THE CONCEALING AND PROTECTING MIST.

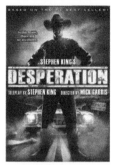

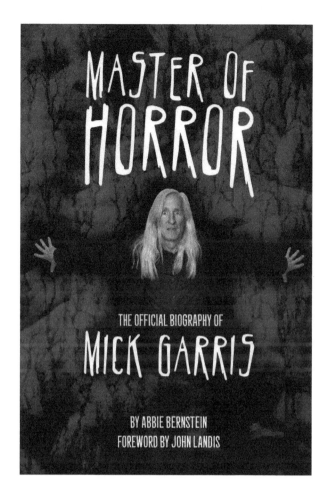

MASTER OF HORROR

Official Biography of **Mick Garris**

Director and screenwriter Mick Garris has produced more Stephen King adaptations to film and TV than any other filmmaker. Thanks to Stephen King Mick Garris's work in film has placed him in a prominent position in Stephen King history. Master of Horror explores the worlds that Mick Garris has created and been a part of in Hollywood, and in fiction, for decades. *Master of Horror* includes guests: Clive Barker, Joe Dante, John Landis, R.C. Matheson, David Schow, Ryûhei Kitamura, William Malone, and Tom McLoughlin; actors Mädchen Amick, John Billingsley, Robert Carlyle, Matt Frewer, Annabeth Gish, Brian Krause, Henry Thomas, Steven Weber, and Lynn Whitfield; makeup effects artists Howard Berger and Bill Corso; composer Richard Band; Garris' wife, Cynthia Garris; and more!

Order a *Signed copy* by **Mick Garris** and **Abbie Bernstein** and all Mick Garris Stephen King films at **StephenKingCatalog.com**

Slipping Back Into *The Mist*

by L.L. Soares

Let's go back to 2007. My wife Laura and I are in mid-town Manhattan, visiting family, and have decided to go see the new Stephen King movie, *The Mist*, which I'd been hearing good things about. We see it at the Regal multiplex theater on 42nd Street (all I can remember is lots of escalators going up, up up!). Little did I know at the time that this movie would have a profound effect on me and become one of my all-time favorite King adaptations.

And it's all because of that damned ending!

Back when I was in middle school, a kid three times my size punched me in the stomach. All of the air went out of me, and I just sat there for a while, trying to get air back into my lungs.

That's what the ending of *The Mist* felt like that first time.

Chances are good if you're reading this, you already know the storyline. But in a nutshell, a small town in Maine (called Bridgton in King's novella and the movie, and Bridgeville in the TV series) experiences a strange fog/mist that comes down from the Arrowhead military facility. With the mist, comes various horrors. A group of characters who live in the town are caught in the middle of it all, and are forced to fight for their lives.

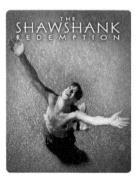

I remember reading King's original novella in the excellent anthology *Dark Forces*, (1980, edited by Kirby McCauley, and still considered one of the all-time best horror anthologies), and enjoying it, so I was looking forward to the movie version. Even more so when I found out it was directed by Frank Darabont, who had previously made two other movies based on King's books that are beloved by a lot of fans – *The Shawshank Redemption* (1994) and *The Green Mile* (1999). Hell, I know a lot of non-horror fans who think *Shawshank* is one of the best movies of all time. So, the fact that Darabont was directing *The Mist* was good news. Also, it would finally be a chance to see Darabont tackle a King story that involved lots of monsters, unlike his previous, more dramatic adaptations.

The movie's cast is pretty terrific. Thomas Jane, who plays lead David Drayton, had previously starred in a flawed comics movie (*The Punisher*, 2004) and was in another Stephen King movie I enjoyed, *Dreamcatcher* (2003). He is well cast here. Andre Braugher, as Drayton's neighbor, Brent Norton, was coming off a career-defining role as Det. Frank Pembleton on the series *Homicide: Life on the Street*, (1993 – 1999) and was in the 2004 TV miniseries *'Salem's Lot*. Toby Jones

had just played Truman Capote to much acclaim in the movie *Infamous* (2006), and Marcia Gay Harden had won an Oscar for Best Supporting Actress in 2001 for *Pollock*.

The Mist movie is also significant for its

television connections. Several of the film's actors would show up again in Darabont's series for AMC, *The Walking Dead* (TWD) which began in 2010,

including Laurie Holden (Amanda Dunfrey in *The Mist*, and Andrea Harrison in TWD), Jeffrey DeMunn (Dan Miller in *The Mist*, and Dale Horvath on TWD), and Melissa McBride (Woman with Kids at Home in *The Mist*, and Carol Peletier on TWD). Also, creature design and makeup effects master Greg Nicotero worked his monster-making magic on *The Mist*, and then went to become the special makeup effects artist on TWD.

One of the most important relationships, right from the start, in *The Mist*, is the one between Jane's David Drayton and his son, Billy (played by Nathan Gamble). You know right

away that Drayton is a good dad, and that he and his son are very close. Billy relies on his dad to keep him safe, and Drayton is put to the ultimate test.

Most of the movie takes place in "The Food House" supermarket. It's just big enough to give the characters room to move around, but small enough to create a strong sense of dread and claustrophobia. Even when these people think they are safe, they're still prisoners, and that huge wall of glass that is the front of the store puts them in a fishbowl that always seems to be on verge of cracking.

The movie's ending, where Drayton kills everyone in the car (including his son) to spare them the horrors of a world overrun with violent monsters – only to find out if he had waited just a little bit longer, the military would have saved them – is the gut punch. And the

movie ends with Jane's anguished screams in response to what he's done.

Darabont changed the ending of King's original novella, and word has

it that King was impressed with the new direction. He wasn't alone.

There's also a 2017 television series of *The Mist*, that aired on the (now defunct) Spike TV Channel for ten episodes. I wanted to check it out and see how it compared to the Darabont movie. The Spike series, in contrast, is bigger, has more characters and story arcs, and seeks to open the horror onto a larger canvas. It also has a much different take on the monsters.

I guess the TV series would fall under the category of "reimaginings," since it not only takes a lot of liberties with the storyline, the characters also have different names. Only the concept of The Mist itself is the same. This makes sense – the movie was a decade old, but fresh enough in people's minds where a faithful remake would have been a slog.

The first character we see in *The Mist* series is Jonah (Okezie Morro), a soldier from the notorious Arrowhead facility. He wakes up in the mist, not remembering his name or who he is. A dog is beside him when he wakes, and it runs into the mist. Soon after, Jonah finds the dog torn apart, but we never know what killed the animal. He then goes to the local jail to beg Sheriff Heisel for help, telling him there's something awful coming with the mist. Jonah is locked up in a cell for his trouble, because the police think he is drunk or on drugs. Later, he gets some company when Mia Lambert (Danica Curcic), a junkie with a mysterious past, is put in the cell beside him.

Also in the first episode, we are introduced to the Copeland family – Kevin (Morgan Spector, *The Gilded Age* 2022, and *The Plot Against America* 2020), Eve (Alyssa Sutherland, *Vikings*, *Evil Dead Rise* 2023) and their daughter Alex (Gus Birney, *Dickinson* 2019 - 2021). They are clearly the stand-ins for the Draytons here, with young Billy now replaced with a teenage girl. Alex and her friend Adrian Garf (Russell Posner, who also made an appearance in *Castle Rock*) go to a party being thrown by their high school's quarterback Jay Heisel (Luke Cosgrove), who Alex has a crush on. That night, Alex is drugged and wakes up in a bed upstairs, having been raped. The suspect becomes Jay when Adrian tells the police that he saw Jay

bring Alex upstairs. Oh, and Jay also happens to be the son of the town's sheriff, Connor Heisel (Darren Pettie, *Evil*, *New Amsterdam*).

Also in the series, Frances Conroy (*Six Feet Under*, *American Horror Story*) plays Mrs. Carmody's counterpart, Nathalie Raven. Instead of being a fervent Christian, Nathalie is more of a "new age" priestess. She has a deep reverence for nature, and sees the mist also as a punishment, but instead of being from God, it's Mother Nature's way of cleansing the world of humans who are killing her. This variant is actually the most interesting in the series, because while Mrs. Raven is just as outspoken about her beliefs, she is more sympathetic than Mrs. Carmody, and appears to be one of the "good guys" until she starts her gradual descent into madness, which grows as her confidence grows that she is serving the right "master."

There actually *is* a character named Mrs. Carmody in the series, played by Mary Bacon, but she's a minor character – a judgmental parent who is angry Eve taught sex education to her students, including her son, Eric. Mrs. Carmody and Eric, in fact, are the first people to leave the mall after the mist has descended. Soon after, Mrs. Carmody slams against the glass door, bloody with her jaw gone, and then is pulled back into the mist by some unseen force. After that, no one wants to leave the mall.

Once the mist actually comes into town, strange things start happening, and Kevin,

who is at the precinct to report his daughter's assault (with witness Adrian along), ends up freeing the prisoners when the police abandon the building. Kevin hopes that, with their help, he can get to the mall where Eve and Alex are.

It's a small town, and things can't be that far apart, and yet it takes the rest of the series for Kevin to finally reach the mall.

There are constant power outages, and they even affect most cars. The explanation is that more modern cars with computers are vulnerable for some reason, but sturdier cars without the technology are spared. Sometimes the mist is a very dangerous place, but other times it just seems to be an especially foggy day. The series does not share the same sense of constant danger that the movie does so well. There's also no barrage of oversized insects and monsters. Instead, the horror seems to be coming from people's fears/regrets, that have somehow come to life.

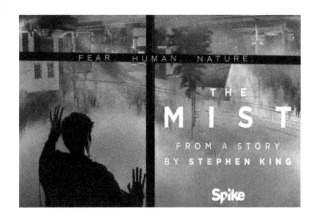

By mid-season, the characters are holed up in different places. Eve and Alex are trapped in the mall with a group of other people (including Jay Heisel!), some of whom are helpful, but most seem to be always on the verge of panic. These people are led by the manager of the mall, Gus Bradley, played by Isiah Whitlock, Jr., who was also Senator Clay Davis in *The Wire* – I kept waiting for him to say his catchphrase "Sheeee-it" from that show here. He was also in the Stephen King adaptation *1408* (2007). The group in the mall votes to create a mini community with its own rules, the first of which is that anyone who endangers the group will be forced to leave, into the mist.

Meanwhile, Sheriff Heisel has found himself in the town's church, where Nathalie has also made her way to, after her husband is killed right in front of her by a terrified man with a gun, who emerges from the mist. The church appears to be a haven, until it's clear that there is a rivalry between Nathalie and the priest, Father Romanov (Dan Butler). Like Mrs. Carmody, Father Romanov is sure that the mist is an instrument of God to punish sinners, and he finally feels a renewed sense of purpose in protecting his flock, but Mrs. Raven challenges his assertion by bringing up the Mother Nature argument again. Some of the people trapped in the church follow the priest, while others (including the Sheriff) gravitate to Nathalie. Kevin, Adrian, Jonah (we later learn his real name is Bryan) and Mia also find themselves at the church briefly, then leave to find an abandoned garage - while looking for gas -and then make their way to the local hospital. At the hospital, they come across Kevin's estranged brother, Mike (Peter Murnik), who can't forgive Eve for her past and treated her with disrespect, which led to their falling out. We also meet Dr. Bailey (Neal Huff), who appears to have gone insane and is performing experiments on patients to test the limits of the mist.

I'm a big fan of imagery, especially if it's unusual or powerful, and Darabont's movie version has several unforgettable moments, including:

- The scene in the movie where a stinging insect (that looks like a cross between a dragonfly and a scorpion) comes into the supermarket via a hole in the glass, and rests on Marcia Gay Harden's chest. It slowly crawls up her, but ends up stopping and flying away before it can do her any harm. In the movie, it's the moment that convinces Mrs. Carmody that she is protected by God and has been spared during these "end times" to do his work.

- The scene where tentacles attack Drayton and some locals in the loading dock – they're vicious looking – especially when one arm grabs stockboy Bobby Eagleton (Brandon O'Dell) and rips strips of flesh from him.

- The feet and legs of soldiers who have hung themselves rather than deal with the mist – one of the few haunting images that both the movie and series share.

- When they find a soldier in the pharmacy, wrapped up in webbing, and try to free him, he cracks open and lets out thousands of baby spiders.

- The monster towards the end that is so huge that the car Drayton and the other survivors are in looks like a pebble as the creature thunders by. This happens just before "the ending."

In the TV show, there aren't as many powerful images, but there are some effective scenes.

Several of these involve Mrs. Raven going out into the mist with other people, and surviving when they don't. The fact that she is spared

more than once confirms in her mind that, like her counterpart Mrs. Carmody in the movie, she has a special purpose here.

An ex-con named Mikhail (Steven Yaffee) talks to Mrs. Raven about what's going on. She mentions a similar event that happened in 1860, that people have come to call "the Black Spring." There aren't a lot of facts about it, but Mrs. Raven is convinced that whatever is happening now is the same thing. She then decides to go home.

It's the first time Mrs. Raven leaves the church on her own, and Mikhail goes after her. While he begs her to turn back, a moth flies into his ear and he screams as a death's head moth tattooed on his back seems to come alive, moving under his skin, until he sprouts wings. He crouches, winged, and hundreds of moths emerge from his mouth. It's one of the best images in the series. But where he dies an awful death, Mrs. Raven is spared.

Later, when Mrs. Raven and Father Romanov go outside to prove which one is right about the mist's intentions to other people hiding in the church. Father Romanov is approached and murdered by figures on horseback that are the Four Horsemen of the Apocalypse, while Mrs. Raven is again spared, going so far as to enter the mist naked and unarmed, to prove her invulnerability, to the others.

There's also a very effective scene that takes place in the hospital, when Kevin and his allies make their way to the wing that is a mental hospital, and its sole inhabitant, Nash, who first seems helpful and pretends to be a nurse, turns out to be a patient. He claims to be able to "see the evil" in people, and immediately fixates on Adrian (foreshadowing future revelations), claiming he is evil, and wanting to kill him. To talk him out of it, Kevin tells the man the darkest fantasies he can think of, of what he would do if he could get ahold of his daughter's rapist. The fact that a character who has been shown to be good throughout the series would suddenly admit to such violent urges makes his character more interesting (and more human), while also adding another layer to Kevin's personality.

I wasn't really sure what to make of the monsters in the series, because there aren't many of them. There are insects, tattoos coming alive, and dead relatives, but they all seem to be things that are extracted from the minds of the victims themselves. One of the few real monsters is a smoky looking creature that kills a little girl in a bookstore in the mall. Alex is with the girl at the time, but the monster spares her, which instantly puts a target on Alex's back.

There is this constant feeling of dread whenever someone looks out into the fog, or physically enters it, but it's never really clear just what the mist is. Is it a kind of nerve gas that makes people hallucinate? Early on, Mia sees her dead mother several times, and at one point Nathalie sees her dead husband again. But they don't seem to be hallucinations, because other people can see them, too. Or does it bring actual creatures with it (the insects that emerge from Deputy Pudnick in Episode 1, The moths that kill Mikhail, the Four Horsemen)? In Episode 9, Kevin even confronts a doppelganger of himself and they fight to the death.

In the movie, it is theorized that the mist has come from another dimension (just one of several similarities between King's work and the Netflix series *Stranger Things*) – a bit of atmosphere brought in from another world, where the giant insects and monsters came from. They are a very real threat to the humans' health and lives.

I'm sure that if the series had been renewed, it would have slowly revealed what the mist was all about, but when Episode 10 ends, it's still a mystery. For me, the movie worked a lot better, with real threats constantly ready to pounce, instead of the slow burn of the series, that was full of inconsistencies.

In the movie, the suspense builds more and ramps up as the story goes on. In the series, there are lulls where the focus is on the human storylines, and we practically forget about the mist. It certainly loses its sense of menace at certain points, especially when characters spend long periods of time outside and yet survive (for example, Vic, a guy who worked in a video store at the mall, was the first person to be exiled "for the good of the group," and yet he's able to stay alive on his own for a long time).

In the series, the most interesting characters are those who undergo changes. Adrian, Alex's best friend, who is gay and treated badly by his father – the man won't even speak to him or acknowledge him in his own house – becomes a very different person by the end of the season. Tyler Denton (Chris Gray), a bully from the high school who had been making Adrian's life miserable, and who was at that fateful party at the Heisel house where Alex was raped, is also seeking refuge at the hospital. They have a tense and violent meeting in a public restroom that ends in a sexual tryst, which changes their relationship dramatically. Mrs. Raven turns from a benign hippy to a vengeful Earth Goddess.

Kevin, who tries to always do the right thing and is our hero here, reveals a very dark side of his personality. Eve, who is an ultra-controlling mother to Alex, reveals that she was very promiscuous when she was her daughter's age, which is why she is so protective of her. Father Romanov turns from a man of God who wants to help, to someone who wants to control his parishioners and exact vengeance on those who would oppose him, with tools like a kid named Link (Dylan Authors) with a dark past, who at one point tries to kill Mrs. Raven for the priest.

But the biggest difference is the ending. In the movie, the ending is one of the bleakest I can think of in modern cinema. Literally, a big, howling cry of grief. The show, in contrast, ends on an intriguing note, but since we never find out more, it's also unsatisfying. A thud instead of a howl.

The ending makes the movie version of *The Mist* a complete, satisfying storyline, with a shocking final twist. The show, with its ambiguity and unresolved ending, is lackluster in comparison, but not completely without worth. Showrunner Christian Torpe and his writing team (Amanda Segel, Andrew Wilder, and others) at least try to do a completely different take on the material, but it's uneven at best. The sense of danger comes and goes. The horror is definitely on the movie's side – the monsters are effective and provide visceral, real danger all the time. The horrors in the series are less defined, and therefore less terrifying.

Frances Conroy (who has been excellent in other shows) shines here as Mrs. Raven. She's the most interesting character in the series, and the one who most defines *The Mist*. Spector's Kevin Copeland is a strong and sympathetic lead. Alyssa Sutherland's Eve is just as strong

a character, but isn't given enough to do, except constantly try to keep Alex and Jay apart when they start to gravitate toward each other. And while Kevin has a close bond with his daughter (he's always the "good cop" to his wife's "bad cop" when it comes to disciplining her), their relationship never seems as urgent and desperate as it does between Drayton and Billy. When Drayton makes his tragic decision at the movie's end, this bond is what makes the ending so dramatically agonizing.

Some of the other characters, especially Alex, Adrian, Mia and Bryan, are also interesting in the series, but in the movie it's much more of a solid ensemble, even though Thomas Jane's Drayton is clearly our hero. There are stronger performances in the movie, which also elevates it when that ending comes around. It feels like there's more to lose in the movie, that the stakes are higher.

It's also not a big surprise that the TV series didn't make it past one season. With its more hallucinogenic approach (whether to save money on effects or just to be something different) it's not as visually or psychologically adept as the movie. Too many things don't make sense. And it's not as emotionally satisfying. By stretching the story out, the series dilutes it, and while I would have watched a second season, I was glad that I didn't have to.

Ultimately, it's not much of a comparison. The movie is a powerful piece of work. The series is adequate, but meandering and often vague about what is going on. So, they sought to give us something different enough to keep us guessing. Unfortunately, the story just isn't as good as the original. If the series sounds interesting to you, you should seek it out. But your time would be better spent re-watching Darabont's original film.

I was (and am) a big *Mist* fan from the get-go. I Read the story when it first appeared. Also, back in those days' audio books were something of a unique and nifty item. The local video store had a small section of audio books. They were all packaged up with cool covers like the VHS flicks of the time. One box stood out: *The Mist*, featuring shrouded tentacles entwining around the title. In big bold font was written "featuring 3D sound!". I grabbed it and spent the afternoon idling around the local back roads with a six pack of cheap beer (forgive me, I was a scamp in those days) listening to it. The book had a full cast of actors and creepy sound effects, and to this day it holds up as great fun. Time marched on. Years later I wound up being lucky enough to illustrate some King stories in the *Secretary of Dreams*

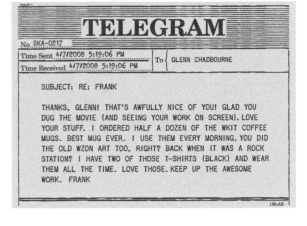

books, and from there being asked to create a sort of mascot character for Stephen King's radio station WKIT. That character became Doug Graves and he's still kicking to this day. As far as *The Mist* movie, when it was first announced then debuted, Sheila (aka, The Hon) and I hit the first showing at the local theater. We settled in and watched things unfold. I thought it had the perfect atmosphere, everything about it loyal to the story. So, I'm sitting there, watching, and something caught my eye. The groceries store bag boy at the checkout line is wearing a WKIT T-shirt featuring the character I did for the station. For a moment I wondered if I'd imagined it. Then, shortly after I first noticed it the kid gets snared by a giant tentacle and killed in great detail! The first victim of *The Mist*! I stood up, not realizing what I was doing and shrieked out THAT'S MY SHIRT!!! I got icy stares for this from the audience but I couldn't help myself. I was shocked, and overjoyed. Not long after this I was telling Rich Chizmar at Cemetery Dance about the experience and he gave me Frank Darabont's email. I told him I'd guard it with my life, and I have. I emailed him, not expecting, understandably (who the hell was I? Some loon from God knew where) A response, but he did respond with some very kind words. It was one of those life experiences that I'll always cherish.

– Glenn Chadbourne

The Mist: When Darkness Came – Centipede Decapitated

by **Pete Von Sholly**   Introduction by **Dave Hinchberger**

Pete Von Sholly created the storyboard art for The Mist film, and all the Frank Darabont Stephen King helmed films. We have been given special permission to print here, for the first time anywhere, a deleted scene from The Mist only available as a storyboard, as well as a color sample never-before seen. There are sections within the storyboards with titles. This section, "When Darkness Came," features a scene of a monstrous centipede that found it's way into the grocery store through a hole in the front of the store's window, created by another flying beastie that crashed through it. Here you get to see what was plotted out for this part of the scene but ultimately was not used. We're not sure why this scene wasn't filmed but possibly it over extended this section of the story and it just wasn't needed.

This colorized storyboard below was created to see if it was feasible to do the boards in color for the whole film. "Turns out it would have taken too long, so we didn't. This is also from the discarded centipede stuff."
– Pete Von Sholly

WHEN DARKNESS CAME

ARC around
and head
back around
over the
aisles...

See Mrs.
Carmody...

Fly over her...

Bird gains
into shot

THE MIST

36
cont'd

NON
drawn
shots

MEN BLASTING FLAMES
WITH FIRE EXTINGUISHERS-
JOE GETS PULLED FROM
THE FIRE.

37

VFX

Two guys
put out
flames
on dead
Tom

WHIP past
them to the
hole in the
glass...

WHEN DARKNESS CAME

37 cont'd

VFX

PUSH IN
on hole...

As a HUGE
MONSTER
CENTIPEDE
comes through!

Men run as
centipede
crawls down
and over dead
Tom...

... and
into the
market.

37
cont'd

VFX

Centipede flows up over counter...

...and moves into the store...

TILT UP past centipede to Reveal Hattie and Billy in the chaos as other people run across frame.

They see the centipede coming!

THE MIST

38

VFX

Centipede coming!

39

VFX

HANDHELD of Hattie and Billy with centipede coming...

PUSH IN on Hattie and Billy-frozen in terror!

40

VFX

Centipede rises up to reveal hideous mouths on underside!

41

VFX

Centipede
looms
close...

Irene
pops into
frame
and blasts
it with twin
cans of
RAID!

42

VFX

Centipede
recoils,
poisoned!

43

VFX

Hattie runs
away
with
Billy in
her arms.

43 cont'd

VFX

WHIP PAN
to Irene
spraying
the centipede.

44

VFX

Irene
strikes
match...

... and
turns the
spray can
into a
flame
thrower!

45

Centipede
burns
and
dies.

Misty Memories

by *Constantine Nasr*

I recall arriving to Shreveport, Louisiana in February 2007 and making my way over to the convention hall (or something to that effect) which had been recently converted into a movie production facility. This was where we were going to be filming *The Mist*, Frank Darabont's next film and his top-secret adaptation of Stephen King's classic novella. I say top secret because nobody – not even the cast – knew the ending. Okay, some people knew. I knew. I was one of the few, but I am really good at keeping secrets, and I didn't say a peep to anyone. (Come to think of it, it was quite possible more people knew the ending than they would admit to.) Why would we? We were all fortunate to be a part of this movie, something many of us King fans (and Frank fans) had been hoping would come to pass for many, many years. And I do believe that now, looking back 16 years after its theatrical release, it couldn't have gone any better.

Sure, we could have had more money, more time, maybe a few things here or there could have been done to make the film a little easier to make. But it would not have been made the way it was made. "What do you mean?" I hear you ask. Well, let's just say that when movies are made, they are definitely the product of their exact time.

Frank had the rights to *The Mist* for quite a long time, maybe as long back as when he

shared his *Shawshank* script with Steve, and he had been developing it for years. The only issue was the ending, which he couldn't crack. But in the many years between when he first starting writing it, and all the challenges he faced in between (including the financial failure of *The*

L to R: Laurie Holden, William Sadler, Sam Witwer, and Constantine Nasr

Majestic and some very complicated creative experiences in the business), Frank's anger seemed to point him in the right direction, at least for this story. As he has said many times, had he been a happier person at the time he was focusing on this story, the raw, unnerving, and damaging ending would not have occurred to him. Like the very best writers, Frank's personal experiences fueled that incredible talent of his. The bleakness of what he saw all around him in the world, especially post 9-11, opened him up in ways that even Stephen King, in the Reagan era, couldn't have imagined. And out came that gut punch finale.

Couple this was with Frank went through in his post-*Majestic* years — in which he directed a TV pilot (*Raines*, starring Jeff Goldblum) and an episode of one of his favorite TV shows (*The Shield*) — and he was driven to push himself behind the camera in new, energetic ways. *The Shawshank Redemption*, *The Green Mile* and *The Majestic* were carefully constructed and lensed films, and it is telling that Frank's inspirations were perfectionists like Stanley Kubrick and Ridley Scott. *The Mist* was never meant to be

made in that manner of storytelling. On the page, it read intense, dire, immediate — the style he knew he needed to bring – and the style discovered when he was directing TV. *The Shield* was not just "TV;" it was riveting, dramatic and unpredictable. That is what *The Mist* needed, and by 2006, he was ready, he was eager and he was – yes – angry.

The Shield also gave Frank the chance to work with a new Director of Photography, Rohn Schmidt, who brought a sharp precision to the "on-the-fly" handheld look that Frank found to be on the mark. He asked Rohn to shoot *The Mist*, and the plan would be to shoot the movie

Frank Darabont and Rohn Schmidt, director of photography

in the small window of time between seasons, so he could also bring on Rohn's two key collaborators, the camera operators Richard Cantu and Billy Gierhart. This trio was critical for Frank's creative vision.

Another thing was the budget. It is hard to believe that *The Mist* was shot for approximately $17 to 18 million, over just seven weeks. All true. And, it didn't have to be that way had Frank been willing to change his ending. But Frank knows what he wants, and that is why he's an artist at heart. He's also very economical, and very aware of the business of making movies. But money ain't everything. When a very big, influential and respected producer offered him nearly twice the budget in CASH to make the film with a different ending, Frank turned it down. He wouldn't give up on what he felt was the right ending, especially once Steve gave his enthusiastic blessing. Fortunately, the company that did come in and support him did so without any such reservations, and Frank made the movie he wanted. Sure, more time and money would always help and is always welcome. But there

was an intensive drive to complete this movie in the time we had, which ratcheted up the stakes for actors and their performances, crew artists and their ambitious creativity and productivity, and the poor assistant directors who had to keep the train on the tracks and make all station stops, each and every day. Seven six-day weeks and $17 million was a small amount in the grand scheme of indie filmmaking, and I think we can see that the result was worth it.

I have so many memories of long, long hours on the iconic grocery set, built by our

incredible production designer (and one of Frank's best friends) Gregory Melton. It was amazing to see something as seemingly mundane and innocent as a grocery store turn into the heart of the apocalypse. Where's the beef indeed? How long can lettuce and bananas hang out under the hot lights before they not only wilt but start to stink? Which books on the spinner rack haven't we looked at this week between setups? Sadly, none of the beer was real. But it was fun, and funny, to start observing how the aisles were arranged, and then start guessing what food was selected and why. I recall how we ran out of craft service at one point towards the end of filming, and

Thomas Jane and Constantine Nasr inside the Food House

food started disappearing from the shelves because extras needed their snacks. The poor team did the best they could, but remember, Constant Readers, er, Viewers, we were on a budget! Oh, don't get me started on all the smoke machines….

The Mist was a welcome reunion for so many of Frank's Friends, from First Assistant Director KC Colwell to script supervisor Susie Malerstein-Watkins (now cast as "Hattie"), from Greg Nicotero and the whole KNB team to Frank's lucky charms actors Jeffrey DeMunn and Brian Libby. We lucked out working with deeply committed superstars like Andre Braugher and Marcia Gay Harden, amazing supporting actors like the brilliant Toby Jones and the always game William Sadler, dear Laurie Holden and of course, the tough guy with a heart of gold (and a nerdy heart at that), Tom Jane! Tom was always ready to pick up an ax and chop heads off those monsters – many of which were designed by our amazing friend, the late and GREAT Bernie Wrightson. And nothing could have gotten done with the dynamic duo of producers Denise Huth and Anna Garduno, who were Frank's right and left hands!

I remember seeing grotesque pterodactyls being set on fire by Tom, watching Sam Witwer put his bloodied hand on the glass for the first time, and finding dead bodies covered in spiderwebs and other goopy, nasty slime. I recall Chris Owen being yanked time and time again by tentacles under the freight door. Crew members shaking the set to create an effective earthquake (including our old buddy, *Goon* creator Eric Powell, who came to visit that week). I remember my parents, brother and soon-to-be fiancée always visiting the set, welcomed by Frank and his extended crew family. I remember the weekends, gambling at the Shreveport casino, down the street, and all the good food we had (which was certainly better than the craft service). I also remember my cameo. Frank positioned me as one of the onlookers as David and his friends make their final escape. I had a great closeup in the pan across the worried, soon-to-be-dead faces inside the building. Unfortunately, that shot hit the cutting room floor, although I know the back of my head when I see it and I know the reverse shot made it in.

There are so many wonderful memories, many more than I could share, but the truth

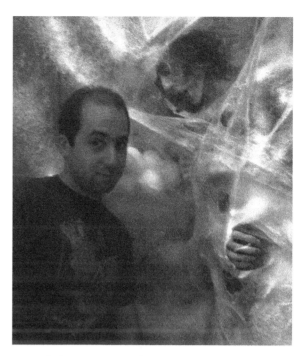

force evil incarnate. Frank could not have been happier. He knew he had something special in the can. And so did we. Those were great days indeed.

When Dave Hinchberger asked me to whip up some memories, I had no idea what I would share, but I knew they would all be good. I was so proud of my pal, Frank, for sticking to his guns, and for finding the best team to stand by him and stick by him to the very end. Frank

Team Darkwoods: L to R: Juan Francisco, co-producers Anna Garduño and Denise Huth, Frank Darabont

is that everyone – EVERYONE – was fully committed to this movie, to Frank's vision (not just the end, but the entirety of the piece). Those of us who grew up on Stephen King's original work wanted to do it justice. I remember how passionate Marcia was when delivering some of Mrs. Carmody's most vicious lines. It was scary just watching her go full

wanted to film the movie in black and white, and we all knew that would never happen. But thanks to the value of home entertainment, Frank got to fulfill that part of his vision. He would do it again with *The Walking Dead* pilot. But it wasn't as effective as it was here, in my humble opinion.

My memories also have a very odd component about them, because I was walking around and filming everyone, every day, for those seven weeks and beyond. I think some of what I have noted has been captured for posterity and revealed in some of the documentary work that we produced for our Saturn award-winning Blu-ray release. What I personally enjoyed most was the freedom and trust that Frank gave to me to work my craft and "do my thing." That's what he does when he works with friends, whether it be artist Drew Struzan, still photographer Ralph Nelson or editor Hunter Via. He surrounds himself with craftspeople and artists at the top of their game, creates a collaborative and open environment and offers an experience in which we all can contribute to the whole tapestry of the movie-making process. The experience is deeply personal, and one I will never forget,

On *The Mist* set: Frank Darabont with Constantine Nasr.

much like the novella.

I have not actually watched the film since I became a father. I always said that David's choice in the film is one that I was sure I wouldn't make if I was in his place. Easy to say if you don't have kids, right? But now that I do, and they are the age of little Billy, I keep wondering, what would I have done? Will I watch the film again? Sure, I will. But how will the ending impact me now. Would I make that choice now? That answer is the thing I may be terrified of most.

The Mist director, Frank Darabont and actor, Thomas Jane (as David Drayton) on the set in *The Mist*.

STEPHEN KING
RARE & ORIGINAL FICTION!

Never heard of these stories? We're not surprised. They're difficult to find but we have copies in stock! In fact we have a lot of items in stock for you to check out, including these Stephen King toy characters here to adorn your Stephen King library!

"The Glass Floor" in *Weird Tales*

"The Blue Air Compressor" in *Shining in the Dark*

"The Luckey Quarter" in *USA Weekend*

"Willie the Weirdo" in *McSweeneys*

Find these and more rare items at:

STEPHEN KING CATALOG.COM

The Shining Opera

by *Dave Hinchberger*

The Alliance Theatre– Atlanta, September 15 – October 1, 2023

The Shining… as an opera? From a dramatic perspective I could see how this could be a possibility but remember this novel has a major supernatural bent. Maybe because of these elements *The Shining* was more suited to this than I'd previously considered. Now, here it was, being produced in my town by the Atlanta Opera making its East Coast premiere. It was originally presented by Ordway Music Theater in Saint Paul, Minnesota. My history with *The Shining* should be evident by our company name, The Overlook Connection. As my first Stephen King novel it made such an impact at the age of fourteen, well, it literally changed the rest of my life. It's been a wonderful ride and now, here I am with at the Atlanta Opera about to attend *another* unique vision of Stephen King's opus, at the Overlook Hotel.

The Shining was greeted by a very healthy start to the new Opera season with the Atlanta audience making this a sold-out two week run! My wife and I attended with life-long friends, John and Carol Thomas for the September 28th performance. As we entered the Woodruff Arts Center it was abuzz with excitement for the evening's performance. You could feel the anticipation in the air and I found several folks were wearing Stephen King t-shirts. Myself included as you could see a hint of *The Shining* film carpet design peeking out. This was a different kind of energy for an opera. I'd only been to one previously, but it was a different vibe.

L to R: Dave and LeeAnn Hinchberger, Carol and John Thomas, Alliance Theatre, Sept 28, 2023

Once the performance began I was completely put to rest as they were performing in English, and with subtitles displayed. My whole group appreciated this and it made the show that much more enjoyable.

Craig Irvin as Jack Torrance and Kearstin Piper Brown as Wendy Torrance performed splendidly in their roles. Irvin was quite distinctive in his delivery, with Brown giving a resounding, and emotive performance. The opera follows the storyline of Stephen King's novel beginning with Jack Torrance taking the job as caretaker for The Overlook Hotel in Colorado, his family in tow. Danny gets a better understanding of his ESP abilities from the hotel cook, Dick Hallorann, who also has these abilities. Dick explains that the Overlook also has entities within and warns him in how to protect himself. Once the Torrance's are on their own the Overlook slowly reveals itself causing havoc with Jack's fragile alcohol instability. Danny is traumatized by an unknown assailant, and Wendy is distraught in the middle with her family's unexplainable issues.

The ghost scenes in Act II were eerie, effective, especially when the ghostly inhabitants of the Overlook all come out

Craig Irvin as Jack Torrance

you knew who was in charge… and it wasn't the living. The whole cast were very confident in their roles. The set, featuring two floors and a grand staircase with additional rooms underneath, had quick minor changes. This saved time and were remarkably inventive. They used several stage-wide screens with projections, sometimes several at one time covering the whole stage, that were see-thru and very effective. This especially was evident withthe grand display at the end, when the Overlook exploded (the boiler had gone red) and it was quite the light show with plenty of booming effects. It was an impressive finale and a crowd pleaser, a standing ovation success.

The opera was performed in two acts within 2 hours and 20 minutes which included a 25-minute intermission. As this was an operatic stage performance there are limitations on how much you can deliver in that amount of time. When singing in a drawn-out fashion, like opera, it's going to take more time to deliver the story. It's obvious the story had to be abbreviated where finer details were not utilized due to these time constraints. Even so, many in the audience knew this story from the novel, film, and TV series and it was easy to relate to this version. Even folks new to The Shining could easily understand the Torrance's

plight of dealing with this haunted hotel. Honestly, I didn't know what to expect, but I enjoyed this version of The Shining, as well as the group with me found it entertaining. We watched the whole performance with rapt attention. Act I was the buildup, and Act II was the payoff. With the intense finale came a realization that this Shining opera… shines.

The Shining was a co-production with The

Thomas Glass as Jack Torrance

Alliance theatre here. Which leads me to point out that there's also a play for Misery that has been making the rounds in theatre for years. I already put my vote in that the Alliance / Atlanta Opera should go forward with that idea. After a two-week sold-out performance of The Shining, I think there's a strong possibility that Annie Wilkes would be a big… smash!

Full cast with Thomas Glass as Jack Torrance

Stephen King Is Still... Having Fun

by *Ariel Bosi*

We're not that far from celebrating ten years since we met Holly Gibney for the first time. If you don't remember, it was almost halfway through *Mr. Mercedes* when Janey Patterson tells Bill about this "weird cousin" who shows up for the first time at the hospital after Elizabeth Wharton's passing. The first description we have states that Holly is "a spinster roughly Janey's age but with none of Janey's looks" and that she never speaks above a mutter and seems to have a problem making eye contact". But that shy woman who was "supposed to be a walk-on character" turned into one of the most important characters created by Stephen King. Wouldn't you agree?

Putting aside *The Dark Tower* saga, for obvious reasons, if you know of another Stephen King main character that leads or co-leads in six books. Go ahead. I'll wait. In 2020 Stephen King himself said (to Terry Gross on NPR) that Holly "just kind of stole the book (about *Mr. Mercedes*) and stole my heart". Not a truer statement could be said since Holly ended up being one of the most important characters in *Mr. Mercedes*, and kept on growing in her leadership within *Finders Keepers* and *End of Watch*. And when we thought that was all, by next year, once again, we were reunited with Holly Gibney in one of the darkest books ever written by Stephen King: *The Outsider*. Did you think that was all? Wrong again. In those early days of the Covid pandemic, a new book by Stephen King hit the shelves. *If It Bleeds*, published in April 2020, featured four new novellas. The main one, the one that gave the book its title, featured a character we all knew very well by this time, a character that

most of us Constant Readers already adored, like Stephen King does: Holly Gibney. If It Bleeds is not a sequel to The Outsider, but it's in the same, dark, neighborhood as that book published in 2018, and I could not have embraced it more. In those tough days, a familiar voice such as Stephen King's made me feel better. I liked Holly Gibney (a lot, actually) but If It Bleeds made me fall in love with her again, and I eagerly awaited for her return. Now, luckily, only three years have passed and Stephen King has brought her back in *Holly*, his new novel, published on September 5th, 2023. This book will be the first one where Holly Gibney is the main character of a novel and she surely deserves it.

Holly starts with an excerpt that was originally published by *Entertainment Weekly* (January 23, 2023). Jorge Castro, a university teacher of creative writing and Latin American Lit in an old city that's hasn't been kept up anymore but there are parts that are still pretty nice, and decides that the fine drizzle outside won't stop him from his evening's run. That turns out to be a mistake, the last one he'll ever make.

Jorge is missing and you know why but the rest of the world doesn't. Ten years pass by, we're in 2021, the world's population continues to move on, while surviving Covid's pandemic, and a desperate woman named Penny Dahl calls Finders Keepers, Holly Gibney's detective agency, seeking help to find her missing daughter. Holly isn't sure if she should pick up the case. Her mother just passed away and she needs to stop and think about her future. But there's something in

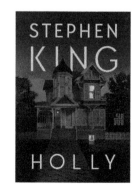

Penny's voice that makes her decide to help her. As she'll soon discover, Jorge and Bonnie Dahl are not the only persons gone missing in this area during the last few years.

Not far from the place where Bonnie was seen for the last time, are where married octogenarian Professors, Rodney and Emily Harris, live. They are semi-retired academics and well respected... however... no one knows about the secret they keep in the basement of their big house filled with books, a secret that might be related to Bonnie's disappearance.

Now take another look at the cover art. It begins to make more sense, doesn't it?

When Stephen King started working on this story, he didn't have the plot in mind but just one very clear scene: Holly Gibney, her mother's passing, the Covid pandemic and the best friend we had in 2020 and 2021: the Zoom app. He started writing the story with that scene in his mind without knowing what else was going to happen but sure that he'd unveil and discover what lay ahead. The answer soon arrived when he read a tabloid's headline that I won't divulge here but would have probably made me sick and smile at the same time. From that moment on, the story was clear in King's mind.

We know Holly; we saw her grow, evolve and improve through her adventures. And while her previous appearances showed us the most important aspects of her personality and life, there were questions in her life, and Stephen King answered several of them in this novel. Through the 464 pages there are parts of her story that act as interludes between those disappearances she investigates, and I found those pauses necessary because, if not, I'd not been able to put the book down. I consider The Outsider one of Stephen King's darkest books, one of those that shows us that while he got a little perceptive after surviving his terrible accident, he still could have fun while scaring us, but this one goes a lot deeper. There are chapters in Holly that made me feel physically sick, where I said out loud "Come on, Stephen. You can't be such an as*hole with ***** (a character I won't name). I had to face that awful feeling of inevitable loss that King knows how to present so well (and that we hate so much).

But not everything is bleak and dark: darkness can also make us grin. One thing is for sure about *Holly*: Stephen King had fun writing it. He clearly enjoyed those passages with Rodney and Emily, with their conversations and plans, with health issues knocking on the door of their Victorian house every now and then. Politics are also present. Yes, you're going to meet characters against vaccination, masks, and Trump supporters. Stephen King has always had strong opions about politics, since his college days, you may not like some of these passages, but it's obvious that Stephen King had fun writing those parts of the story as well.

The Holly Gibney Universe (yeah, we can use that term from now on. Six books allows us) also brings back other characters from previous tales. Some earned more space, like Barbara, and other stories were not relevant in *Holly*, such as Jerome's. Their fathers are barely mentioned and that's okay. Every single character in *Holly* has the perfect space and that's not a surprise. Stephen King has been a master creating characters since the 70s. Be aware that there are "spoilers" from all previous Holly Gibney appearances in *Holly*, so bear that in mind before reading this novel.

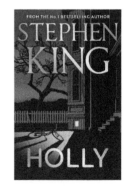

Last but not least is that this book is just *demanding* a Stephen King adaptation. A movie adaptation might be a better fit but if someone wants to expand the plot and characters, a streaming series would be as great. But please, nothing that's below a Mature rating. This story deserves its darkness to be respected.

Stephen King is about to turn 76 and he's still on top of his game. *Holly* is, once again, a perfect example that he's hit his target, dead center.

2023

The major King event in 2023 was the release of *Holly*, a crime novel involving an elderly couple who, every three years or so, kidnap someone and then…well, I won't go into the gruesome details of what they

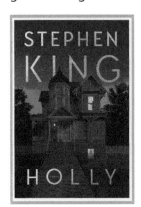

do next. The novel is set in the middle of the pandemic. Holly Gibney, a self-confessed hypochondriac, loses her Covid-denying mother to the disease and her partner, Pete Huntley, is also out of commission because of the virus although, thanks to his vaccinated status, he's faring somewhat better. The novel reflects the sociopolitics of the period, as well as being a bang-up "whydunit." Justine Lupe, who played Holly in the *Mr. Mercedes* series, read the audiobook. A few weeks before it was released in September, King took to YouTube to read a passage. Molly, the Thing of Evil, made a cameo appearance in this video.

This was a rare year with no short story

publications from King. None yet, at least.

Centipede Press's lovely hardcover edition of *The Long Walk* was released this year. I wrote the book's introduction and signed a couple of editions.

Stephen and Tabitha King were the keynote speakers at a Maine Library Association fundraiser in May, discussing their role as authors, philanthropists, and library advocates. The audio recording of their interview can be found online. King participated in an hour-long interview on the *Talking Scared* podcast in August, which was both interesting and informative, about which, more later.

This was different—King took on the role of "agony aunt," doling out advice in response to questions from readers of *Slate's* "Dear Prudie" column. He took his job seriously, without a hint of a wink or a nudge. He also penned a brief tribute to Cormac McCarthy after that author's death and reviewed S.A. Cosby's novel *All the Sinners Bleed* for *The New York Times*.

The umpteenth film based on "Children of the Corn" hit theaters briefly in March, switching to digital rentals later that same month. There isn't enough popcorn on the planet to get me to watch that one.

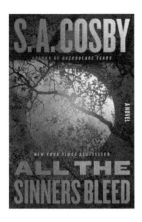

The Boogeyman was originally slated to be released directly to Hulu. The studio had a change of heart after positive test-screening response and decided to put it out in theaters in June. Based on the change and the trailer, it looked promising, but the early reviews were scathing and the film died a quick death. I watched it when it showed up on Hulu and was pleasantly surprised. It has a good backstory, great performances and is effectively creepy.

I always find it interesting to review my essay from the previous year, particularly the list of "forthcoming" projects. Last year, I itemized nine possible adaptations of which exactly one has come to fruition: *Pet Sematary: Bloodlines*, the prequel film that launched on Paramount+ in early October (which I disliked intensely). Thanks to the WGA and SAG strikes, the latter of which is still ongoing as of this writing, all productions have come to a screeching halt, which means we might not see many adaptations for a while. It makes me wonder how bad the *'Salem's Lot* feature film has to be that Warner Bros has refused to even

make it available on streaming.

King on Screen, the documentary in which directors of adaptations of King's work are interviewed, had a limited run in theaters before hitting OnDemand and physical media release in early September.

The opening section is for fans of Easter eggs. The seven-minute segment features over 300 objects and references to King's work.

Brian Keene and Christopher Golden are editing an original anthology of stories based on *The Stand*. The book will be called *The End of the World as We Know It: Tales of Stephen King's The Stand*. Contributors include: Josh Malerman, Paul Tremblay, Richard Chizmar, S. A. Cosby, Tananarive Due, Alma Katsu, Caroline Kepnes, Michael Koryta, Scott Ian, Joe R. Lansdale, Maurice Broaddus and Wayne Brady, Bryan Smith, Somer Canon, Hailey Piper, Jonathan Janz and me! King will write an introduction for the anthology.

2024

For most of last year, we had no news about what would follow *Holly*. Then, in his appearance on the *Talking Scared* podcast, King revealed details about forthcoming publications and what he was currently working on.

The next book will be *You Like It Darker*, a title that summons to mind the Leonard Cohen song "You Want It Darker." King says the book is a collection of stories, mostly longer and mostly new, and says it's about 600 pages long. We can probably expect to see some of his recent, uncollected stories in it. He wanted to include a poem, but his publisher didn't agree. During the podcast, King described a story called "The Dreamer" in detail. It was inspired by both Lovecraft and Cormac McCarthy, who he was reading at the time, and it sounds positively creepy. I wouldn't be surprised to find "Rattlesnake" in this book, too, the novella King calls a sequel to *Cujo*, but that's just speculation on my part.

At the time of the podcast, King said he was working on a long novel called *We Think Not* that features Holly Gibney but also a large

THE GUNSLINGER

Box lately, but it's something we might see in 2024. Most of the recent movie/TV news is about things that won't be happening. For example, André Øvredal said that he is no longer attached to direct an adaptation of *The Long Walk*. The writer's room was working on *Welcome to Derry* for Max, but that ground to a halt because of the strikes. Mike Flanagan had completed his script for *Life of Chuck* before the writer's strike, but the actor strike meant it couldn't go into production. However, there were reports filming was to begin on October 16, coupled with a call for hundreds of extras.

Theo James was announced as the lead in *The Monkey*, adapted and directed by Osgood Perkins, but that is presumably stalled, too. Although previously announced as a limited series, *Billy Summers* was acquired by Warner Bros., possibly as a project for J.J. Abrams to direct and Leonardo DiCaprio to star in. Rob Savage revealed he is considering remaking *The Langoliers*, although there are issues with the rights. Mike Flanagan is still talking about adapting *The Dark Tower* series and seems enthusiastic about the project, but nothing can happen until the SAG strike is settled.

cast of other characters. He set the internet on fire when he said he has a third Talisman novel in his active file, although he has not begun work on it and may never. Before Peter Straub died, he sent King a long letter with a cool idea for the book.

I haven't heard anything about Brian Keene's graphic novel adaptation of *Gwendy's Button*

So, unlike in recent articles, I don't have a bulleted list of properties that have been acquired but will probably never go into production. All that popcorn is going to get stale if you're saving it for the next King adaptation, alas.

ON THE SET: *The Mist*

L to R: Mist actor Sam Witwer with author David Schow

L to R: Chris Hewitt (*Empire Magazine* UK), author Bev Vincent, actor Johnathon Schaech, and Cemetery Dance's Rich Chizmar.

STEPHEN KING

2025 ANNUAL

STEPHEN KING ON TOUR!

WOULD **YOU** LIKE TO APPEAR IN **THE 2025 ANNUAL!?**

The 2025 Annual theme is **Stephen King on Tour**. Have you seen Stephen King at a reading? A bookstore signing? Did you see the *Rock Bottom Remainders* Tour? Maybe you've met him at a Red Sox game or on a film set? We're looking for anyone that would like to write 500 words or less and / or any photos you might like to share (with notes on the photos). Everyone who responds will **receive a special gift set we've created exclusively** for this participation. If you are published in the 2025 edition you will receive a free copy of the *2025 Stephen King Annual!* E-mail us at **ServiceOverlook@gmail.com** for more details or go ahead and send your written piece, and any high-rez scans of your photos. I'm looking forward to your exciting stories! – **Dave Hinchberger**

Written and Edited by Dave Hinchberger
Also features Artwork by Glenn Chadbourne

Coming Fall 2024

Available to order at
StephenKingCatalog.com

Published by
Overlook Connection Press

The Monkey (2023)
Spencer Sherry's Dollar Baby

by **Anthony Northrup**

Anthony Northrup has taken on the herculean task of keeping track of all the Stephen King "Dollar Baby" films. Stephen King began the tradition of giving permission, at the contract cost of one dollar, for filmmakers to create a film based on his fiction. These films cannot be sold in any media format and can only be shown at film festivals, etc. Northrup's first book, Stephen King Dollar Baby: The Book, *is now available, with a second edition almost completed, taking an in-depth look at each film and the filmmakers. This year's review of* The Monkey *is the first in a series of Dollar Baby films for the Stephen King Annual, and his input in this area is invaluable for Stephen King fans and we're glad to have him on board in this capacity. – Dave Hinchberger, Editor.*

When it comes to demonic dolls in cinema one thinks of Annabelle, Puppet Master, 'Talking Tina' from the old *Twilight Zone* episode...and more. However, leave it to the "Master of Horror", Stephen King, to bring his own take on an evil doll (of sorts) to life. In 1980 he brought us one of his most terrifying tales ever..."The Monkey"!

Spencer Sherry has done what no other "Dollar Baby" filmmaker has ever done before. He was persistent enough to get Stephen

King's office to approve a Dollar Baby short film adaptation of, "The Monkey." This film was not on the approved list of short stories to adapt, but with King's blessings, Spencer brought his vision of this nightmare to life on the big screen in 2023. Spencer Sherry is a filmmaker who hails from New York, and we hope to see many more fine films from him in the future.

The Monkey...
Stephen King's terrifying nightmare of a story, "The Monkey" was first published in *Gallery* Magazine, in 1980. It was later published in King's short story collection, *Skeleton Crew*, in 1985. This story is about an evil cursed toy monkey, a doll if you will, found in the attic in an old chest by two brothers, Peter, and Dennis, at their uncle's house. The story

surrounds their father, Hal, who first discovered the monkey years before, and it was cursed. Soon Hal himself feels cursed, as those near him begin dying. He eventually gets rid of the toy monkey by throwing it down a well at his uncle's house, but later it again shows up. This time Hal goes to Crystal Lake where he throws the monkey in the water, believing that this is the end of it. Not long after a local newspaper runs an article of fish mysteriously dying in Crystal Lake, and so the story continues...

In Spencer Sherry's film version of King's short story, Pete (Peter from King's story) is now married. He and his wife are about to have their first child. Pete has been having recurring nightmares of a deadly toy monkey since his childhood. Meanwhile, his father is on the verge of death, and is also having these same nightmares. Pete's brother, Dennis, who has been estranged for years, still refuses to make amends with their dying father. Pete is left with the task of changing that, and is also set on putting an end to these hellish nightmares... once and for all.

To find out what happens in this great film adaptation of King's short story, I urge you to look for a short film festival near you that also features Dollar Baby Films. Or you can pick up

my first book *Stephen King Dollar Baby: The Book* and read about many great Dollar Baby films available to view at fan film fests. My second book *Stephen King Dollar Baby: The Sequel* will be published soon by Bear Manor Media press and available at **StephenKingCatalog.com**, and online through many fine booksellers. This new volume will feature a full biography of Spencer Sherry, an in-depth interview, and complete film review as well.

For now, to whet your appetite, here's a little of what Spencer had to say about his decision to choose "The Monkey" as his Dollar Baby short film production.

AN: Let's talk about your Stephen King Dollar Baby film, *The Monkey*. This particular short story wasn't available for a long time on the Dollar Baby film list. How, and why did you pick this terrifying tale?

SS: Well, I picked it mostly because I thought it *was* on the list. I'd read that quote from him talking about how any, and all, of his short stories were up for grabs for the program and never bothered to check to see if that was still the case. When I read it, I immediately knew it was the story I wanted to take a swing at.

I definitely lean more towards creep than gore when it comes to horror, and the narrative device of "The Monkey" perfectly lends itself to the type of suspense I try to write into scripts. I lean heavily into this cursed entity

being a stand-in for the inevitable, and the fear of it that we all share. I also really love a good drama, and the way King incorporates these themes about fatherhood and favoritism really made this something that I thought was deeper and more meaningful than a lot of the other dollar baby stories.

AN: Which film festivals so far has *The Monkey* played at?

SS: Two. As I write this, we're headed up to

our most exciting showing so far: The Magic Lantern Theatre in Bridgton, Maine (ironically the town where *The Mist* takes place – Ed.) where *The Shining* premiered in 1980. It takes time to get into festivals, so we've been doing a grassroots tour of it; screening it locally and all-over Upstate New York, showing it at whatever venue is interested. Probably the biggest so far was at the Malta Drive-In. To see it on the huge screen in that nostalgic environment was such a surreal experience. The crowd was great, and the reception was overwhelmingly positive. Some of my favorite compliments have been that the film perfectly captures the tone and themes of a Stephen King story, and that "it's like, a *real* movie!" I think I'm most proud when people watch it and realize the quality is that of a big budget film. In general, though, everyone that's seen it has been extremely impressed and supportive, and tell me it left them wanting more.

To enjoy a more in-depth look at Spencer Sherry's short film *The Monkey*, as well as the more extensive interview, please look for a copy of *Stephen King Dollar Baby: The Sequel*, by Anthony Northrup, coming soon.

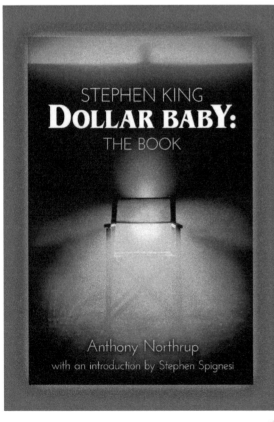

Stephen King Dollar Baby: The Book

by **Anthony Northrup**
Introduction by **Stephen Spignesi**

In the late 1970s, Stephen King had the idea of selling his short stories for one dollar and a contract to let young filmmakers make their own films based on his works. For the last forty-plus years and over hundreds of films made, with King's approval.

In this book, readers will learn all about the Dollar Baby program, fun facts, trivia, personal stories from the fans themselves, special guests contributors, essays, Where Are They Now?, 55 exclusive interviews with the Dollar Baby filmmakers and reviews of their films, and a whole lot more!

Available at **StephenKingCatalog.com**

We invite you to join author Marsha DeFilippo and her unique mysteries of the paranormal Cozy Quilts Club!

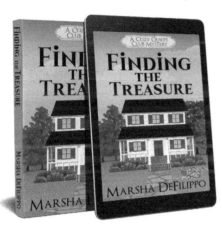

When four friends start the Cozy Quilts Club, the last thing they expect to be discussing at their meetings is their paranormal abilities. Even less likely — using them to find a killer. Follow Eva, Annalise, Jennifer, and Sarah as they stitch together quilts and clues to solve crimes.

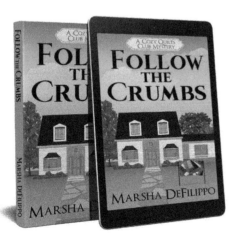

After retiring from her day job of nearly 33 years as Stephen King's personal assistant, Marsha DeFilippo has embarked on a new career of writing mystery novels. She is also a quilter and lifelong avid crafter who has yet to try a craft she doesn't like. She spends her winters in Arizona and the remainder of the year in Maine.

King's Garbage Truck

by *Tyson Blue*

During his four years as a student at the University of Maine at Orono, Stephen King continued moving his writing career forward. In 1966, he wrote the first half of *Rage*, the first of the Richard Bachman books. The following year, *Startling Mystery Stories* published his first professionally-sold short story, "The Glass Floor", and he completed *The Long Walk*, the second Bachman book. In 1968, King began a novel about a race riot, *Sword in the Darkness* (or *Babylon Here*), and the short stories "Cain Rose Up" and "Here There Be Tigers", "Strawberry Spring", and the poem, "Harrison State Park '68".

This trend continued in 1969, King's junior year, with the publication of "The Reaper's Image" in *Startling Mystery Stories* reprinted in *Skeleton Crew*, while UMO's literary magazine, *Ubris*, published "Night Surf", a precursor of *The Stand*, later reprinted in *Night Shift*, "Stud City", which was incorporated into the novella *The Body*, published in the 1982 collection *Different Seasons* as a Gordie LaChance story, and "The Dark Man", a poem published in book form in 2013 by Cemetery Dance Press.

Most of King's writing from February, 1969, until his graduation in 1970, was two bodies of work written for UMO's campus newspaper, *The Maine Campus*. There were two series of columns —"King's Garbage Truck" (February 20, 1969, to May 21, 1970) and an eight-part Western spoof called "Slade" (June to August, 1970).

One reason these columns have not more widely read is that they have not been widely available. In 2016, King allowed the University of Maine Press to publish four of the columns in *Hearts in Suspension*, a book dealing with King's college experiences, that should be enough to get readers to pick up this most interesting book.

The "Garbage Truck" columns gave King a chance to hone his skills of writing on more general subjects, covering a plethora of subjects from media reviews to philosophical ruminations, as well as the evolution of a writer's persona.

Reading the "Garbage Truck" columns with this in mind, it is relatively easy to see King already evolving this conversational style that makes readers feel more comfortable with him.

An example — in the March 26, 1970 column (#42), King is talking about some of his ideas for improving things around UMO that have occurred to him while he had been student teaching:

"Yeah, yeah", some guy is yelling from the balcony.

'But what about the drip who would never get out of his rut if you didn't force him to? If you leave off requirements, the idea of a liberal education goes right down the drain.' The guy from the balcony is wrong."

(Stephen King, "King's Garbage Truck", *The Maine Campus*, March 26, 1970, p.5)

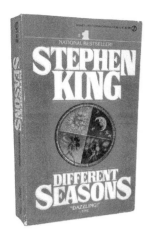

And now, this, from the "Afterword" to *Different Seasons*: Subtract elegance from the author's craft and one finds himself left with only one good leg to stand on, and that leg is good weight. As a result, I've tried as hard as I can, always, to give good weight.

Put another way, if you find out you can't run like a thoroughbred, you can still pull your brains out (a voice rises from the balcony: "What brains, King? Ha-ha, very funny, you can leave now.

(Stephen King, "Afterword," *Different Seasons* (Signet Edition), p. 504.)

In both excerpts, King uses the device of dealing with a fictitious heckler from the balcony to give a humorous twist to what he is saying and to get his point across.

Not that King can't put on an attitude with the best of them. When King turns to reviewing films, he can wipe on his all-knowing film-reviewer's cloak with amazing skill, as in his February 26, 1970 review of the George Kennedy film *Tick…Tick…Tick…* a review which would have done Siskel and Ebert (two prominent film-reviewers of the day) proud (Column # 40).

But when there are holes in his omniscience, it can trip him up. For example, in one column (February 19, 1970, #39), King talks about the film *Frankenstein Meets the Werewolf*, with Boris Karloff and Lon Chaney, jr. King appears to have been lucky, since there is no record that anyone at UMO ever noticed that the film was actually called *Frankenstein Meets the Wolf Man*, and that it starred not Karloff (who is not in the picture) but Bela Lugosi as the

Frankenstein Monster (no amount of makeup could hide that famous nose!) after playing Ygor in the two previous films in the series, *Son of Frankenstein* (Karloff's final bow as the Monster) and *The Ghost of Frankenstein* (in which Lon Chaney Jr. played the Monster), before going on to play the Wolf Man in next film.

But such lapses in doing one's homework are understandable — this is, after all, a college newspaper, and not *The New York Times* — and at that time, access to these films was limited to late-night movie shows, as opposed to the DVD and Blu-ray sets of the entire Universal Monster library available today. This is probably one reason why King is somewhat embarrassed by some of these early columns, and remains reluctant to see them appear in a mass-market edition. What is most significant about the "Garbage Truck" columns in the long run are those columns which, one way or another, give hints or motifs or ideas which show up in his later, published work.

In Column #34, which appeared on December 18, 1969, King described a number of strange things that have happened in the world.

Among them are the disappearances of Judge Crater and Ambrose Bierce, an image which resonates through King's short story "The Reaper's Image", already published in *Startling Mystery Stories* by the time this column ran. Another powerful image appears in the same column:

"In the early 1800s, the Shakers, a rather strange religious persuasion at best, disappeared from their village (Jeremiah's Lot) in Vermont. The town remains uninhabited to this day."
(Stephen King, "King's Garbage Truck", *The Maine Times*, December 18, 1969, p.6)

It's not hard to agree with Collings that this incident served as a foundation for both King's short story "Jerusalem's Lot" and his second published novel, 'Salem's Lot. If nothing else, the similarity in the names of the Shaker village and King's fictional town would bear this out, along with the deserted status of both towns, not so much for the stories already mentioned, as it is in the short story "One For The Road," which was, like "Jerusalem's Lot," collected in Night Shift.

In the same paragraph with King's description of the desertion of Jeremiah's Lot is another vignette of a nightmare King had on the night a friend died in a car accident:

"I dreamed of a hideous man with a scarred face hanging from a black gibbet against a green sky. The incident sticks in my mind because the hanged man was wearing a card around his neck bearing this friend's name. I woke with the sweaty premonition that on the night before I kicked off I would dream the dream again, only this time the card would bear my name."

This story connects with a scene in 'Salem's Lot wherein Ben Mears says:

"No, I'm telling you the truth," he insisted. "The truth of what a nine-year-old boy saw and what the man remembers twenty-four years later, anyway. Hubie was hanging there, and his face wasn't black at all. It was green. The eyes were puffed shut. His hands were livid...ghastly. And then he opened his eyes."
(Stephen King, 'Salem's Lot, Signet Edition , p.29)

The hanged man dream resonates powerfully with the image of Hubie Marston hanging in the Marston House, a connection also suggested by King in interviews from time to time.

This same column also discusses Shirley Jackson's novel The Haunting of Hill House, whose premise of living houses reflecting the evil which goes on within them King took for his own in The Shining. And in this same essay are found two images, one of a rain of frogs over Oklahoma in 1936, and another of a 1964 incident in which a Long Island family were forced to leave their home after being pelted with flying bottles, ashtrays, vases and stereos, the last of which was flung at one of the family's teenage daughters — which will not seem unfamiliar to anyone who recalls the rain of stones Carrie White brought down on her house as a child or the telekinetic displays that take place in the early chapters of King's first novel.

More than any of the others, this column proves the importance to King scholars of the "Garbage Truck" columns. In this single example alone are found major ideas that suggest importance foundation stones for King's first three novels.

Another column conjures up images which resonate powerfully in a number of King's fictional works. The "snow" column (#41), which ran on March 19, 1970, reprints a letter King had written a year before and never sent, detailing some of the "strange thoughts" set off in his head by a heavy winter storm. Of particular importance is the image of a group of twenty people stranded by the snow in The Den, a local hangout.

At first, the atmosphere is festive, but as the windows white out and pale tendrils of snow intrude into the place, and ice fingers rattle around the windows, the "gayness...slowly (changes) to sobriety, sobriety to solemnity, solemnity to silence". The power fails, and soon all is still.

For me, this article suggests the basic elements of The Mist.

A couple of the columns bear on themes addressed in The Bachman Books as well. Column #3, published March 6, 1969, deals with network television, and with game shows in particular. King argues that most of the game shows then available on the tube were geared strictly to a young audience, and offered several suggestions for game shows aimed at an older crowd. Among them were such gems as "The Brutality Game", where Chicago policemen are pitted against a studio audience of young people, and "The Burial Game", in which living and dead contestants are teamed up in a race to the grave.

The bizarre games suggested in this column reflected some of the equally bizarre and brutal games that were being televised in the future-world of *The Long Walk* and *The Running Man*, and also presages some of the bizarre games shows which appear in the expanded version of *The Stand*, as well as the uncompleted online serial novel *The Plant*.

In the May 15, 1969 (#12) column, an account of King's participation in the March To End The War, King describes how his fellow marchers are vilified, beaten and pelted with eggs, with the word "ugly" appearing between paragraphs as an ongoing motif. It is a well-written, impassioned column, one of the columns King permitted to be included in *Hearts In Suspension*.

There is a subtext to the article as well, dealing with a group of people marching down a road, surrounded by a hostile crowd, not knowing where they are going or what is going to happen to them. It echoes *The Long Walk*. Since the novel was completed in 1967, it may have suggested the subtext for this column, rather than vice-versa.

Another strong narrative column also details one of King's experiences as a political activist. Column #44 (April 16. 1970) begins with King's account of a confrontation with a little old lady while handing out flyers before a free-speech rally. The old charmer "let the flyer fall

to the floor, and grated 'I don't want anything from you, you scummy radical bastard.'" The column goes on into a consideration of King's personal political beliefs, from the perspective of a conservative Republican in the process of being alienated by Richard Nixon.

Many of the columns concern lists — favorite films, favorite books, favorite people — and they are important not just as precursors to King's radio "Lists That Matter" — but for other reasons. They indicate King's broad-based interest in the things that make up our popular culture, one of the key elements that helps to make his writing accessible to so many people.

The last two columns are interesting for the picture they paint of King, just about to graduate, poised on the edge of adulthood, looking back to assess "Where We Are At" in Column #46 and forward to "march(ing) along with the Class of '70 into the Outside World, shining of eye (as long as I'm not hung over), noble of countenance, a smile on my lips, joy in

Stephen King speaking against the War in Vietnam from the Fogler Library steps, May 1969. Photograph from the 1969 University of Maine *Prism*, reproduced courtesy of Special Collections, the Raymond H. Fogler Library, University of Maine.

my heart, and a cigarette cough in my lungs."

The final "Garbage Truck" column is an announcement of King's "Birth" into the real world, giving an account of his name, real-world date of birth (June 5, 1970), physical description and favorite colors (blue, although recent assassinations and world events make black seem more in vogue), favorite films, university personalities, rock bands etc. He classes his future prospects as hazy, but states that he has shown "evidences of some talent, although at this point it is impossible to tell if he is just a flash in the pan or if he has real possibilities."

In his summation, King offers the following advice to his readers "before driving his garbage truck into the sunset…

1. Live peace.
2. Love a neighbor today.
3. If the Establishment doesn't like it, then screw 'em."

"King's Garbage Truck" is not easy to find. As stated before, they are available on microfilm at UMO, and although there has been talk of their someday being published by the university press, since they remain the property of UMO. But to date only four of the columns have seen print, in *Hearts In Suspension*.

These early "college papers" are not for everyone. For the King fan who enjoys horror and fantasy, they would be of marginal interest at best. But any King scholar worth his salt would be amply repaid by putting on his old clothes and work gloves and sifting deep into the payload section of "King's Garbage Truck".

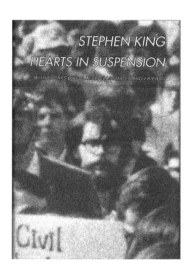

Author's Note: This material has appeared in slightly different form in *The Unseen King*, by Tyson Blue, originally published in 1989 by Starmont House, and subsequently by Borgo Press.

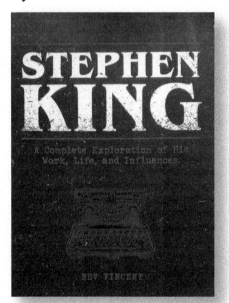

HEARTS IN SUSPENSION:
STEPHEN KING REMEMBERS A LOST ATLANTIS

This publication marks the 50th anniversary of Stephen King's entrance into the University of Maine at Orono in the fall of 1966. The accelerating war in Vietnam and great social upheaval at home exerted a profound impact on students of the period and deeply influenced King's development as a writer and as a man.

Features in *Hearts In Suspension*:

- Stephen King's original story of this experience in his novella "Hearts in Atlantis" is published here.

- In his accompanying essay, "Five to One, One in Five," written expressly for this volume, King sheds his fictional persona and takes on the challenge of a nonfiction return to his undergraduate experience.

- Twelve fellow students and friends from King's college days contribute personal narratives recalling their own experience of those years.

- This book also includes four installments of King's never-before-reprinted student newspaper column, "King's Garbage Truck." These lively examples of King's damn-the-torpedoes style, entertaining and shrewd in their youthful perceptions, more than hint at a talent about to take its place in the American literary landscape.

- A gallery of period photographs and documents augments this volume.

Hearts In Suspension is a unique and one-of-a-kind Stephen King publication.

First printing hardcover available at **StephenKingCatalog.com**

The New Lost Work of Stephen King

by *Stephen Spignesi*

What Stephen King is up to when he's not writing novels... A Look at 8 Uncollected Works

To the memory of Lady Sybil Crawley... (Yes, I'm a titanic (get it?) Downton Abbey *fan)*

A Note About *You Like It Darker*

In Fall 2023, Stephen King announced a new short story collection that would be released in 2024. The title is *You Like It Darker* (an honorific nod to the Leonard Cohen song "You Want It Darker" perhaps?) and we were told that it would be around 600 pages in length.

In November 2023, we learned the release date of the anthology—May 21, 2024—and the titles of the stories included.

I write about six of the *You Like It Darker* stories in "The New Lost Work of Stephen King," which was written for the *2023 Overlook Connection Annual*.

I was very careful to avoid spoilers of any kind in my reviews, so you should be able to read these reviews before the anthology comes out without being spoiled and getting mad at me and Dave.

Stephen King is prolific.

He writes a lot, and he has never limited himself to writing only the stuff he's best known for, i.e., Immense Novels.

The commercial book market being what it is, however, there is something of a marketing template for hugely popular authors like King: publish one, maybe two books a year. (And we're not talking about Stephen King movies. Those are second tier King, since, in the vast majority of cases, King doesn't write them. So changes made to the books for the films are not Canon.)

That said, the obvious question is, what else does Signore King write?

Well, short stories, book reviews, poems, and screenplays, for starters. (Although he's also written recipes, plays, Twitter posts, TV miniseries, cover blurbs, and more.)

This feature looks at eight pieces that are still uncollected: i.e., they have only appeared in the original publication, which was usually a magazine, literary journal, or a website, including King's own site. They're available, but may take a little hunting to find them.

• • •

One of the books I did about Stephen King's work is called The Lost Work of Stephen King.

And before I did that, when I was working on my Complete Stephen King Encyclopedia, the editor of this Annual, Dave Hinchberger, was at Ground Zero with me. During the development of both books, Dave was invaluable to me for sharing some very rare pieces from his collection.

I will never forget the day a copy of Stephen King's self-published, typed, short story collection *People, Places & Things* showed up in my PO box from Dave. At the time, that "anthology" of sorts was probably the rarest known King piece in existence. One original exists, and as you would assume, belongs to Stephen King.

Copies have circulated since its existence became known (King's secretary found it at the bottom of a pile of manuscripts kept in a safe).

But it is still "lost" because it has never been officially published.

And that's what makes "lost work" so important to fans: Unseen Stephen King is sought-after Stephen King.

Special thanks to the aforementioned ***Dave Hinchberger*** *for always understanding and recognizing the staggering interest in All Things King and supporting all of us who are always on the hunt.*

1. "Cookie Jar"
Virginia Quarterly Review, Spring 2016

***The Virginia Quarterly Review* is a literary journal**—an esteemed quarterly publication focused on poetry, fiction, book reviews, essays, photography, and comics by an array of writers.

Sounds grand, right? And also academic, right? So what are we talking about here? An *academic* literary journal that publishes Stephen King?

But wait a minute (*Sarcasm Alert!*): Stephen King is just a *horror* writer. What's he doing in a *literary* journal? He doesn't belong there, right?

Fucking *wrong*. (And as Chris Rock would say, "Yeah, I said it.")

As I and many others have been preaching for, oh, going on five decades now, Stephen King is an underrated, staggeringly talented

writer: He is an unquestionable literary force, and one who started young. He was in his twenties when he wrote the masterpiece *The Shining*, which was published in 1977.

Anyone who can write *The Shining* more than deserves a spot in a literary journal, which brings us to "Cookie Jar."

King has used a specific device or trope a few times in his work: *an elderly relative or friend tells stories to a kid*. And that's exactly what happens in "Cookie Jar." The kid is 13; great-grandpa is 90. This story also seems to foreshadow a similar structure in "Willie the Weirdo," which came out six years later, in 2022. (**Note:** *See the section on "Willie" below.*)

Thirteen-year-old Dale has a school assignment: talk to an elder family member about their past.

Dale brings his iPhone with him when he visits Great-Grandpop, who insists on being called Rhett. "I was a Rhett before there was a Rhett Butler—imagine that," he proclaims to Dale.

After Dale's estranged and somewhat unstable mother's death, her kids are allowed to take something from her house in her memory.

Dale takes the one thing his mother was afraid of: The blue cookie jar.

The blue cookie jar that never ran out of cookies, no matter how many you ate.

Great-Grandpop Rhett knows that the cookie jar is more than a container for cookies: it could very well be a portal. But how would one access it if the jar never emptied of cookies?

Rhett tells Dale how to peer into the other world of the cookie jar and the story ends with Rhett cautioning Dale to be careful, knowing that he won't, telling him, "You're on your own."

Is Dale doomed? Perhaps. Maybe not. Maybe we'll never know...

But if there's a story that warrants a sequel, it's "Cookie Jar."

Because I, for one, am dying to know what, if anything, will Dale do with the blue Cookie Jar?

2. Thin Scenery
Ploughshares, Summer 2017

I lie in bed at night and see headlines. MAN SLAYS WIFE AND DAUGHTER. Or how about "IT WAS OK BECAUSE THEY WEREN'T REAL," SAYS SUBURBAN PSYCHO—that one would sell some newspapers even in this day and age, don't you think?

What is real and what is delusion?

These are the questions Stephen King asks in his superb short play *Thin Scenery*, which appears in the Summer 2017 issue of *Ploughshares*.

I like *Thin Scenery* a lot, and it is the perfect production for a small theater group and high school and college productions.

What is real and what is delusion? These are the questions Stephen King asks in the play and, as he's particularly good at it, he establishes a reality, and then makes us question it. All of it.

Like, maybe that TV is something we can put our hand right through?

Or maybe that wall is cardboard? Or not even

there? But there's a picture hanging on it, isn't there?

Or maybe a child is not who her father believes she is?

This is a chilling, multiple viewpoint tale that literally makes you question who's the audience? And who are the actors? Who are the characters? And is the play even really happening?

Early on, the psychiatrist says, "There's a difference between perception, which is subjective, and empiric reality, which is not."

Yes. There certainly is.

3. "Laurie"
www.stephenking.com (May 17, 2018)

"It was life, you were stuck with it, and all you could do was live it."

This is a story about a man and his dog.

I mean, puppy. A man and his puppy.

Laurie is a dog. The main character Lloyd is a widower whose sister Beth gives him Laurie to help him navigate his grief.

But fear not: Yes, this is a humanistic fable about grief, love, mourning, etc., but it is also a Stephen King story, and this line from the tale hints at what goes on, sort of...

"The top of Don's head was pretty much gone."

Ah, there's the Uncle Stevie we know and love!

There is heartfelt emotion permeating "Laurie," particularly Lloyd's growing bond with his new puppy. But there is also gore galore... which is what happens when a character, y'know, is partially consumed by an alligator. Plus, there are moments that have a real *Jaws* feel to them.

"Laurie" is still uncollected, but is available to read for free on King's website:

stephenking.com/other/stephenking-laurie.pdf

One thing I came away with after reading "Laurie" is the certainty that it was written by an animal lover. King knows animals; he knows how to take care of them; he knows how they think; and he knows what they add to our lives.

King dedicated the story to "Vixen." After the story was published, King posted this on X, the Website Formerly Known as Twitter:

Several people have asked me about the dedication at the end of "Laurie," the story I posted. Vixen was my wife's dog. We all loved her, but she was a one-woman Corgi. A sweeter, gentler dog you'd never meet. She died early this spring.

4. "The Fifth Step"
Harper's (March 2020)

Do you avoid strangers?

Like, *really* avoid them?

Does any of this ring a bell? You will cross the street to avoid contact with someone, you don't go to gatherings of more than two or three people, you don't join anything, and you almost had a stroke when your Caller ID died and you actually had to answer the phone without knowing who was calling.

Sure, this approach to everyday living could be considered a psychopathy, but lots of people are neurotic enough that they'd never talk to a stranger unless it was unavoidable.

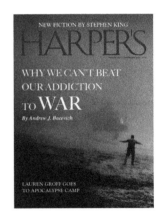

Whether or not you avoid strangers is a good question, because as Stephen King's short story "The Fifth Step" so aptly illustrates, sometimes even a conversation can turn a halcyonic park, complete with iconic park benches, into a crime scene.

"The Fifth Step" is not about walking and taking the step after your fourth. It is about addiction, and guilt, and mayhem, and the title refers to the "fifth step" of the AA program.

"The Fifth Step" could be titled "Autobiography of an Alkie," since the bulk of the story takes place on a park bench in Central

Park. An alcoholic stranger named Jack tells the main character Harold his story, in fulfillment of the aforesaid fifth step. At first, Jack offers Harold $20 to listen, but Harold declines and, somewhat reluctantly, gives Jack the go-ahead to tell his story.

Big mistake. As we soon learn.

Any more deets and we're in Spoiler World, so this is Spig signing off on this one!

5. "On Slide Inn Road"
Esquire (October/November 2020)

"Granpop," she says, "you left Aunt Nan's special baseball bat."
The woods are scary, dark and deep...

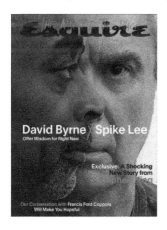

Well, shit, they *are*.

And so are the williwags—a word I learned from this story, thanks to Signore King (The williwags are the boondocks, the sticks, unpaved roads, gullies, trees, abandoned shacks, flooded foundations, etc.).

This story is without a doubt Klassic King. It has hints and tonal elements that remind us of *Deliverance* and even *Inglorious Bastards*. It has that SK mojo we all know and love.

We meet a family on a trip to visit an ailing aunt—Mom, Dad, kids, Granpop—and it isn't long before they all end up in peril.

Granpop is a piece of work and it is his fault the family, in his big-ass "dinosaur of a Buick station wagon," ends up stuck in a gully in the williwags, nearby a flooded foundation that may or may not have something horrible submerged in its depths.

The setup is simple: The son and his wife are pissed at Granpop for insisting on taking the Buick. If that wasn't bad enough, he also insisted they take a "shortcut," which doesn't show up on Google Maps—but it wouldn't have mattered even if it did show up. They had no phone service once they ended up "inland," so to speak.

The kids go exploring the grounds of the long-gone Slide Inn and find a truck with a flat next to the flooded foundation...and then something they can't believe they're actually seeing in the water...and then they meet Galen and Pete. Anyone familiar with King's work knows that these two knuckleheads are a "Yikes!" moment in the tale.

And then the real fun begins.

And it involves a signed baseball bat.

Again, any more details wander into spoiler territory, so we'll leave it at that.

6. "Red Screen"
Humble Bundle ebook (September 2021)

For a moment, no more than a second, the screen of his cell phone flashes red.

This nifty tale, originally published digitally by Humble Bundle in 2021, asks a question we actually can't answer, except within, y'know, the "gestalt" of fiction: What if *Invasion of the Body Snatchers* actually happens one day?

"Red Screen" starts in a detective's home on the morning he is scheduled to interview a guy who stabbed his wife three times in the stomach and killed her.

Our main character, Detective Wilson, has a wife who is...*prickly*: "you didn't put the toilet seat down," "you didn't put the cap back on the toothpaste," etc.

Considering his "at-home" circumstances, it is thus no surprise that Wilson, a classic detective archetype, is jaded, tired, fed up, bored and forgetful.

The killer, Leonard Crocker, has admitted he killed his wife, but it's not for any reasons Wilson could conceive, or even believe. Leonard claims he killed his wife because she had been taken over by an alien and was planning on killing him, and he knew that mankind was under attack as other people were similarly taken over...

...once their phones flashed a red screen.

The story wraps up later that night when Wilson and his wife are in bed.

Could Crocker be right?

Gee, I wonder whose phone shines red next?

7. "Finn"
Scribd (May 2022)

"Elvis has left the building."

This is how "Finn" was teased on King's website pre-publication:

> *In a new short story—characteristically propulsive, wickedly funny, with twists both narrative and literal—"Finn" points straight at our current struggle to differentiate between farce and experience and asks: can 50,000,000 Elvis fans be wrong?*

Finn Murrie—and he makes sure to emphasize that his last name ends with an "ie" not an "ay"—lives in Ireland and has always had bad luck.

As a child, he lost his left pinky toe when someone tossed a cherry bomb his way.

He once fell off the monkey bars at a park and broke his arm.

And once, a bolt of lightning struck the ground close enough to him to char a line down the back of his jacket. He fell and sustained a concussion.

And then, as we learn in "Finn," he was kidnapped and tortured because a psycho who was losing his mind believed he was someone else.

Maybe...

Did Finn's kidnapping and abuse actually take place? Or was it a delusion/hallucination/déjà vu experience that took place on the Twisty at Finn's favorite park?

As noted above, King's site describes Finn's story as something between "farce and experience." What's a farce? The Oxford definition prompts questions about the story...

> *A comic dramatic work using buffoonery and horseplay and typically including crude characterization and ludicrously improbable situations.*

"Comic?" "Ludicrously improbable situations?" Does this mean "Finn" is a comedic satirical story not to be taken seriously?

All good questions, brothers and sisters. The answers lie within. (The story, that is. Check it out.)

8. "Willie the Weirdo"
McSweeney's (May 31, 2022)

"Take a mouthful."

This is how "Willie the Weirdo" was teased on King's website pre-publication:

Willie, by most accounts, is a weirdo: the dead birds, the dead bugs, staring into space for hours. Luckily, there's another weirdo in the house: Grampa, sharing with Willie tales of war, blood, volcanoes, and destruction. In this new short story, Willie finds out if the weird inherit the earth—or something much darker.

"Willie the Weirdo" is a story about a grandson who inherits a... *gift* from his grandpa—James Jonas Fiedler—a guy who happens to be a real piece of work. Granpop is another King classic old guy. a cynical, curmudgeonly type who claimed to have fought for the Confederates in the Civil War, which ended in 1865.

But is what the grandson ultimately receives actually a gift? Or could it be a curse?

Stephen King is one of the greatest short fiction writers of all time. Raymond Carver, Shirley Jackson, Ernest Hemingway, Edgar Allan Poe, Anton Chekhov...King deserves a spot on any list that purports to chronicle the greatest writers in the genre.

I am a fan of everything Stephen King writes (except for the baseball stuff—not interested enough in the sport for prose about it to hold my attention) and on a scale, my adulation of

his work would probably put his short stories at the top, followed by the novellas, and then the novels.

"Willie the Weirdo" has the Stephen King mojo—that "King of Horror" vibe—in spades. "Willie the Weirdo" offers stylistic, structural, and tonal nods to *The Green Mile* and *My Pretty Pony*. Maybe "Gramma" too? It is also notable that King's short story voice hasn't really changed all that much since the early *Night Shift* days.

As the Teaser tells us, Willie is weird as all get-out—He's in the Remedial, after all, as his nasty sister Roxie continually reminds people—but Grandpa? He's a foul piece of work who definitely seems to be more than what everyone sees on the surface.

Is Grandpa eternal? Is his soul evil? What happens when Grandpop bequeaths a "mouthful" of his dying essence into Willie?

King leaves the story open-ended, in the sense that we don't know the answers to those questions at the end of the story...but we can make a pretty good guess as to what might happen.

Let's give a tortured weirdo eternal powers that can likely be used for good or evil...what could go wrong, right?

EXTREME KING

Diana Petroff

Noah Mitchell

DARK FORCES
SKELETON CREW

Welcome to a brand new and exciting column in which we discuss and explore the rarest and most sought-after works of Stephen King. *The Stephen King 2024 Annual* theme is "The Mist", which first appeared in 1980 within *Dark Forces* and was subsequently collected for *Skeleton Crew* in 1985 along with twenty-one other stories. Join us in looking at the original appearances of these stories, poems, and novellas, as well as the limited editions of *Skeleton Crew*.

The collected works in *Skeleton Crew* were written over a period of seventeen years, published in many formats, and, like most Constant Readers, we first discovered them all in one place when Putnam released *Skeleton Crew*.

The book was released as a limited edition in two states: first by Scream Press in 1985 and again by PS Publishing in 2015. *Dark Forces*, which included the first appearance of "The Mist", was also released as a limited edition by Lonely Road in 2007, twenty-six years after first appearing as a trade hardcover in the US and UK.

Skeleton Crew was the first King book that I purchased upon release as a book collector in 1985. I had been a Stephen King fan for several years and had recently decided to upgrade all of my paperback reading copies to hardcovers so that they looked nicer on my shelf. I remember buying two copies of *Skeleton Crew* on release day at the local B. Dalton: one to read and one to collect.

– Noah Mitchell

As a long-time lover of King's short works, I recall picking up the trade paperback of *Skeleton Crew* at a local used book store. I read that book until it was falling apart at the seams. When I began serious collecting, one of the first signed limited editions I purchased was the signed numbered edition from Scream Press. The additional content and artwork from J.K. Potter is legendary.

– Diana Petroff

Let's take a step into our vault and take a closer look, shall we?

US Trade Publication, Putnam 1985 Issued with a dust jacket and price of $18.95. First printings will state
1 2 3 4 5 6 7 8 9 10
on the copyright page.

Limited edition hardcover of 1,000 numbered and 52 lettered copies, signed in silver ink by author and artist, with slipcase (numbered state) and laid-in print by the artist. This edition includes King's "The Revelations of 'Becka Paulson," which is unique to both this release and the PS Publishing limited editions. There were also 25 zippered copies not signed by King, of which 8 were offered for sale.

One of the most unique designs in the lettered Stephen King market is the leather-bound zippered "portfolio" case that is debossed with a skeleton on the front cover. The lettered state is a legendary production among collectors and remains one of the most difficult lettered Stephen King editions to locate on the secondary market. The interior art is by JK Potter, and includes a laid-in 3-page poster - issue price of $75. There is also an accompanying art portfolio which could be purchased separately

UK Trade Publication, MacDonald 1985 UK jacket price is £9.95. Copyright page has no indication of edition or printing.

The Scream Press edition was originally scheduled to be published before the US trade edition by Putnam. The copyright page of the Putnam trade edition states, "A limited first edition of this book has been published by Scream Press."

DEBUNKED! The urban legend about *Skeleton Crew* putting Scream Press out of business is false. In 1985, Scream Press also released an omnibus edition of Clive Barker's *The Books of Blood* (Volumes 1 – 3). This was followed in 1991 by the release of the remaining three volumes in individual signed numbered slipcased editions. Scream Press was still around six years after supposedly closing its doors due to a delay in releasing *Skeleton Crew*.

Skeleton Crew - PS Publishing Anniversary Edition 2015

A lettered edition of 26 copies, signed by Stephen King, Pete Von Sholly and Stephen Jones. Housed in a foil stamped traycase. Pete Von Sholly (who produced storyboards for Frank Darabont's movie adaption of *The Mist*, see his interview in this edition) provided artwork for each story plus covers, slipcases and endpapers, along with 26 pieces of original signed artwork, with one included with each copy of the lettered state. Issue price of £2,295

A numbered edition of 974 copies. Housed in a slipcase with full wraparound artwork. The book was released with two variants of the dust jacket (an unpublished third jacket had been rejected, but makes its first appearance in this 2024 Annual!). It Includes a facsimile signature by King as well as actual signatures by Pete Von Sholly and Stephen Jones. This anniversary edition also includes the additional story "The Revelations of Becka Paulson." Issue price of £59.99

PS Publishing is active on fan forum sites, and does a great job of listening to their customers. Initial feedback to the first dust jacket design was not very positive. So, PS went back and designed a second jacket. The decision was made that anyone who requested the original design during pre-ordering would get it. Otherwise, they would get the new "uncluttered" design. It is believed that there are 100 - 200 copies with the original artwork from Sholly.

Note on the Lettered: The lettered state of PS's limited was published in a print run of 26 copies and is the only state signed by King. PS sells their lettered editions via a rights system; therefore, only collectors who purchased the previous lettered edition directly from the publisher had rights to *Skeleton Crew*. It is thus also quite difficult to acquire on the secondary market, as most collectors have retained their copies.

Dark Forces - 1980 - 1st Trade Editions - contain "The Mist"

When McCauley began to assemble a collection with supernatural works for his anthology, he approached many authors, including Stephen King. King began work on an idea he had had the previous year. What started out as a short story of a few thousand words grew into a novella of over 40,000 words and became what we all know and love: "The Mist."

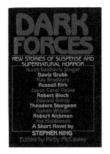

Dark Forces - US 1st edition Viking Press - 1980 : Issue price of $16.95
From the US edition of *Skeleton Crew* (Putnam): "Thanks to Kirby McCauley, my agent, another Irishman who sold most of these, and who pulled the longest of them, 'The Mist', out of me with a chain fall."

Dark Forces - UK 1st edition - MacDonald - 1980 : Issue price of £6.95

Dark Forces - Lonely Road Books - The 25th Anniversary Special Edition 2006

Lettered edition: 26 copies, with all the special features of the limited edition, plus a different type of high-quality binding, a full-color dust jacket with a different design than the numbered edition, all housed in a custom-made deluxe traycase featuring a special magnetic latch. Issue price of $750.

Numbered edition: 300 copies, signed by the editor and artists on an illustrated signature page, bound in a deluxe material, with full-color and black & white interior illustrations, a full-color dust jacket, all housed in a custom-made traycase featuring a special magnetic latch. Issue price of $200. Includes an interview with editor Kirby McCauley in which he discussed the popularity and importance of the book with Kealan Patrick Burke. This special bonus addition to the Lonely Road Books edition of Dark Forces has never been printed anywhere else. Originally intended to be released in 2006, this publication was delayed until 2007.

Ubris - University of Maine literary magazine - Spring 1968 - contains "Here There Be Tygers" and "Cain Rose Up"

Ubris was one of the University of Maine's literary magazines. There were four issues (1968-69) that contained King fiction. All four of these are among the most difficult of all publications that contain original King fiction to find, as likely 99% of the copies printed were discarded by college students either immediately or following graduation. Close to sixty years later, it's doubtful that more than a dozen to 20 copies of these remain in circulation; perhaps not even that many.

Ubris has no issue price, it may have been a free publication for the University of Maine's community. It was published by the students two times during the academic year.

Gallery Magazine - "The Monkey" and "The Raft"

Gallery Magazine published three King stories as booklets that were stapled into the binding of the magazines that contained them: "The Raft," "The Monkey," and "The Jaunt." Of these, it should be noted that the latter is a reprinted story that was first published in *The Twilight Zone* Magazine; therefore, it is not considered collectible by most. Also, it's common to find these booklets removed from the original magazines and sold as a stand-alone. The serious collector should try to seek out only copies that remain bound inside the magazines themselves.

Gallery Magazine November 1980 contains "The Monkey". Issue price of $2.95. It is interesting to note *The Monkey* was revised for its inclusion in *Skeleton Crew*.

Gallery Magazine November 1982 contains "The Raft". Issue price of $3.50

Startling Mystery Stories #12 - 1969 - contains "The Reaper's Image"

Stephen King's first two professionally sold stories appeared in SMS while he was still a college student: "The Glass Floor" (1967) and "The

Reaper's Image" (1969). Both of these undersized digests, whose print runs were small, are still comparatively easy to acquire, although the market value of the 1967 issue continues to rise. The 1969 issue is the first time King's name appears on the cover of a magazine, and he is billed on the first page of the story therein as "the author of 'The Glass Floor'." Issue price of $0.50

Terrors - 1st US mass market paperback original - Playboy Paperbacks 1982 - contains "Survivor Type"

Terrors was originally published in 1982 by Playboy Paperbacks as a mass market paperback original. The book was re-released in 1984 by Berkley Books. This second edition is much more common than the *Playboy* edition and retains the same cover artwork. Collectors should be careful to seek out only the original *Playboy* edition. Issue price of $2.50

Rolling Stone Magazine July 19 - August 2, 1984 issue - contains "The Revelations of Becka Paulson"

"The Revelations of Becka Paulson," a story that was later incorporated into the body of *The Tommyknockers*, is a short story that originally appeared in this *Rolling Stone* Magazine in 1984. This story was collected in the Scream Press limited edition of *Skeleton Crew*, but did not appear in either the US or UK trade edition of the book. Issue Price of $2.50

. . . .

Redbook Magazine May 1984

issue contains "Mrs. Todd's Shortcut" Issue price of $1.50

Twilight Zone Magazine June 1981

issue contains "The Jaunt" Issue price of $2.00

Ellery Queen's Mystery Magazine December 1980

issue contains "The Wedding Gig" Issue price of $1.35

Playboy January 1983

issue contains "The Word Processor"
"The Word Processor" was retitled as "Word Processor of the Gods" in Skeleton Crew. Issue price of $3.50

Shadows 4

1st US trade hardcover edition - Doubleday 1981 - contains "The Man Who Would Not Shake Hands" Issue price of $10.95

Weirdbook #19 - Spring 1984

issue contains "Gramma" Issue price of $5.00

Shadows

1st US trade hardcover edition - Doubleday 1978 - contains "Nona"
Issue price of $7.95

Yankee Magazine October 1983

issue contains "Uncle Otto's Truck" Issue price of $1.50

New Terrors 2

1st UK mass market paperback original - Pan Books 1980 - contains
"Big Wheels: A Tale of the Laundry Game".
"Big Wheels: A Tale of the Laundry Game" was retitled to "Big Wheels
a tale of the Laundry Game (Milkman #2)". Both "Morning Deliveries"
and "Big Wheels" were originally excerpted from an unfinished novel
titled The Milkman. Issue price of £1.79

Weird Tales Fall 1984

issue contains "Beachworld" Issue price of $2.50

The Magazine of Fantasy & Science Fiction June 1984

issue contains "The Ballad of the Flexible Bullet" Issue price of $1.75

Yankee Magazine November 1981

issue contains "Do the Dead Sing"
"Do the Dead Sing" was retitled as "The Reach" for inclusion in
Skeleton Crew. Issue price of $1.75

Some of these stories in their original appearance, such as "Mrs. Todd's Shortcut" in Redbook Magazine, remain quite difficult to find on the secondary market, while others, including "Gramma" in Weirdbook, the print run and distribution of which was much smaller than that of Redbook, can be found and acquired very easily and inexpensively. Unlike some of the stories in Night Shift and Nightmares & Dreamscapes, most of the stories that appear in Skeleton Crew can be tracked down and acquired by determined collectors, perhaps, with the exception of the stories appearing in Ubris, which remains elusive even to the determined collector. It took Noah decades of searching before he was able to complete his collection of all four issues.

Previously unpublished works appearing for the first time in Skeleton Crew: "Paranoid: A Chant", "For Owen", "Morning Deliveries (Milkman #1)".

Thanks for taking a look back at 1985's Skeleton Crew with us! We hope you enjoyed your visit to our vault to see the first appearances, limited, and trade editions. We hope you have enjoyed visiting with Skeleton Crew as much as we have enjoyed sharing its contents. If you've enjoyed this article, and if you are a King collector or even a novice collector or a reader with an interest in rare King, please join us on FaceBook at Stephen King Rare Book Collecting.

We look forward to seeing you next year for more from Extreme Stephen King!

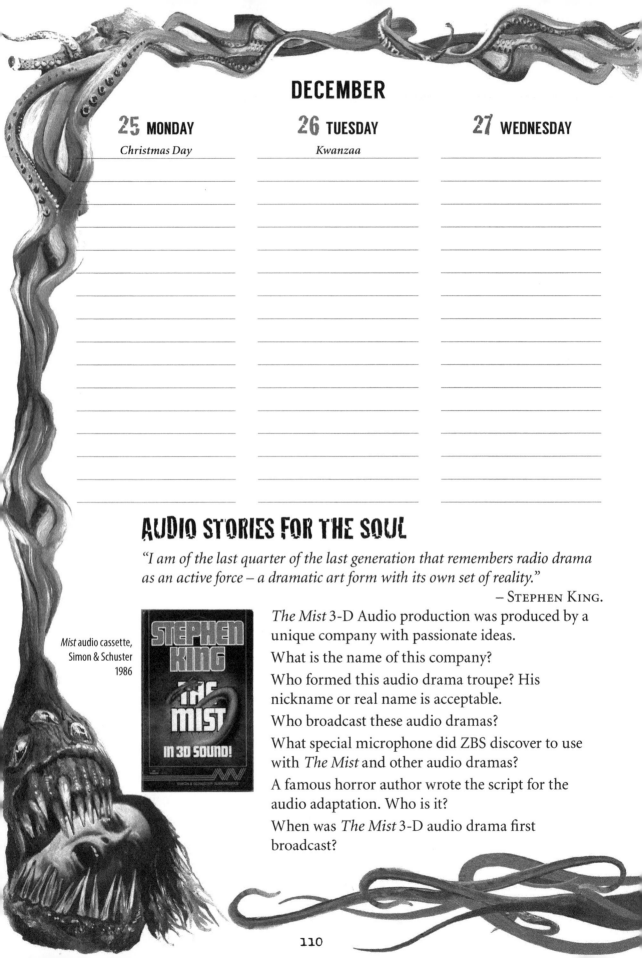

DECEMBER

25 MONDAY
Christmas Day

26 TUESDAY
Kwanzaa

27 WEDNESDAY

AUDIO STORIES FOR THE SOUL

"I am of the last quarter of the last generation that remembers radio drama as an active force – a dramatic art form with its own set of reality."

— STEPHEN KING.

Mist audio cassette,
Simon & Schuster
1986

The Mist 3-D Audio production was produced by a unique company with passionate ideas.

What is the name of this company?

Who formed this audio drama troupe? His nickname or real name is acceptable.

Who broadcast these audio dramas?

What special microphone did ZBS discover to use with *The Mist* and other audio dramas?

A famous horror author wrote the script for the audio adaptation. Who is it?

When was *The Mist* 3-D audio drama first broadcast?

DECEMBER

28 THURSDAY

29 FRIDAY

30 SATURDAY

31 SUNDAY

New Year's Eve

Answers:

A1: ZBS Foundation.

A2: Meatball Fulton, aka Thomas Manuel Lopez.

A3: NPR broadcast these ZBS dramas throughout the 1980s.

A4: Kunstkopf binaural microphone and dubbed "Mr. Fritz" at ZBS.

A5: Dennis Etchison. Etchison was considerable help to Stephen King during the writing of *Danse Macabre* due to his extensive knowledge of the horror genre.

A6: It was serialized on NPR on the ZBS program *The Cabinet of Dr. Fritz* on October 2, 9, and 16th, 1984

The Mist audio cassette, ZBS Corp. 1984

JANUARY

1 MONDAY
New Year's Day

2 TUESDAY

3 WEDNESDAY

Artwork by Drew Struzen, 2007, *The Mist*.

DID YOU KNOW?

THE MIST FEATURED STUNT... PAINTINGS?

The Mist film used *Dark Tower* prop paintings. Giclee print on 24 x 36 in. canvas stretched over frame, of Drew Struzan's art from the opening of the film. The painting depicts poster art for a fictional *Dark Tower* movie with a shadowy Western gunfighter figure suggestive of a young Clint Eastwood (chosen by director Frank Darabont as homage to both Stephen King and Eastwood). While multiple prints were created in several degrees of distress, this version was auctioned and is in the light distress stage closer to that seen in the opening scene as artist "David Drayton" (Thomas Jane) puts finishing touches on his work before the storm hits. In production used very good condition. (Dimension Films, 2007).

Sold on Dec 15, 2012 for $1,168.50.

JANUARY

4 THURSDAY

5 FRIDAY

6 SATURDAY

7 SUNDAY

Thomas Jayne "David Drayton" screen used "destroyed" *The Dark Tower* prop painting and framed Drew Struzan art print from *The Mist*. (Dimension, 2007) Original screen used prop painting consisting of a color print on linen affixed to wooden framing bars, being Drew Struzan's portrait of "Roland 'The Gunslinger' Deschain" from Stephen King's *The Dark Tower* saga. The linen has been slashed with additional paint drips and smears added. Framing bars exhibit studio distress, soiling and breakage. This is "destroyed" version of the painting that Drayton is working on at the beginning of the film, ravaged by the elements when he leaves the window to his studio open. Also includes a giclée print on fine art paper of the original Struzan artwork with 23.5 x 35.5 in. visible through mat. Presented in a dark wood 37.5 x 49.75 in. frame. Prop in production used condition.

Artwork by Drew Struzen, 2007, *The Mist*.

8 MONDAY	**9** TUESDAY	**10** WEDNESDAY

King Kong, RKO Pictures,
1933 theater poster.

DID YOU KNOW?

BEHIND THE SCENES

"I had the nutty feeling that I was watching some extra-good piece of visual effects, something dreamed up by Willys O'Brian or Douglas Trumbull." – **Stephen King**, *The Mist*.

Stephen King is grand when it comes to acknowledging personal influences in his own stories. Willis O'Brien (the correct spelling) and Douglas Trumbull were filmmakers, pinnacles in their fields of visual effects and directing. In his story, *The Mist*, character David Drayton mentions these creators and its fitting that you should know who they are.

Willis O'Brien's ground-breaking stop motion animation work on the 1933 film *King Kong* introduced a worthy adversary to audiences the world over. In 1949 O'Brien worked as Chief Technician on another gorilla film titled *Mighty Joe Young*. A young Ray Harryhausen (later an award-winning master in stop motion film) would do most of the animation, but O'Brien did come up with the designs for the film. At the 1950 Academy Awards, O'Brien was awarded an Oscar for Best Visual Effects for *Mighty Joe Young*. This, along

JANUARY

11 THURSDAY

_____
_____
_____
_____
_____
_____
_____
_____
_____
_____
_____
_____

12 FRIDAY

_____
_____
_____
_____
_____
_____
_____
_____
_____
_____
_____
_____

13 SATURDAY

_____
_____
_____
_____
_____
_____

14 SUNDAY

_____
_____
_____
_____
_____

with _King Kong_, are often considered his greatest achievements. Interestingly he spent significant pre-production time on various film projects that were never made, one in particular was Emilio and Guloso a.k.a. _Valley of the Mist_ (1950).

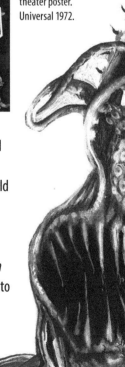

Silent Running theater poster. Universal 1972.

Douglas Trumbull co-created a film for the 1964 World's Fair, _To the Moon and Beyond_. Director Stanley Kubrick hired him for the ground breaking 1968 film _2001: A Space Odyssey_. A job that certainly changed his life. In 1972 he directed and produced the special photographic effects for _Silent Running_, the excellent ecology in space film with Bruce Dern, that featured three robots: Huey, Dewey, and Louie, named after Donald Duck's nephews. He was the Visual Effects Supervisor on the momentous classic films _Close Encounters of the Third Kind_, _Star Trek: The Motion Picture_, and _Blade Runner_, all earning him Academy Award nomination for Best Visual Effects. His visual effects can also be seen in _The Andromeda Strain_, and his last film that he also produced, _The Man Who Killed Hitler and Then Bigfoot_ with Sam Elliott (it's great!). He did have to turn down George Lucas once though… to work on his film, _Star Wars_, due to other commitments.

JANUARY

15 MONDAY
Martin Luther King, Jr. Day

16 TUESDAY

17 WEDNESDAY

MONARCH THAT IS GLENN

In one scene in *The Mist* someone is wearing a t-shirt by a well-known Maine artist.

Who is the artist?

Who / what is on the t-shirt?

Which character wore the t-shirt? Who was the actor in this part?

Who produced this exclusive t-shirt?

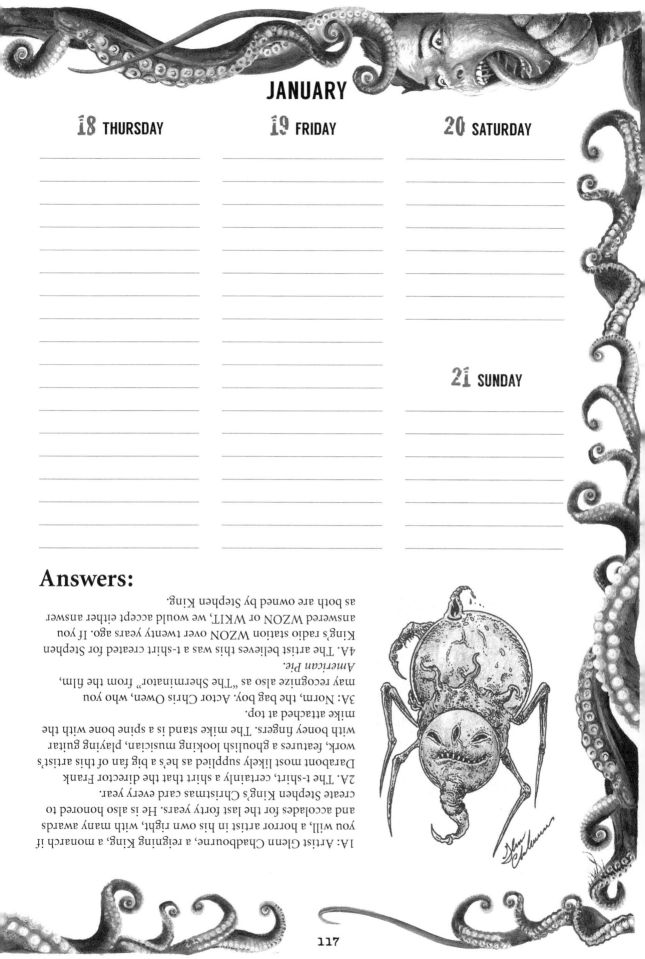

JANUARY

18 THURSDAY

19 FRIDAY

20 SATURDAY

21 SUNDAY

Answers:

1A: Artist Glenn Chadbourne, a reigning King, a monarch if you will, a horror artist in his own right, with many awards and accolades for the last forty years. He is also honored to create Stephen King's Christmas card every year.

2A. The t-shirt, certainly a shirt that the director Frank Darabont most likely supplied as he's a big fan of this artist's work, features a ghoulish looking musician, playing guitar with boney fingers. The mike stand is a spine bone with the mike attached at top.

3A: Norm, the bag boy. Actor Chris Owen, who you may recognize also as "The Sherminator" from the film, *American Pie*.

4A. The artist believes this was a t-shirt created for Stephen King's radio station WZON over twenty years ago. If you answered WZON or WKIT, we would accept either answer as both are owned by Stephen King.

JANUARY

22 MONDAY

23 TUESDAY

24 WEDNESDAY

BLOCKBUSTER *THE MIST* ONLINE CONTEST

In 2008, Blockbuster, the then video rental giant, offered a special online game, for a limited time, which would release special clips and a coupon towards renting *The Mist* for free! Blockbuster contracted to have an exclusive interview with Stephen King and director Frank Darabont features on their copies of *The Mist* DVD.

BLOCKBUSTER PRESS RELEASE:

DALLAS, March 18 (2008)/PRNewswire-FirstCall/ -- "The Mist" is rolling in today, with Blockbuster Inc. launching a free online game inspired by the Stephen King film at its website, http://www.blockbuster.com/. The game pits players against the predatory "Mist" creatures from the movie and highlights that BLOCKBUSTER(R) will have exclusive rentals of The Weinstein Company film when it is released on DVD on March 25.

Now through April 8, "The Mist" game will give gamers a chance to live the movie. Players must defeat a series of predators, battling their way through three levels based on scenes in the film. Those who escape the mist and win the game get a sneak peak of an exclusive interview with Stephen King and director/screenwriter Frank Darabont.

BLOCKBUSTER EXCLUSIVE

STEPHEN KING'S

THE MIST

WRITTEN FOR THE SCREEN AND DIRECTED BY
FRANK DARABONT

Exclusive Bonus Footage

"A MASTERPIECE! ONE OF THE MOST SHOCKING MOVIE ENDINGS EVER!"

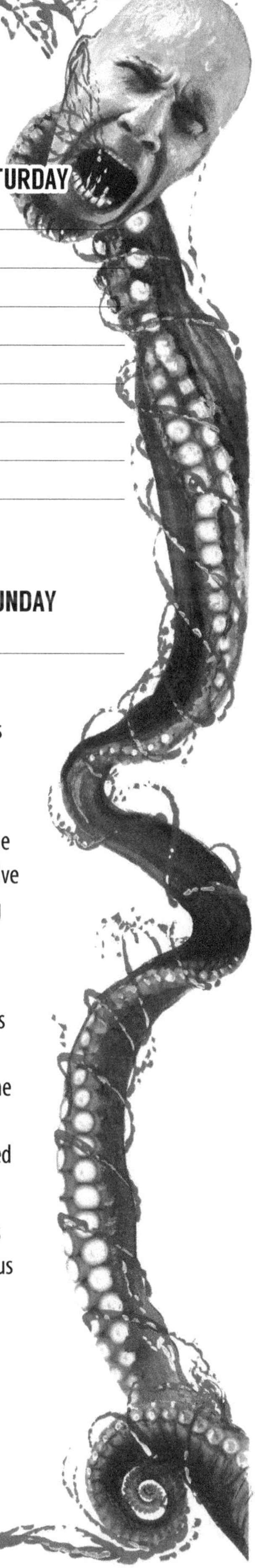

JANUARY

25 THURSDAY

26 FRIDAY

27 SATURDAY

28 SUNDAY

The full version of this interview will be featured on the rental DVD, exclusively available at participating BLOCKBUSTER stores and online at http://www.blockbuster.com/.

The public can access the game at http://www.blockbuster.com/. In addition to the game, the landing page will feature the movie trailer, an option to rent the DVD and the option to receive a coupon redeemable for one $1.99 DVD rental at participating BLOCKBUSTER stores.

Based on the horror novella by Stephen King, "The Mist" tells the story of a mysterious mist that rolls into the town of Bridgton, Maine. David Drayton and his young son Billy are among a group of terrified townspeople who are trapped in a local grocery store by a strange, otherworldly mist. David is the first to realize there are "things" lurking in the mist -- deadly, horrifying things, not of this world. In this legendary tale of terror from master storyteller Stephen King, the thin veneer of civilization is stripped away, the masks are discarded and the true horror is revealed as us.

"The Mist" is part of an agreement that provides BLOCKBUSTER with exclusive U.S. rental rights to The Weinstein Company's theatrical and direct-to-video films, which are distributed by Genius Products, LLC. Other recent Weinstein Company releases made available for rent exclusively through Blockbuster also include the Stephen King/Frank Darabont film "1408."

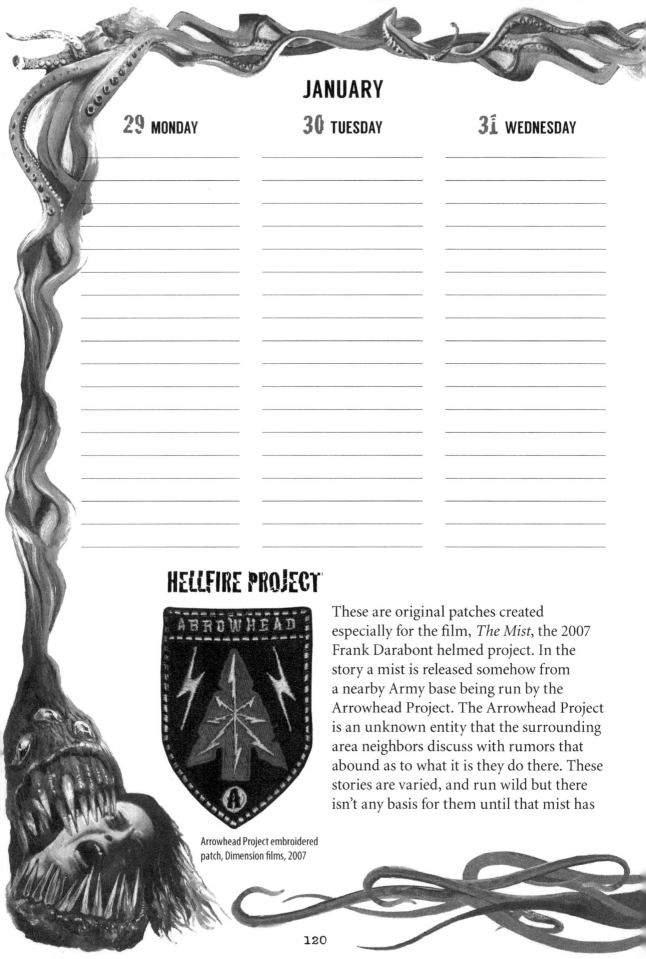

JANUARY

29 MONDAY

30 TUESDAY

31 WEDNESDAY

HELLFIRE PROJECT

Arrowhead Project embroidered
patch, Dimension films, 2007

These are original patches created
especially for the film, *The Mist*, the 2007
Frank Darabont helmed project. In the
story a mist is released somehow from
a nearby Army base being run by the
Arrowhead Project. The Arrowhead Project
is an unknown entity that the surrounding
area neighbors discuss with rumors that
abound as to what it is they do there. These
stories are varied, and run wild but there
isn't any basis for them until that mist has

FEBRUARY

1 THURSDAY

2 FRIDAY
Groundhog Day

3 SATURDAY

4 SUNDAY

been released. The uniforms created for the film included these original patches of art worn in the movie by Army Special Forces, known as Hellfire Squads. Also shown is a patch for the Arrowhead Project used on the other side of these uniforms. You can see them on the soldiers at the end of the movie while they're burning creatures and debris. A very rare find to be sure. These patches shown are official patches that were offered for sale on Ebay by one of the seamstresses from the film.

Arrowhead Project embroidered
patch, Dimension films, 2007

FEBRUARY

5 MONDAY   **6** TUESDAY   **7** WEDNESDAY

MEET THE DRAYTON'S

Time to meet the family! The Drayton's are at the center of this creature feature and this trivia is based on Stephen King's original novella. Time to dig deep, gang!

What type of chairs were the Drayton family sitting in at home?

What is printed on the back of the miniature version of this chair for their son?

What town is on the "far side of the lake" where the Drayton's live?

Who were the Drayton's neighbors at the lake house?

FEBRUARY

8 THURSDAY

9 FRIDAY

10 SATURDAY
Lunar New Year

11 SUNDAY

Answers:

A1: All had director's chairs
A2: Billy. (page 3, Scribners 2018)
A3: Harrison, a real town in Maine.
A4: Brent Norton on the right and the Bibbers on the left.

The Mist TP,
Sperling & Kupfer,
Italy 2018.

FEBRUARY

12 MONDAY

13 TUESDAY
Mardis Gras

14 WEDNESDAY
Ash Wednesday
Valentine's Day

THE MIST, SPIKED!

Advance press kits sent to the media can be very attractive and involved, featuring unique boxes produced to get the attention of outlets that will review and promote these shows. *The Mist* TV series had high expectations from media and the audience and this press kit reflects this, with embossing's on the folder, and uniquely printed DVDs. Here someone was offering *The Mist* TV series press kit on Ebay. The listing is well thought out and fun so I thought I'd offer a truncated version of their listing (this one is long sold, but I bet another will show up before you can say "creature feature.")

The Mist Stephen King DVD TV Show Press Kit. Attention Stephen King

FEBRUARY

15 THURSDAY

16 FRIDAY

17 SATURDAY

18 SUNDAY

collectors! This is the sensational, beautifully rendered press kit from the Spike TV production of "The Mist" based on a story by Stephen King. Press kit is complete with all original components, unused and all in the original box as shown. Included is a hardcover book that has a slipcover that reads: "Fear Human Nature." The hardcover book inside is filled with images from the show, as well as descriptive text of the principal characters. Also included is a folio that holds a thumb drive with high resolution images from the show, a card that shows the images available, and a DVD with the Pilot Episode. All comes packaged in the original box. Press kit is complete and in perfect, unused condition. The outer box is included and has the original mailing label removed. Originally produced by Dimension Television for Spike TV in 2017.

FEBRUARY

19 MONDAY
President's Day

_____
_____
_____
_____
_____
_____
_____
_____
_____
_____
_____
_____
_____
_____
_____
_____

20 TUESDAY

_____
_____
_____
_____
_____
_____
_____
_____
_____
_____
_____
_____
_____
_____
_____
_____

21 WEDNESDAY

_____
_____
_____
_____
_____
_____
_____
_____
_____
_____
_____
_____
_____
_____
_____
_____

Der Nebel (The Mist),
German TP, Heyne

WHITE NOISE

Going back to the source, Stephen King's original novella text is where you will find the answers to these here questions, but you may only drudge up "white noise" depending on how long ago it was when you read "The Mist."

What is the name of the local rock station that Steph cannot get on the radio?

Is this a real radio station in Maine?

What radio station did Steph finally find that was broadcasting?

Is this a also a real radio station in Maine, or is it something cooked up by Stephen King during a BBQ?

FEBRUARY

22 THURSDAY

23 FRIDAY

24 SATURDAY

25 SUNDAY

Answers:

A1: WOXO. It was located beyond the mist that was slowly encroaching over the lake toward the Drayton's.

A2: Yes! During the mid-1970's WOXO was a top forty radio station covering the Norway, Maine area. It eventually shifted to country music format but due to Covid they shut the station down in 2020.

A3: WJBQ, covering the Portland, Maine area and opposite of where the mist was.

A4: Yes, this too is a real radio station operating out of Portland, Maine. I don't think BBQ is on the menu, but JBQ BBQ is kinda catchy.

THE MIST

Glenn Chadbourne Art 2015

FEBRUARY

26 MONDAY

27 TUESDAY

28 WEDNESDAY

DID YOU KNOW?

MAN HOLE TENTACLES, ALLIGATORS IN THE SEWERS

In the novel, *The Mist*, Stephen King described the tentacles that appeared under the stockroom door and into the stockroom as "The big ones had candy-pink suckers that seemed the size of manhole covers." Frank Darabont, the director of *The Mist*, with his team of artists (check out

THE MIST

WHAT HAPPENED TO THE BAG BOY

9

23
VFX

First tentacle biting down

PAN to another one as it rears and opens mouth

BAM! It his Norm's other leg at the knee!

And tears away a hunk of cloth and flesh!

Cont'd

Mist storyboard art by Pete Von Sholly, 2007.

MARCH

29 THURSDAY

1 FRIDAY

2 SATURDAY

3 SUNDAY

Pete Von Shollys art in this edition) and special effects teams created a very elaborate tentacle that opened up at the end of it, like a mouth, not only with suckers surrounding it, but with teeth that could bite and devour chunks of its prey. A lot more involved than the description in the story. These movie CGI tentacles were very menacing and effective on the movie screen.

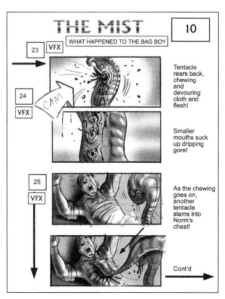

(?, Spanish edition, 2019)

Mist storyboard art by Pete Von Sholly, 2007.

MARCH

4 MONDAY   **5** TUESDAY   **6** WEDNESDAY

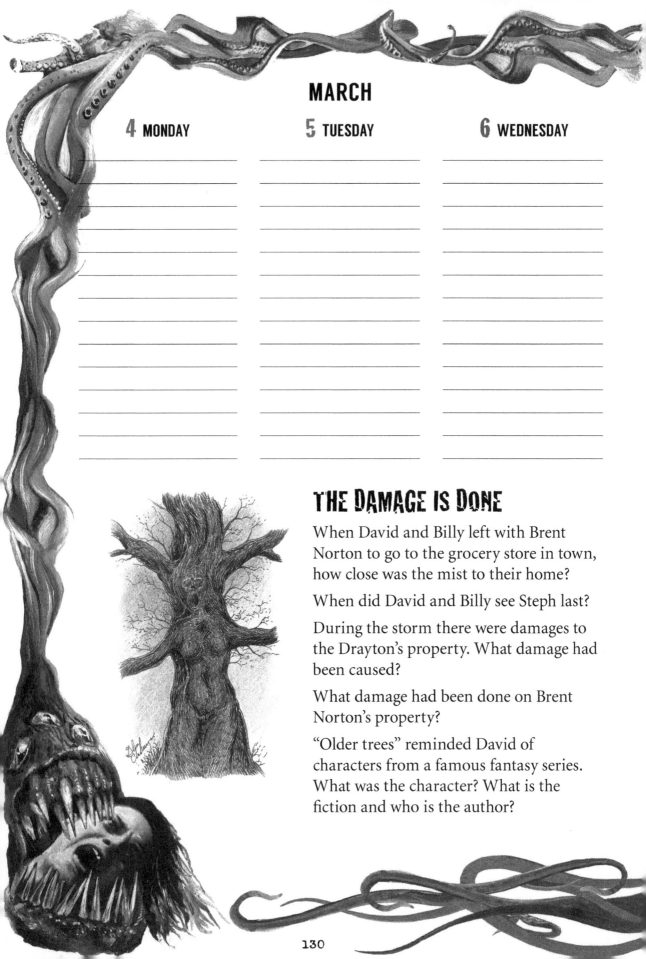

THE DAMAGE IS DONE

When David and Billy left with Brent Norton to go to the grocery store in town, how close was the mist to their home?

When did David and Billy see Steph last?

During the storm there were damages to the Drayton's property. What damage had been caused?

What damage had been done on Brent Norton's property?

"Older trees" reminded David of characters from a famous fantasy series. What was the character? What is the fiction and who is the author?

MARCH

7 THURSDAY

8 FRIDAY

9 SATURDAY

10 SUNDAY
Daylight Saving begins

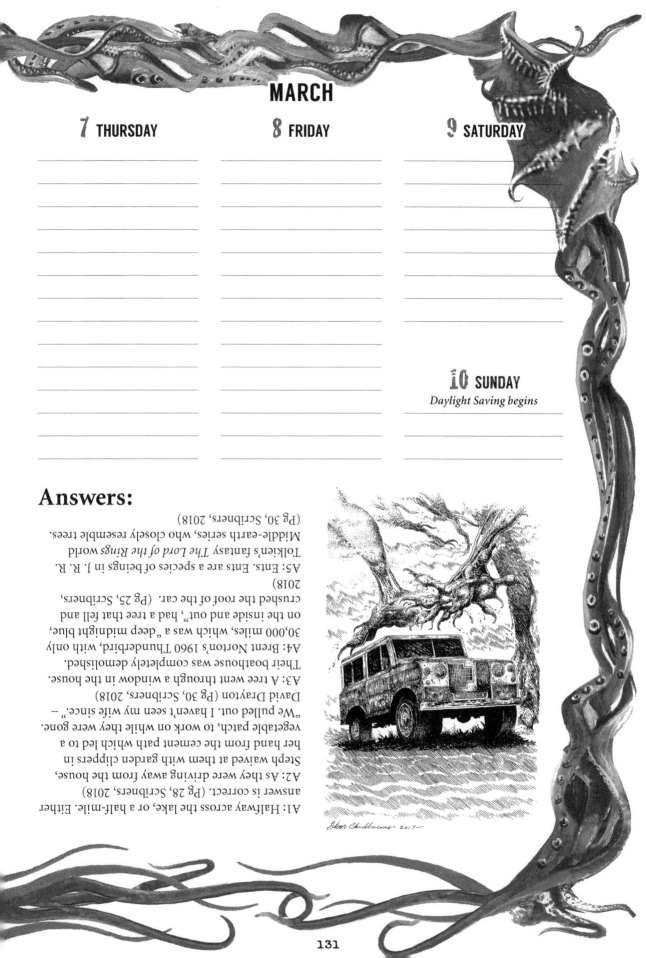

Answers:

A1: Halfway across the lake, or a half-mile. Either answer is correct. (Pg 28, Scribners, 2018)

A2: As they were driving away from the house, Steph waved at them with garden clippers in her hand from the cement path which led to a vegetable patch, to work on while they were gone. "We pulled out, I haven't seen my wife since." – David Drayton (Pg 30, Scribners, 2018)

A3: A tree went through a window in the house. Their boathouse was completely demolished.

A4: Brent Norton's 1960 Thunderbird, with only 30,000 miles, which was a "deep midnight blue, on the inside and out", had a tree that fell and crushed the roof of the car. (Pg 25, Scribners, 2018)

A5: Ents. Ents are a species of beings in J. R. R. Tolkien's fantasy *The Lord of the Rings* world Middle-earth series, who closely resemble trees. (Pg 30, Scribners, 2018)

MARCH

LICENSE TO KILL

The license plate from *The Mist* film (2007) for the Drayton's vehicle went on the auction block in June 2023. This screen-Matched License Plate Display had a winning bid:$1,250.

David Drayton's (Thomas Jane) license plate display from Frank Darabont's 2007 sci-fi horror *The Mist*. This plate screen-matches to the back of Drayton's van when the mist's survivors attempted to gather medical supplies and when they left the food store to venture out.

License Plate from
The Mist film, 2007.

MARCH

14 THURSDAY

15 FRIDAY

16 SATURDAY

17 SUNDAY
St. Patrick's Day

This white aluminum Maine license plate numbered "M8 270" is affixed with "DEC" and "MAINE 08" decals on front and labeled "David" on the reverse with metal screws glued into its top holes. It comes inside a custom-made wood display case with an acrylic cover and two stills from the film. The plate exhibits intentional red grime applied by production. Dimensions: 21.75" x 20" x 3" (55 cm x 50.5 cm x 7.25 cm)

Drayton's Scout vehicle,
The Mist film, 2007

MARCH

18 MONDAY   **19** TUESDAY   **20** WEDNESDAY

The Mist Japan DVD 2008.

"I'VE GOT TO GET HOME TO SEE MY KIDS"

There is a poignant moment in the story and the film of The Mist when a woman tells the crowd stuck in the grocery store this statement.

What is this woman's name?

What are her kids names that she has too get home too?

What happens to the woman in the story version of The Mist?

What happens to the woman in the film version of The Mist?

MARCH

21 THURSDAY	**22** FRIDAY	**23** SATURDAY

24 SUNDAY
Palm Sunday

Answers:

A1: In the story, she is only described as "a blond woman with a tired, pretty face", no name is ever given.

A2: Wanda, who is only eight, and little Victor.

A3: After no one would respond to her call for help to go with her to find her kids she disappeared through the door and entered the mist, "only the misty remnants of her red summer dress remained, seeming to dance in white limbo." (Pg 51, Scribners 2018)

A4: After she left the store and disappeared in the mist outside, (spoiler alert) she appeared again at the end of the film riding in the back of an army truck, along with her kids. They made it out alive, when so many others did not survive the creatures they encountered in the mist.

THE ULTIMATE STORYTELLER

STEPHEN KING

THE MIST

What lies within

The Mist UK Hodder paperback, 2021.

The Green Mile
Advance movie
one sheet poster
announcing
CHRISTMAS as
a future release.
Warner Bros. 1999

25 MONDAY

26 TUESDAY

27 WEDNESDAY

1980 anthology, *Dark Forces*, edited by Kirby McCauley.

ORIGINS OF THE MIST

The Mist made its first published appearance in *Dark Forces: New Stories of Suspense and Supernatural Horror*. New York: The Viking Press, [August 29th,1980]. A first edition, first printing copy inscribed by the editor, Kirby McCauley, on the half-title page. Also inscribed or signed by contributors Edward Bryant, Gene Wolfe, Charles L. Grant and Stephen King at each author's chapter heading. Octavo. 551 pages. Publisher's black cloth with stamped Edward Gorey device on front and red titles on spine.

The description of this particular copy sold for $1,280.00 June 26th, 2017.

MARCH

28 THURSDAY

29 FRIDAY
Good Friday

30 SATURDAY

31 SUNDAY
Easter

The signed and dated title page, shown in the photo here, of *The Mist* in *Dark Forces*, dated November 1, 1980 by Stephen King is only eight weeks after the release date of the anthology. This photo courtesy of Michael Hamel's personal copy.

APRIL

1 MONDAY
April Fools' Day

2 TUESDAY

3 WEDNESDAY

THE HOUSE OF FOOD

Literally. Not only for the folks trapped within a store full of groceries, but for the creatures outside who would like to dine on the folks trapped within. Blood for gravy.

The Mist, Glenn Chadbourne, 2007

What is the name of the grocery store in the novel, *The Mist*?

What is the name of the grocery store in the film version of *The Mist*?

Where did they film the grocery store scenes?

Can you name most of the characters that ended up in the grocery store?

After much debate who was elected to go outside to clear the exhaust for the backup generator that sealed their fate?

APRIL

4 THURSDAY

5 FRIDAY

6 SATURDAY

7 SUNDAY

Answers:

A1: Federal Foods market.

A2: The Food House. While on the set of *The Mist* I asked the director why he changed the name of the store for the film. He said the Food House was a local grocery store he grew up with and saw the opportunity to include the business he so frequented when growing up.

A3: The outside was filmed at Tom's Market in Vivian, Louisiana. The store was always an independent but closed in 2016. The inside was shot on a sound stage built in the Shreveport Conference Center where it was turned into studios, three levels worth, after hurricane Katrina forced New Orleans filming up north to Shreveport.

A4: Mrs. Carmody, Brent Norton, David and Billy Drayton, Bud Weeks, Ollie Weeks, Norm the bag boy, Buddy Eagleton, Bud Brown, John Lee Frovin (although he wasn't there long), Sally the checker, Jim Grondin, Myron LaFleur, Amanda Dunfrey, Mike Hatlen, Ambrose Cornell, Amanda Dumfries (local, housewife), Dan Miller (new local), Hattie Turman, Mr. McVey (the butcher), Arnie Simms, Walter (no last name), Tom Smalley, Mrs. Reppler (Hilda), Lou Tattinger (ran the Pine Tree Car Wash), Hank Vannerman, Mrs. Clapham (the lady who had been trampled on by the panic folks running from the bug attack).

A5: Norm the bag boy. He was eighteen.

Toms Market, 212 N. Pine St, Vivian Louisiana.

139

APRIL

8 MONDAY

9 TUESDAY

10 WEDNESDAY

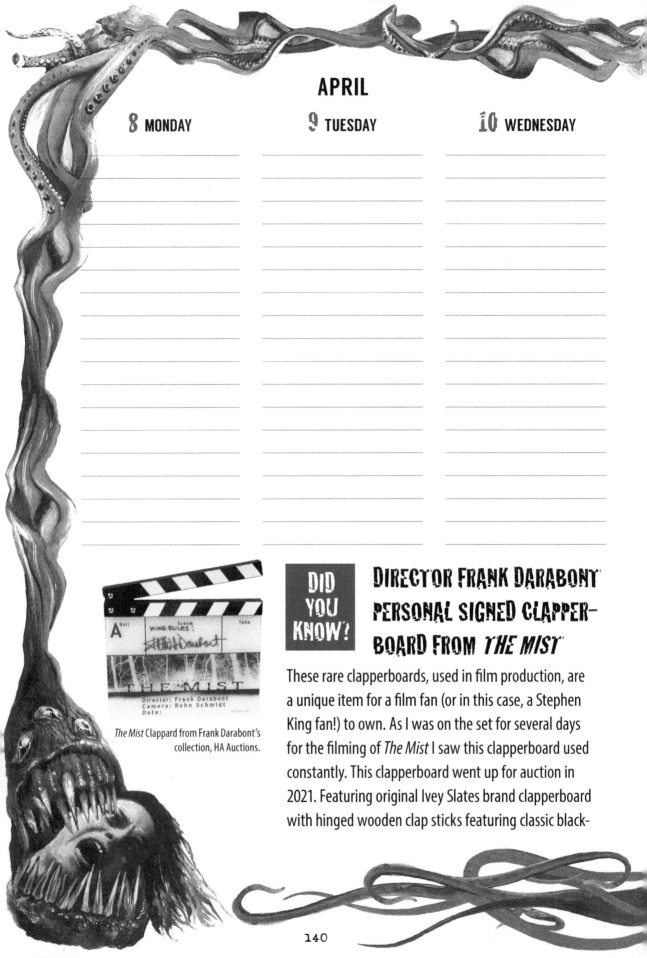

The Mist Clappard from Frank Darabont's collection, HA Auctions.

DIRECTOR FRANK DARABONT PERSONAL SIGNED CLAPPERBOARD FROM *THE MIST*

These rare clapperboards, used in film production, are a unique item for a film fan (or in this case, a Stephen King fan!) to own. As I was on the set for several days for the filming of *The Mist* I saw this clapperboard used constantly. This clapperboard went up for auction in 2021. Featuring original Ivey Slates brand clapperboard with hinged wooden clap sticks featuring classic black-

APRIL

and-white pattern and small round magnets, lower with unique printed background with movie title and graphic, Director: Frank Darabont, Camera: Rohn Schmidt, Date:, A Roll, Scene, and Take, with a thick colorless plexiglass overlay, upon which is written, "King Rules / Frank Darabont" in permanent black ink. Measures approx. 11" x 9.5" Exhibiting only minor production wear. In Fine condition. Came with a certificate of authenticity. It originally sold on Jul 16, 2021 for: 937.50. It was then turned around and resold just two months later for **$2,200** on September 22, 2021.

A photo included with *The Mist* Clappard Board auction. From Frank Darabont's Collection, HA Auctions

APRIL

15 MONDAY
Tax Day

16 TUESDAY

17 WEDNESDAY

Long Lake illustration
by Joanne Kollman, Etsy.

REAL OR NOT REAL. THAT...
IS THE QUESTION

In any Stephen King fiction the author uses many places that are real places, cities, and towns. He also invents fictional locales when creating his worlds. In *The Mist* can you discover which is which?

Is Long Lake real?

Is the Vicki-Linn Campground Real?

What famous author of children's and non-fiction books had a summer lake house here?

What fantastic books did he create?

APRIL

18 THURSDAY

19 FRIDAY

20 SATURDAY

21 SUNDAY

Answers:

A1: Yes, Long Lake, where the Drayton's have a summer lake home, is real and is located in Bridgton, Maine.

A2: The Vicki Lin (correct spelling) Campground is real and is located at 70 Weymouth Rd, Bridgton, Maine, 04009 and is located on ... you guessed it ... Long Lake.

A3: Author E.B. White had a summer home on the North Bridgton section of Long Lake.

A4: He wrote the children's books *Charlotte's Web* and *Stuart Little* among many others, including the non-fiction *The Elements of Style*, with William Strunk, Jr. on writing. Stephen King wrote in his non-fiction book, *On Writing* (2000), that he observed, "There is little or no detectable bullshit in that book. (Of course, it's short, at 85 pages it's much shorter than this one.) I'll tell you right now that every aspiring writer should read *The Elements of Style*." I have found no record that White and King have met, but being they were possibly in the vicinity at times, you have to ponder. White passed away in 1985.

This fragrance, dedicated to Vicki Lyn Camping Area can be found at: luckyscent.com

APRIL

22 MONDAY
Passover
Earth Day

23 TUESDAY

24 WEDNESDAY

GRAY WIDOWER LIGHTING STAND-IN AUCTION

A grey widower lighting stand-in from the production of Frank Darabont and Stephen King's horror film *The Mist*. Grey widowers were spider-like creatures which, along with other monsters appearing out of the mist, terrorised a group of people hiding in a supermarket. Lighting stand-ins are used to give special effects artists lighting references for the CGI creatures appearing in a film.

Widower stand-in, *The Mist*, 2007.
propstoreauction.com

APRIL

25 THURSDAY

26 FRIDAY

27 SATURDAY

28 SUNDAY

The hand-painted creature has resin legs, a foam-rubber body and head, and wooden spines. It has some minor cracks in the foam rubber and is missing three fangs around the mouth. Dimensions: 27 cm x 38 cm x 17 cm (10 3/4" x 15" x 6 3/4") Lot # 1167 : MIST, THE (2007). Estimated to bring in £1,500 - £2,500 the winning bid was much higher at £4,375. Listed at propstoreauction.com

Widower stand-in, *The Mist*, 2007.
propstoreauction.com

MAY

29 MONDAY

_____
_____
_____
_____
_____
_____
_____
_____
_____
_____
_____
_____
_____
_____
_____
_____
_____
_____

30 TUESDAY

_____
_____
_____
_____
_____
_____
_____
_____
_____
_____
_____
_____
_____
_____
_____
_____
_____
_____

1 WEDNESDAY

_____
_____
_____
_____
_____
_____
_____
_____
_____
_____
_____
_____
_____
_____
_____
_____
_____
_____

I SQUIRMED WHEN I SAW THE SHERM!

In the film, _The Mist_, the actor Chris Owen is featured in a small, but memorable role.

What character does Chris Own play in _The Mist_?

In what film series is Chris Owen primarily known for?

In _The Mist_, Chris Owen is wearing a t-shirt, that from the back displays an important artist's artwork. Fans of his can tell who created this artwork immediately.

Who is the artist?

The t-shirt was produced exclusively for... who?

Why was this shirt featured in the movie?

2 THURSDAY

3 FRIDAY

4 SATURDAY
Kentucky Derby Day

5 SUNDAY
Cinco de Mayo

Answers:

A1: Norm, the bag boy.

A2: In 1999, Chris Owen appeared in the hit comedy film *American Pie* as Chuck Sherman, a teenager that boasts himself of being a "ladie's man" and goes by "The Sherminator". He reprised his role in all of the sequels of the *American Pie* film franchise, including one of the straight-to-DVD spin-offs called *American Pie Presents: Band Camp.*

A3: Why our very own, Glenn Chadbourne! Mr. Chadbourne is the artist for The Stephen King Annuals, cover and interior, and has been a part of the Overlook Connection Press (the publisher of SKA) for almost thirty years.

A4: Glenn Chadbourne was commissioned to create art for a series of t-shirts for Stephen King's radio station, WKIT, in Bangor, Maine. This is one of those shirts.

A5: *The Mist* director, Frank Darabont, is a fan of Mr. Chadbourne's work and this was a personal shirt from his collection to honor the artist. Now how cool is that?

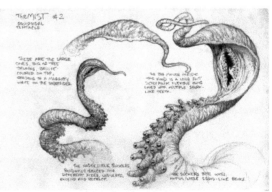

The Mist #2 art, "Squidoidal Tentacle" by Bernie Wrightston, 2006.

MAY

6 MONDAY   **7** TUESDAY   **8** WEDNESDAY

SPIDER SNOW GLOBE

DID YOU KNOW?

Blockbuster video announced an exclusive promotional "snow globe" that would be released in 2008 in conjunction with the then upcoming DVD/Blu-ray release of The Mist in their stores. This option was only available in select stores. These snow globes were unique for their "inside" contents. Instead of snow these globes had black "bugs" and "spiders." Actually, a very cool globe. The whole piece is approximately 3.5 tall x 3" wide. The white spot in all pics is from my overhead square, fluorescent light.

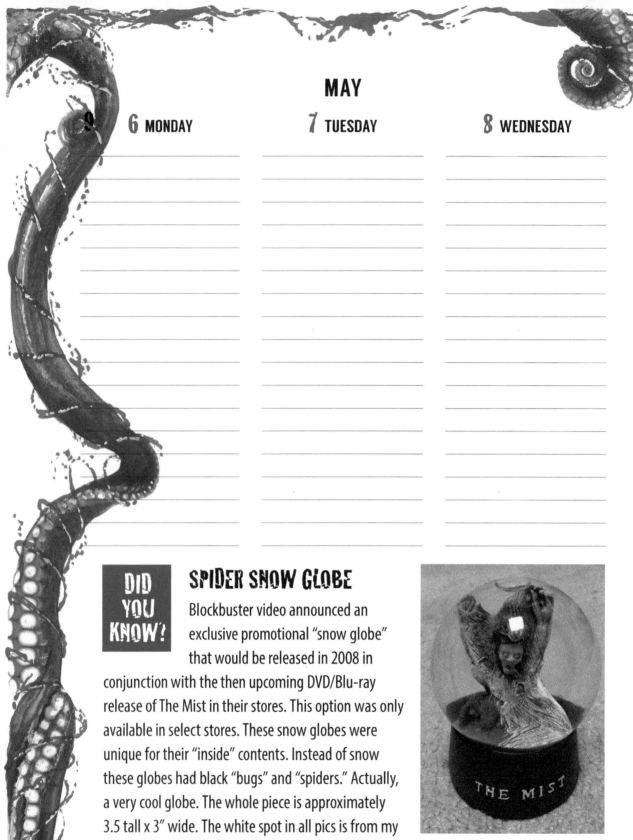

The Mist snow globe, Blockbuster Video, 2008

MAY

9 THURSDAY

10 FRIDAY

11 SATURDAY

12 SUNDAY
Mother's Day

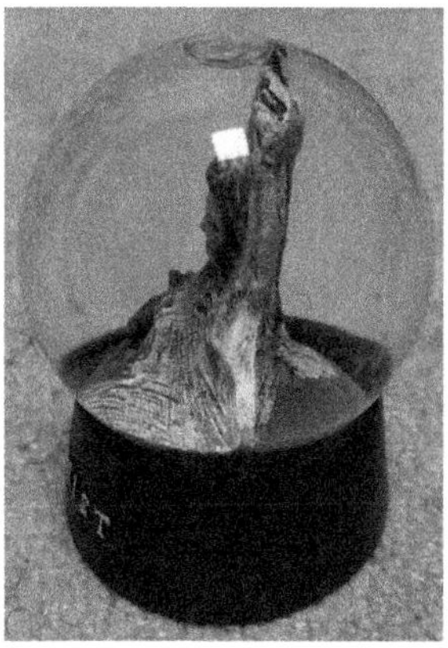

The Mist snow globe, Blockbuster Video, 2008

MAY

13 MONDAY

14 TUESDAY

15 WEDNESDAY

The Mist, trade paper,
Scribners 2018

WELL, IT ISN'T THE ALAN PARSON'S PROJECT...

What is the name of the Army facility where the mist came from?

What area is this facility located in Maine?

Who was found hanging in the back storage area of the grocery?

Who discovered them?

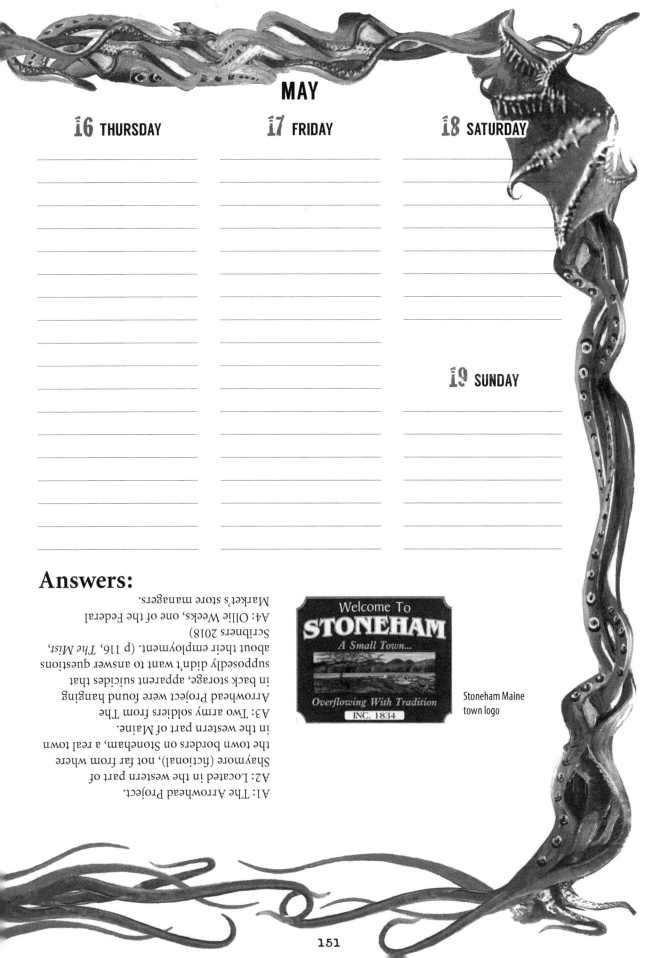

MAY

16 THURSDAY

17 FRIDAY

18 SATURDAY

19 SUNDAY

Answers:

A1: The Arrowhead Project.

A2: Located in the western part of Shaymore (fictional), not far from where the town borders on Stoneham, a real town in the western part of Maine.

A3: Two army soldiers from The Arrowhead Project were found hanging in back storage, apparent suicides that supposedly didn't want to answer questions about their employment. (p 116, *The Mist*, Scribners 2018)

A4: Ollie Weeks, one of the Federal Market's store managers.

Welcome To **STONEHAM** A Small Town... Overflowing With Tradition INC. 1834

Stoneham Maine town logo

MAY

20 MONDAY | **21** TUESDAY | **22** WEDNESDAY

The Mist UK Hodder paperback, 2007.

BY THE NUMBERS

The Mist film opened nationwide in the US November 21, 2007.

It had a film budget of 18,000,000.

The US opening garnered $8,931,973 in it's first weekend.

The total US tickets sales were $25,594,957.

Total international sales were $31,875,263.

This brings a grand worldwide total receipts to $57,470,220.

23 THURSDAY

24 FRIDAY

25 SATURDAY

26 SUNDAY

Stephen King *Short Fiction* boxed set, Scribners, 2021

Available at **StephenKingCatalog.com**

MAY

27 MONDAY
Memorial Day

28 TUESDAY

29 WEDNESDAY

The Mist theater poster, Turkey.

ROUND AND ROUND

What did David Drayton call the group headed by Brent Norton in the grocery store?

As Brent Norton's group was getting ready to leave the grocery store, David Drayton asked Brent Norton if he would do something for him. What was it and what was the reason?

What was the name of the man who responded to David's request?

Who killed one of the flying monster bugs with a spray, when it broke through the stores front window?

What did they use to kill the bug?

JUNE

30 THURSDAY

31 FRIDAY

1 SATURDAY

2 SUNDAY

Answers:

All answers with page references are from *The Mist*, Scribners, 2018 trade paperback.

A1: The Flat-Earth Society (pg 81), later referenced as the Flat-Earthers (pg 94)

A2: A clothesline. To take the 300 ft clothesline available in the store and tie it to something once it they came to the end of it so David would know they had reached at least 300 feet outside the store in the mist.

A3: He was simply called "Golf Cap" in the story and he had tied the clothesline around his waist so he wouldn't lose it outside by dropping it, etc.

A4: Mrs. Reppler, the third-grade teacher. "Mrs. Reppler stood over her kill, her thin chest rising and falling rapidly." (p 109)

A5: "She had a can of Raid in each hand like some crazy gunslinger in an existential comedy." (p 108)

155

JUNE

3 MONDAY

4 TUESDAY

5 WEDNESDAY

NOVA SCOTIA COMES THROUGH *THE MIST*

When *The Mist* TV series was given the green light to film the series the Nova Scotia government stepped up and contributed $5.9 million as they were filming in their area. They filmed in and around Halifax and in the Bedford Place Mall, which had been transformed into the Bridgeville Mall for the series. It's the biggest production to ever shoot in that province, with an estimated production cost of $22.8 million. Nova Scotia Minister of Business, Mark Furey said "we're very encouraged by the confidence producers have in the Nova Scotia film industry." "We've worked very hard with the film industry representatives to restore confidence in the industry," said Furey.

The production used as a studio an

The Mist TV series, Spike TV, 2017.

JUNE

6 THURSDAY

7 FRIDAY

8 SATURDAY

9 SUNDAY

abandoned Target store located in Bedford Place Mall. The crew built up to 10 sets there, including a sewer system, forest sets, and replicas of rooms of a Dartmouth house they filmed in.

Both interiors and exteriors of the temple were filmed at Christ Church in Dartmouth. The town of Windsor was used for some exterior shots with Morgan driving around Bridgeville. Some establishing shots for *The Mist* were recorded on location at Lockview High School in Fall River. Production started on July 18th, 2016 and completed Nov. 18th, 2016.

Bedford Mall, Nova Scotia, @halifaxretales 2017.

JUNE

10 MONDAY   **11** TUESDAY   **12** WEDNESDAY

SEX, DRUGS, AND BUGS

What is the name of the pharmacy in Stephen King's *The Mist*?

What is the name of the pharmacy in the film of *The Mist*?

The pharmacy, as well as the Federal Foods market, were very busy after the storm. What happened to the folks in the pharmacy?

Who snuck up to the empty office in the grocery store? What was their mission?

The Mist, window bug, Dimension Films, 2007.

JUNE

13 THURSDAY

14 FRIDAY
Flag Day

15 SATURDAY

16 SUNDAY
Father's Day

Answers:

A1: Bridgton Pharmacy

A2: King Pharmacy. An obvious tribute to Stephen King from director Frank Darabont.

A3: The grocery store had an automatic door, and was constantly kept shut. The pharmacy had both doors open. "...but the drugstore had been wide open, the doors chocked with rubber doorstops to let in a little cool air...." everyone in the drugstore met their demise from the creatures of the mist.

A4: David and Amanda. Of course, sex was their mission, "I've just been up to the office. It's empty and there's a lock on the door."

The Mist DVD, special sleeve art, 2008.

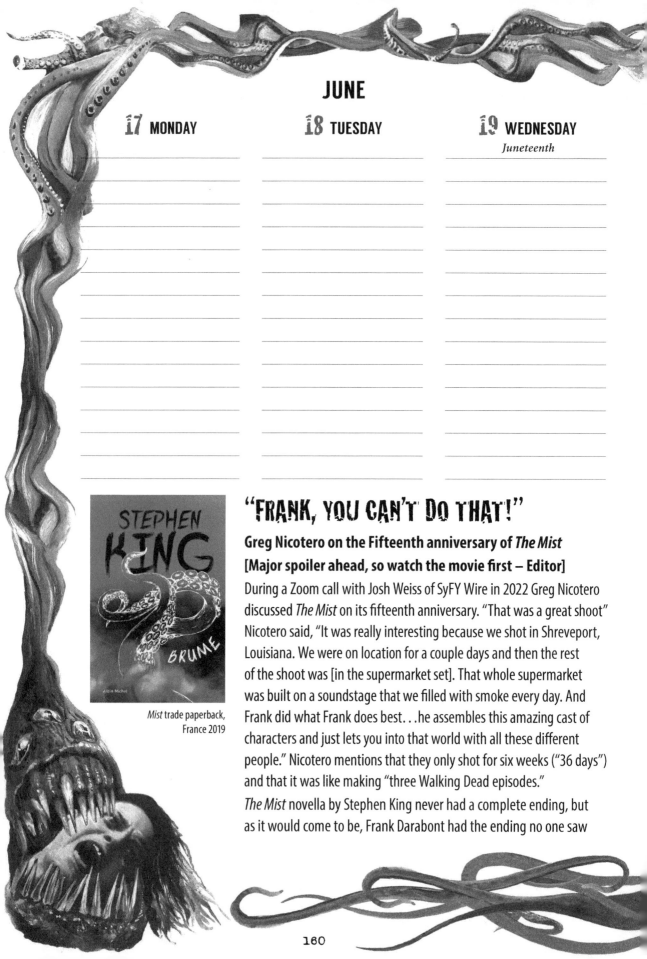

JUNE

17 MONDAY

18 TUESDAY

19 WEDNESDAY
Juneteenth

Mist trade paperback,
France 2019

"FRANK, YOU CAN'T DO THAT!"

Greg Nicotero on the Fifteenth anniversary of *The Mist*
[Major spoiler ahead, so watch the movie first – Editor]

During a Zoom call with Josh Weiss of SyFY Wire in 2022 Greg Nicotero discussed *The Mist* on its fifteenth anniversary. "That was a great shoot" Nicotero said, "It was really interesting because we shot in Shreveport, Louisiana. We were on location for a couple days and then the rest of the shoot was [in the supermarket set]. That whole supermarket was built on a soundstage that we filled with smoke every day. And Frank did what Frank does best. . .he assembles this amazing cast of characters and just lets you into that world with all these different people." Nicotero mentions that they only shot for six weeks ("36 days") and that it was like making "three Walking Dead episodes."

The Mist novella by Stephen King never had a complete ending, but as it would come to be, Frank Darabont had the ending no one saw

JUNE

20 THURSDAY

21 FRIDAY

22 SATURDAY

23 SUNDAY

coming. Almost everyone in the Drayton Scout dies(I won't spoil how), including his young son Billy, except for David Drayton, who staggers outside only to learn that no one had to die and he screams the scream of the forever damned. Greg Nicotero said "I remember reading the script for the first time and I'm like, 'Frank, you can't do that.' And he did it."

"I'll never forget going to the premiere in New York and Stephen King saying, 'Man, I wish I would have thought to end the book that way,'" Nicotero says. "Because in the book, they kind of just drive off.

This conclusion horrified a lot of people at the time, going against the usual Hollywood traditional happy ending. Most studios want audiences to leave the theater with some sort of warm and fuzzy feeling. Through Darabont's deal with the studio, they left his original vision to him, and its end reveal that gives the film its lasting impact. That ending is why we still discuss *The Mist* today.

JUNE

24 MONDAY

25 TUESDAY

26 WEDNESDAY

IT'S A RAID! IT'S A RAID!

When the group of volunteers from the grocery, went to the pharmacy next door. How many feet was it between the grocery door and the pharmacy door?

As part of the group, Hilda Reppler carried a canvas bag of items in one hand. What was in the bag?

Hilda held something else in her free hand, what was that?

What creature did the grocery store group find in the pharmacy next door in the story?

JUNE

27 THURSDAY

28 FRIDAY

29 SATURDAY

30 SUNDAY

Answers:

All page references refer to *The Mist* trade paperback, Scribners 2018 edition.

A1: It was estimated to be about 20 feet.

A2: Black Flag and Raid bug spray cans.

A3: "…she held a Spaulding Jimmy Connors tennis racket from a display of sporting goods in Aisle 2." (pg 131) When Stephen King wrote this Jimmy Connors was an American World No. 1 tennis player in the late 70's. This inclusion is definitely a sign of that time.

A4: Spiders the size of dogs that emitted cable-like webs that cut an acid burn whatever it touched.

CHADBOURNE 2018

| 1 MONDAY | 2 TUESDAY | 3 WEDNESDAY |

The Mist, Der Nebel,
German BluRay.

"...IT WAS SO ANTI-HOLLYWOOD — ANTI-EVERYTHING, REALLY! IT WAS NIHILISTIC."

An interview Stephen King gave in 2017 on Yahoo Entertainment he discussed the lack of an ending of his original novella and Frank Darabont's film that finally gave us his gut-punch of an ending none of us saw coming. Writer Nick Schager had interviewed Frank Darabont in 2016 and spoke about the "brutal" ending to the film. In this 2017 interview he asked Stephen King what he thought about Darabont's ending vision. I remember asking Frank Darabont on *The Mist* set in Shreveport, Louisiana, about this ending — an ending we didn't know yet as it wasn't in the script that producer Denise Huth had given me a "secret" she said — and asked if Stephen King had approved it. He said "Steve loves the ending and he's completely behind it."

"When Frank was interested in *The Mist*, one of the things that he insisted on was that it would have some kind of an ending, which the

JULY

4 THURSDAY
Independence Day

5 FRIDAY

6 SATURDAY

7 SUNDAY

story doesn't have — it just sort of fades off into nothing, where these people are stuck in the mist, and they're out of gas, and the monsters are around, and you don't know what's going to happen next. When Frank said that he wanted to create the ending that he was going to do, I was totally down with that. I thought that was terrific. And it was so anti-Hollywood — anti-everything, really! It was nihilistic. I liked that. So, I said you go ahead and do it. The critics and fans both kind of excoriated him for that. And now, when you read retrospective pieces about *The Mist*, people are, 'Wow, that's one of the great ones.' They like it. They just had to get used to it."

The Mist, UK Steelbook Bluray.

"...I mean, there's nothing wrong with a movie that has a nice happy ending, and everybody walks off into the sunset, and Red gets together with what's-his-name down in Mexico and they build boats together. That's great — everybody likes that. They go out of the theater, they're on cloud nine.

But it doesn't have to be that way. It does not have to be that way. Think of *Carrie* — the hand comes out of the ground, and Sue Snell wakes up and you know that that girl is going to be traumatized for the rest of her life. And that movie was a success."

JULY

8 MONDAY

9 TUESDAY

10 WEDNESDAY

MUDDING IN *THE MIST*

In the novella, what type of vehicle does David Drayton use to go into town after the storm?

What is unique about this vehicle in a Stephen King story?

What vehicle is used for the film version of *The Mist*?

JULY

11 THURSDAY

12 FRIDAY

13 SATURDAY

14 SUNDAY

Answers:

A1: In the novella Stephen King used an International Scout.

A2. The International Harvester Scout is an off-road vehicle produced by International Harvester from 1961 to 1980. Actually, Stephen King has used the Scout land cruiser in many of his novels and stories. One would assume that because Stephen King's home in Maine you would need to utilize a vehicle like this during heavy winter months with ice, snow, and mud. Scout's feature four-wheel drive and have been a popular vehicle in those climates.

A3: A 1968 Toyota Land Cruiser.

JULY

15 MONDAY

16 TUESDAY

17 WEDNESDAY

BERNIE WRIGHTSON'S ORIGINAL "WINDOW BUG"

Bernie Wrightson was hired by Frank Darabont, the director of *The Mist*, to create creatures for the film. This was one of the concept art pieces for Frank Darabont's *The Mist* (Darkwoods Productions, 2007).

Accomplished in pencil 12" x 17" artist's leaf. Hand-titled at top, "The MIST #15 Window Bug-" and signed at lower right, "Bernie Wrightson." A detailed and

18 THURSDAY

19 FRIDAY

20 SATURDAY

21 SUNDAY

finished pencil study for a winged creature used in the Frank Darabont film adaptation of Stephen King's novella, *The Mist*. Light production handling. In Fine condition. It came with a Certificate of Authenticity from Heritage Auctions. From the Personal Collection of Frank Darabont. "Window Bug" sold on Jul 18, 2021 for: $4,750.00

The Mist DVD, Korea

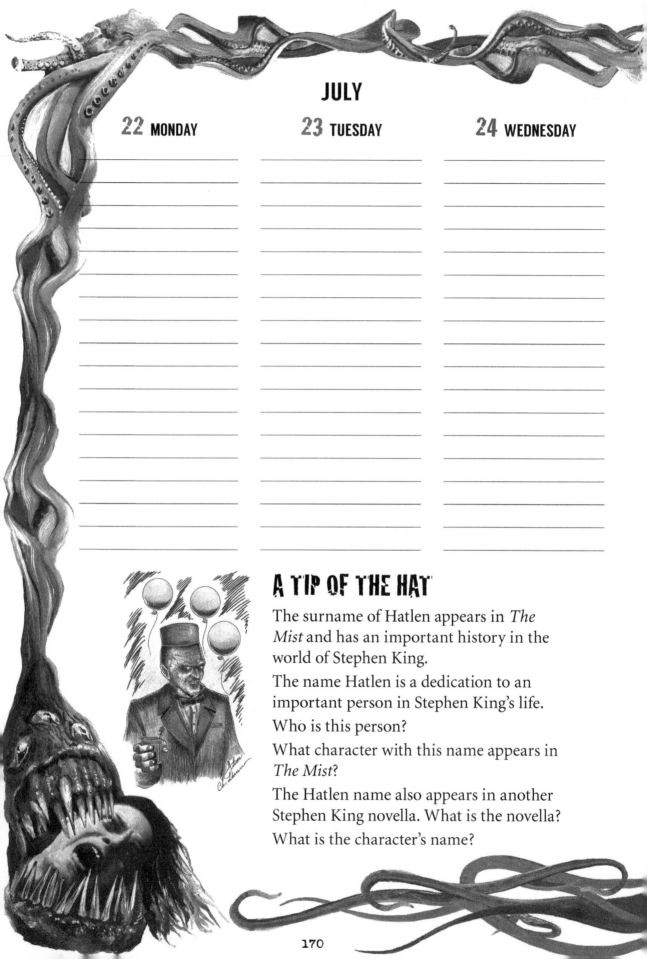

JULY

22 MONDAY

23 TUESDAY

24 WEDNESDAY

A TIP OF THE HAT

The surname of Hatlen appears in *The Mist* and has an important history in the world of Stephen King.

The name Hatlen is a dedication to an important person in Stephen King's life.

Who is this person?

What character with this name appears in *The Mist*?

The Hatlen name also appears in another Stephen King novella. What is the novella?

What is the character's name?

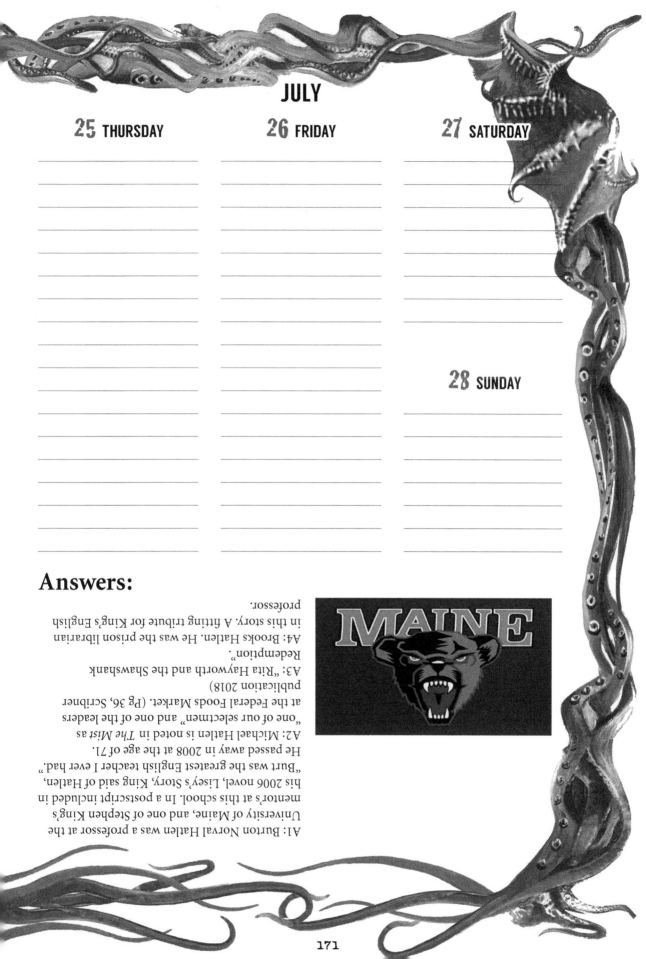

JULY

25 THURSDAY

26 FRIDAY

27 SATURDAY

28 SUNDAY

Answers:

A1: Burton Norval Hatlen was a professor at the University of Maine, and one of Stephen King's mentor's at this school. In a postscript included in his 2006 novel, Lisey's Story, King said of Hatlen, "Burt was the greatest English teacher I ever had." He passed away in 2008 at the age of 71.

A2: Michael Hatlen is noted in *The Mist* as "one of our selectmen" and one of the leaders at the Federal Foods Market. (Pg 36, Scribner publication 2018)

A3: "Rita Hayworth and the Shawshank Redemption".

A4: Brooks Hatlen. He was the prison librarian in this story. A fitting tribute for King's English professor.

JULY

29 MONDAY

30 TUESDAY

31 WEDNESDAY

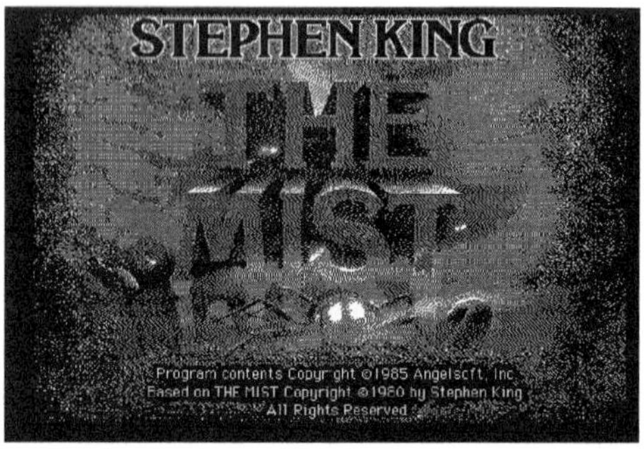

STEPHEN KING

THE MIST

Program contents Copyright ©1985 Angelsoft, Inc.
Based on THE MIST Copyright ©1980 by Stephen King
All Rights Reserved

DID YOU KNOW?

THE MIST – 1985 GAME by ANGELSOFT

I discussed in length about *The Mist* game from Angelsoft earlier in this year's annual. Did you know that you can still access the game online? And did you know there is reportedly a typo you had to know to complete the game?

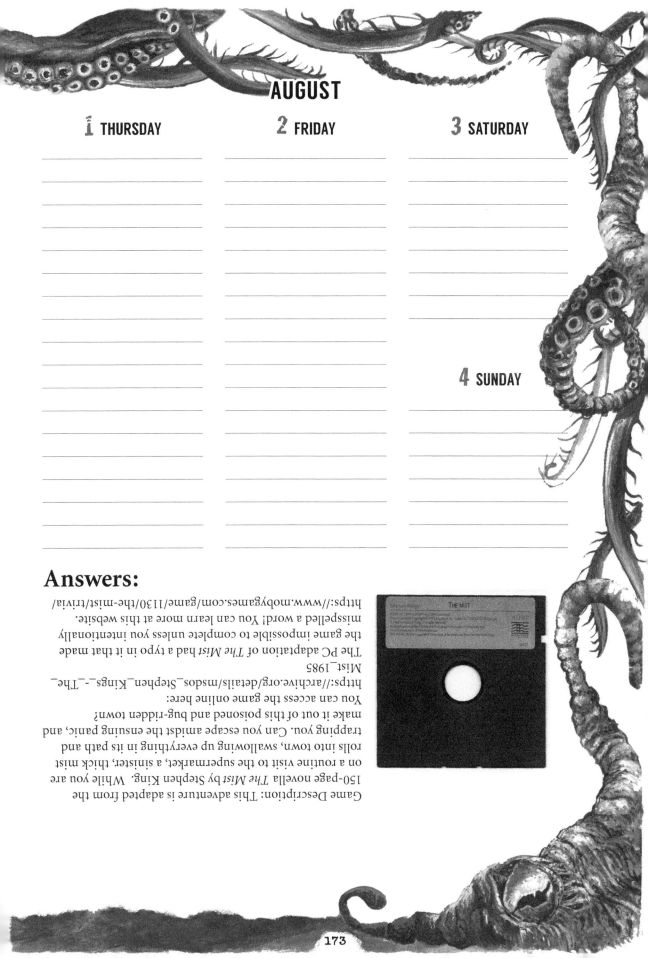

AUGUST

1 THURSDAY

2 FRIDAY

3 SATURDAY

4 SUNDAY

Answers:

Game Description: This adventure is adapted from the 150-page novella *The Mist* by Stephen King. While you are on a routine visit to the supermarket, a sinister, thick mist rolls into town, swallowing up everything in its path and trapping you. Can you escape amidst the ensuing panic, and make it out of this poisoned and bug-ridden town?

You can access the game online here:
https://archive.org/details/msdos_Stephen_Kings_-_The_Mist_1985

The PC adaptation of *The Mist* had a typo in it that made the game impossible to complete unless you intentionally misspelled a word! You can learn more at this website.
https://www.mobygames.com/game/1130/the-mist/trivia/

AUGUST

5 MONDAY

6 TUESDAY

7 WEDNESDAY

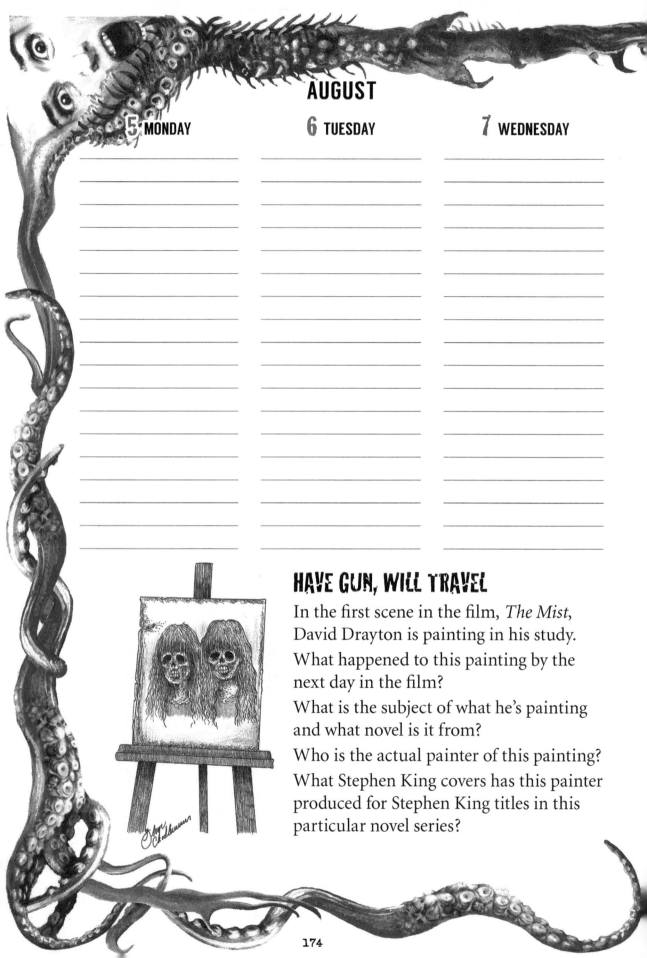

HAVE GUN, WILL TRAVEL

In the first scene in the film, *The Mist*, David Drayton is painting in his study.

What happened to this painting by the next day in the film?

What is the subject of what he's painting and what novel is it from?

Who is the actual painter of this painting?

What Stephen King covers has this painter produced for Stephen King titles in this particular novel series?

AUGUST

8 THURSDAY

9 FRIDAY

10 SATURDAY

11 SUNDAY

Answers:

A1: The Gunslinger from *The Dark Tower*.

A2: Clint Eastwood. Eastwood was apparently the original idea when it came to who should play "the gunslinger" in film, in this futuristic western opera Stephen King had begun. In *The Dark Tower: The Wastelands* (No. 3) Clint Eastwood is even mentioned when Jake sees the actor in a movie poster hanging at the theater: "Eastwood was wearing a Mexican serape. A cigar was clamped in his teeth." (Pg. 179-180). This would make sense as Stephen King grew up with all the Eastwood spaghetti westerns that made him a movie star and he was the epitome of the "western stranger" who strolled in and out of these films.

A3: Michael Whelan

A4: *The Dark Tower : The Gunslinger* (No. 1), *The Dark Tower* (No. 7)

A5: After the storm, the Drayton's are examining any damage in and around the house. David Drayton discovers the same painting from the night before in the front yard, torn and tattered.

AUGUST

12 MONDAY

13 TUESDAY

14 WEDNESDAY

A CONVERSATION:

STEPHEN KING and FRANK DARABONT on *THE MIST*

This conversation between Stephen King and Frank Darabont was produced for the special features on the disc release. It was exclusively available on the Blockbuster rental for about a month before it was seen/heard anywhere else. This is an abridged version of the interview. You can see the interview on the special features from the discs and/or possibly at YouTube.

This is a little insight between the text and film creators I thought you might enjoy.

SK: It is funny isn't it? How much like a prison story *The Mist* is when you think about it.

FD: Yeah, it really is, it's just it's a remake of *Shawshank* is what it is.

SK: That's what it is, with Mrs. Carmody as the warden!

FD: That's right (laughs), no these themes do, do, do, keep popping out, and *The Long Walk* is also, in a sense, a prison, that road, and that group of kids on the road, that they're imprisoned in that situation, you do that really well.

Two Disc Collector's Edition
DVD 2008

SK: "life is a prison" it's what (Eugène) Ionesco said in *Rhinoceros* (laughs). I don't think either of us really knew how to end it for a long time. We talked about that, we kicked it back and forth, the story has no ending. Frank finally came up with an ending. Once the ending was there... Say this about the ending, say that about the ending, I hope people realized that there's like two hours before the ending, but they will talk about it.

FD: Right, exactly and a damn good ride along the way thanks to you, rich material. I mean it's a movie about fear sending people off a precipice and it, it just felt intuitive to me and I'm really glad that you agreed and felt it was true to the story.

FD: Shot it in Louisiana in 6 weeks, 37 days...

SK: I almost came down. I got on the computer and I did like MapQuest and everything, and it was about 600 miles further than I thought but I thought I was gonna jump in my car and drive, from Sarasota to wherever it was, ya know, and jump and surprise you. I couldn't.

AUGUST

15 THURSDAY

16 FRIDAY

17 SATURDAY

18 SUNDAY

FD: Are you kidding me? I would have done a jig, man, it would have delighted me.

SK: ...you got me in *The Mist*, one time, and I mean I had seen the film in a rough cut and it still got me!

FD: My favorite moment, possibly in life, but certainly the whole experience of *The Mist*, was we were at the New Jersey test screening. You flew in for that,... I was sitting right next to you... and there's just one moment in the movie something happens. Stephen King jumped three feet out of his chair!

SK: I did!

FD: You landed and crunched down, and I thought man, I rule! I scared Stephen King, but fresh scared!

SK: I mean scaring Stephen King...

FD: With his own story!

FD: I read *The Mist* in 1980, which was the year that I sent you that letter saying 'Dear Mister King do you mind if I make a short film out of "The Woman in the Room."' I was flabbergasted but you were generous enough to say yes. I didn't realize at the time you had this policy...

SK: I didn't have a policy then, Frank. You were the guy who made the policy possible.

FD: Well, I always thought it was incredibly generous of you to grant those kinds of rights to young filmmakers. Was I the first, really?

SK: I think you were probably the first because that's a very, very, early story, and it was never published in a magazine. It was only published in *Nightshift*, because nobody would take it, because I had a reputation for horror stories, and that one was something a little bit different. When you sent me a copy of the film, I thought it was so fantastic, I thought, you know what, this is really interesting. These people can go and make small films out of short stories and you just never know what they're gonna come up with.

Famous last words considering what Frank Darabont wrote for the ending to... *The Mist*.

The Mist Audio compact disc 2008

19 MONDAY

20 TUESDAY

21 WEDNESDAY

1922 trade paperback, Scribners 2019

HOW DEEP IT GOES

Let's see if you know your actors from *The Mist*, and their place in the land of Stephen King.

Who plays David Drayton? What other Stephen King projects has he acted?

Who plays Mrs. Drayton, Billy's mom? She has been in one other King project. Do you know it?

Who plays Jim Grondin? In what other King films has he appeared?

Who plays Dan Miller? What other King appearances has he had?

AUGUST

22 THURSDAY

23 FRIDAY

24 SATURDAY

25 SUNDAY

Answers:

A1: Thomas Jane. He was Henry in *Dreamcatcher* (2003) and starred as Wilfred James in 1922, a Netflix original movie.

A2: Kelly Collins Lintz portrays Steff Drayton. She is Monica Porter in *Mr. Mercedes*, Season 3, Episode 8, as Kelly Lintz.

A3: William Sadler, has become a veteran acting in King and Darabont films. He first played Heywood, a member of Red's gang, serving a long sentence in Shawshank prison. He then was Klaus Detterick, the father of the two dead girls in *The Green Mile*. He is slated to be in the new *Salem's Lot* film from Warner Bros, but no character update has been given. It has been delayed from it's 2023 release. We do understand it is completed and now we wait.

A4: Jeffrey DeMunn. Another Frank Darabont favorite and Stephen King film actor. He played Andy Dufresne's prosecuting attorney in *Shawshank Redemption*. He played Harry Terwilliger as an E Block guard at Cold Mountain Penitentiary in *The Green Mile*, and Robbie Beals in *Storm of the Century*.

'Salem's Lot (Movie Tie-in) Anchor 2022

AUGUST

26 MONDAY

27 TUESDAY

28 WEDNESDAY

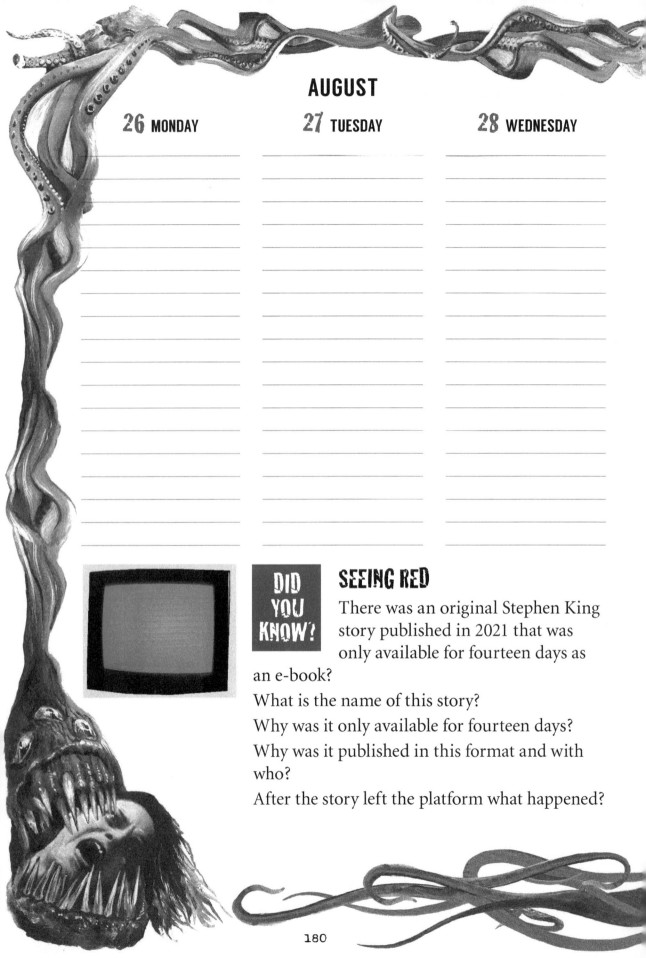

DID YOU KNOW?

SEEING RED

There was an original Stephen King story published in 2021 that was only available for fourteen days as an e-book?

What is the name of this story?

Why was it only available for fourteen days?

Why was it published in this format and with who?

After the story left the platform what happened?

AUGUST

29 THURSDAY

30 FRIDAY

31 SATURDAY

1 SUNDAY

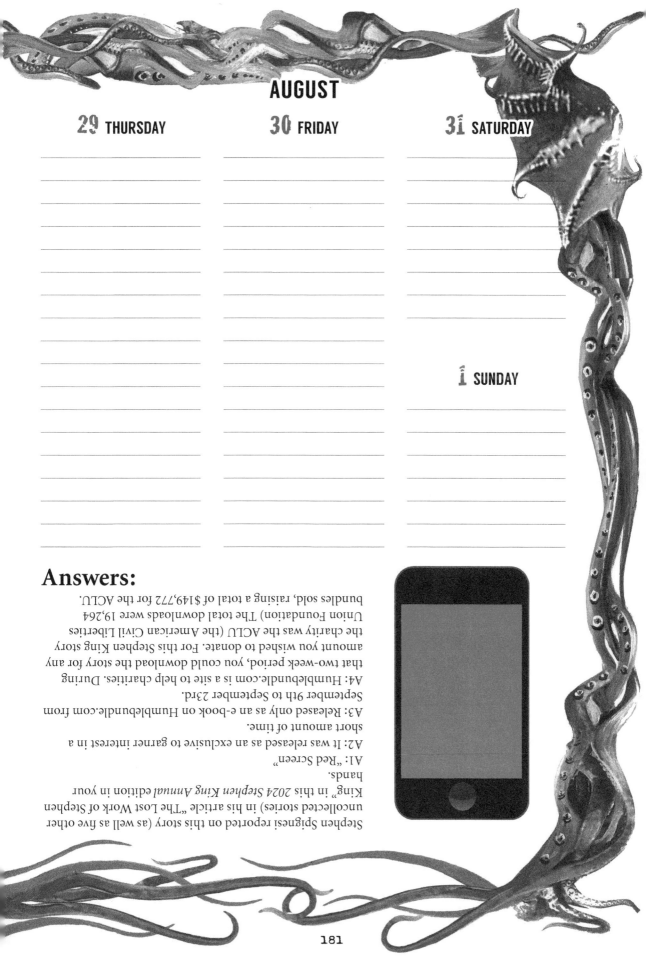

Answers:

Stephen Spignesi reported on this story (as well as five other uncollected stories) in his article "The Lost Work of Stephen King" in this *2024 Stephen King Annual* edition in your hands.

A1: "Red Screen"

A2: It was released as an exclusive to garner interest in a short amount of time.

A3: Released only as an e-book on Humblebundle.com from September 9th to September 23rd.

A4: Humblebundle.com is a site to help charities. During that two-week period, you could download the story for any amount you wished to donate. For this Stephen King story the charity was the ACLU (the American Civil Liberties Union Foundation) The total downloads were 19,264 bundles sold, raising a total of $149,772 for the ACLU.

SEPTEMBER

2 MONDAY
Labor Day

3 TUESDAY

4 WEDNESDAY

This image of a theoretical Planet X by Caltech / R.Hurt

TENTACLES FROM PLANET X

Three soldiers from the Arrowhead Project show up in the grocery store. One of the actors began starring in films and a TV series after *The Mist*. Can you name him?

Can you name a film and / or TV series he was in?

Upon hearing the story of Norm's demise by the multi tentacled creature Brent Norton refers to the news about the creature in the storage room as what?

The MP in the film came to pick up the three soldiers in the store, but left soon after. What happened to the MP?

What did the MP say when he was found?

SEPTEMBER

5 THURSDAY

6 FRIDAY

7 SATURDAY

8 SUNDAY

Answers:

A1: Sam Witwer

A2: Sam Witwer was in Star Wars: Solo and in the SyFy series *Being Human*

A3: "Tentacle he says.... tentacles from Planet X."

A4: The MP was discovered when the group went to check on the pharmacy next door. He was hanging from a store beam, writhing around saying he could "feel them" as baby spiders crawled out of his face and bubbled under his chest.

A5: "It's our fault, it's all our fault", obviously referring to the Arrowhead Project where the creatures appear to have come from.

SEPTEMBER

9 MONDAY

10 TUESDAY

11 WEDNESDAY

I GOT BOSCHED!

"It looked like one of the minor creatures in a Bosch painting-one of his hellacious murals." **– Stephen King**, *The Mist*.

If you're not familiar with Bosch then let us – us including Stephen King since he's brought him into *The Mist* – bring you up to speed. Hieronymus Bosch was a Dutch/Netherlandish painter from Brabant in the 1500's. He is one of the most notable representatives of the Early Netherlandish painting school. His work, generally oil on oak wood, mainly contains fantastic illustrations of religious concepts and narratives. Bosch is seen as a hugely individualistic painter with deep insight into humanity's desires and deepest fears. only about 25 paintings are confidently given to his hand along with eight drawings. About another half-dozen paintings are confidently attributed to his workshop. His most acclaimed works consist of a few triptych altarpieces, including *The Garden of Earthly Delights* which you see here.

SEPTEMBER

12 THURSDAY

13 FRIDAY

14 SATURDAY

15 SUNDAY

A selected pane from *The Garden of Earthly Delights* by Hieronymus Bosch, 1500's.

SEPTEMBER

16 MONDAY

_____
_____
_____
_____
_____
_____
_____
_____
_____
_____
_____
_____
_____
_____
_____
_____
_____
_____
_____

17 TUESDAY

_____
_____
_____
_____
_____
_____
_____
_____
_____
_____
_____
_____
_____
_____
_____
_____
_____
_____
_____

18 WEDNESDAY

_____
_____
_____
_____
_____
_____
_____
_____
_____
_____
_____
_____
_____
_____
_____
_____
_____
_____
_____

SURE, GO OUT IN THE MIST...
SEE WHAT THAT WILL GET YOU!

After his denial about any creatures outside the grocery store, Brent Norton convinces a small group of folks and leads them outside to see what they can discover, and possibly send back help. A biker agrees to David Drayton's request to tie a clothesline around his waist and tie the other end to a stationary object when he comes to the end of it.

Who is the actor that plays the biker?

How long is this clothesline?

What is the relationship between the biker actor and the director Frank Darabont?

What is the name of Frank Darabont's first Stephen King film?

SEPTEMBER

19 THURSDAY

20 FRIDAY

21 SATURDAY

22 SUNDAY

Answers:

A1: Brian Libby.

A2: 300 feet, according to Stephen King's novella.

A3: Brian Libby was hired to be in Frank Darabont's first film, which was also a King story. Like a good luck charm, Brian Libby has been in every Frank Darabont film.

A4: *The Woman in the Room*. Brian Libby photo on the opposite page is from this film.

VHS Granite Entertainment Group, 1996

23 MONDAY

24 TUESDAY

25 WEDNESDAY

WHO MADE WHO?

"A little boy named David Drayton with his father, the famous artist Andrew Drayton, whose painting Christine Standing Alone hung in the White House."
– *The Mist*, Stephen King.

This line, from page 48 in the 2018 Scribner trade paperback release of *The Mist*, may not be obvious to all but as soon as I read this line I recognized the "nod" that Stephen King was giving to Maine artist Andrew Wyeth and his 1948 painting *Christina's World*. This painting is part of the Museum of Modern Art (MOMA) collection in New York City. Christina Olson and her family were neighbors in Cushing, Maine, and this is perhaps Andrew Wyeth's best known work. It depicts Christina Olson,

SEPTEMBER

26 THURSDAY

27 FRIDAY

28 SATURDAY

29 SUNDAY

sprawled on a dry field facing her house in the distance. Wyeth was inspired by Christina, who, crippled from (undiagnosed) Charcot–Marie–Tooth disease, a genetic polyneuropathy, and unable to walk, spent most of her time at home.

The Olson house has been preserved and renovated to match its appearance in *Christina's World*. It is open to the public as a part of the Farnsworth Art Museum.

Wyeth did a number of works and studies of the Olson House and property. Because of Wyeth's profile, the property was designated a National Historic Landmark in June 2011.

OCTOBER

30 MONDAY

1 TUESDAY

2 WEDNESDAY

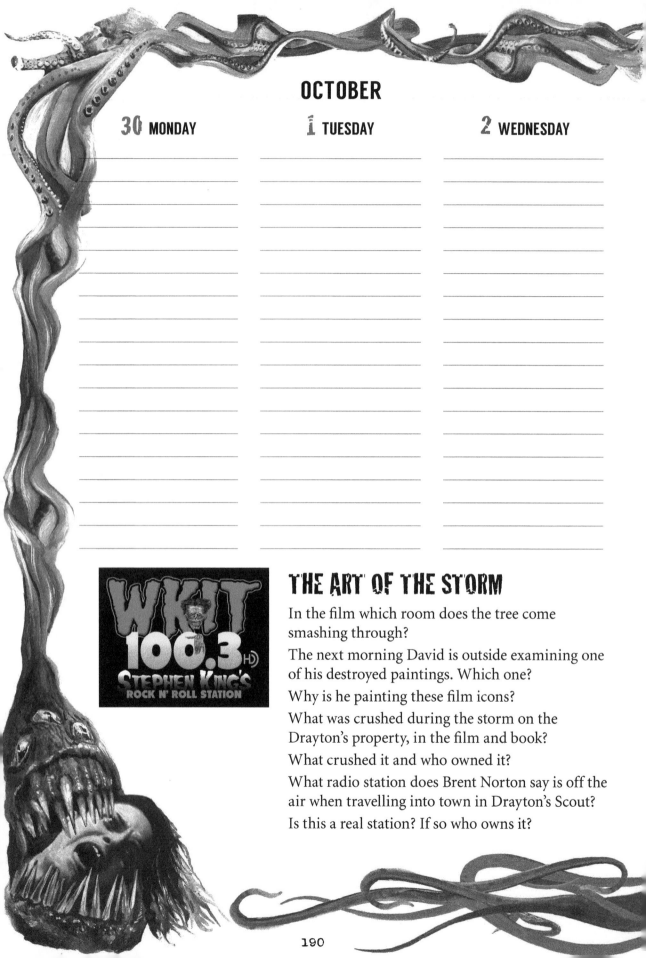

THE ART OF THE STORM

In the film which room does the tree come smashing through?

The next morning David is outside examining one of his destroyed paintings. Which one?

Why is he painting these film icons?

What was crushed during the storm on the Drayton's property, in the film and book?

What crushed it and who owned it?

What radio station does Brent Norton say is off the air when travelling into town in Drayton's Scout?

Is this a real station? If so who owns it?

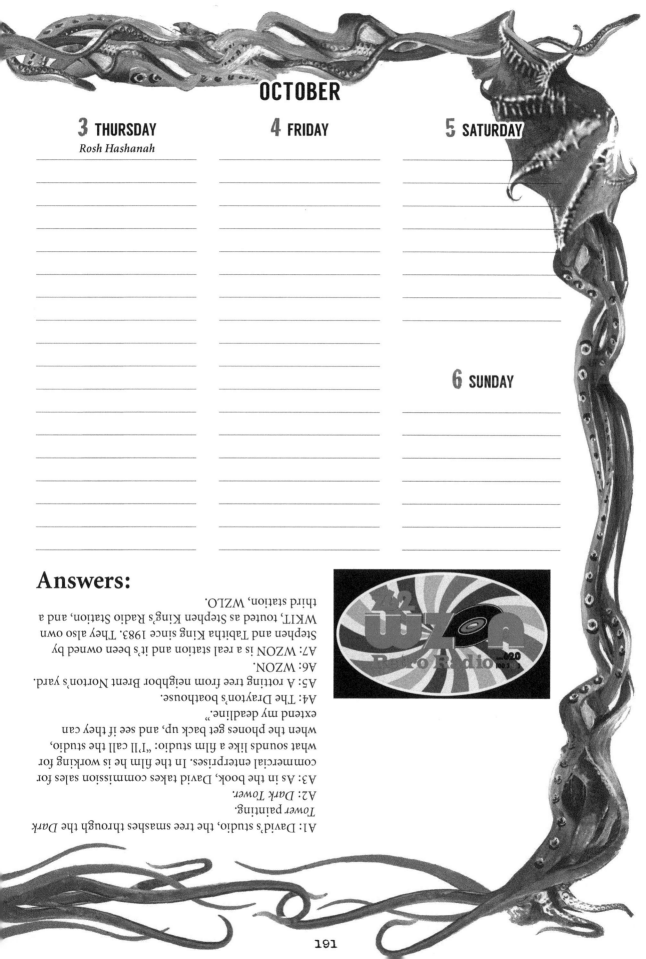

OCTOBER

3 THURSDAY
Rosh Hashanah

4 FRIDAY

5 SATURDAY

6 SUNDAY

Answers:

A1: David's studio, the tree smashes through the *Dark Tower* painting.

A2: *Dark Tower.*

A3: As in the book, David takes commission sales for commercial enterprises. In the film he is working for what sounds like a film studio: "I'll call the studio, when the phones get back up, and see if they can extend my deadline."

A4: The Drayton's boathouse.

A5: A rotting tree from neighbor Brent Norton's yard.

A6: WZON.

A7: WZON is a real station and it's been owned by Stephen and Tabitha King since 1983. They also own WKIT, touted as Stephen King's Radio Station, and a third station, WZLO.

OCTOBER

7 MONDAY

8 TUESDAY

9 WEDNESDAY

FIRST THE KIDS... THEN ZOMBIES

While I was on the set of *The Mist* I'd been experiencing some intense acting in many scenes. I was especially taken aback by one actress on the first day I was there. It's the scene in the grocery store when a woman says, "I can't stay here, I've gotta get home to my kids." She pleads with the group at the front of the store, "won't somebody here see a lady home?." As she begins quietly crying as she looks around, her scene of two minutes and 15 seconds are some of the most powerful moments in the film. The next day I was talking with some of the crew about the scene and a makeup person said that some of crew were crying it had affected them so much.

The Mist theatrical poster, Dimension Films, 2007

The filming was so intense during this shoot that there wasn't a lot of down time, it was a constant filming schedule, unlike the movie sets I'd been on before, there was no time to waste as I discovered this film was on a tight budget. I was able to ask Frank Darabont "who is that actress, the mother that had to leave and get to her kids"? Frank said "Dave, be sure to write about her in your review. We discovered her in Houston and she's bringing a lot to this role for us." Well, I'm finally setting this down for posterity. As it was this was originally to appear in our next print catalog (see my *Entering The Mist* earlier in this edition of why) I'm glad to finally be able to share this.

Fast forward to three years later in 2010. Frank Darabont has brought *The Walking Dead* to life for AMC, and who do we see in the third episode? The

OCTOBER

10 THURSDAY

11 FRIDAY

12 SATURDAY
Yom Kippur

13 SUNDAY

mother from *The Mist*, actress Melissa McBride, now playing character Carol Peletier. My son Trey and I were on the set for *The Walking Dead*, season six, the episode "The Same Boat" (wonderful episode written by Angela Kang) was being filmed. The scene we saw that day featured, you guessed it, Melissa McBride! I had an opportunity to speak to Melissa after filming and I told her I was on the set for her scene in *The Mist*. "You were there?" she said. "Yes, I was. What an intense moment," I told her, "You had some of the crew in tears that day ." I also told her that I brought her performance up to Frank Darabont and mentioned what he said, that I should include her in the review, drifting off with that Frank said she was from "Houston." She laughed, with a grin and said "Frank is always getting that wrong" I came in from North Carolina for *The Mist* filming. It was then that our escort for the day, Julia Hobgood (and assistant to Greg Nicotero), and Melissa learned that they both lived and worked in and around the same area of North Carolina and was surprised working together all these years and just discovered this during our conversation. We all learned a lot that day. Oh, and during our conversation Melissa did have stage blood spots over her face and shirt, but you'd expect that from an actress that takes out zombies for a living. Hell, I remember when she was saving her kids from big ol' *Mist* monsters.

The Walking Dead Official Trading Cards, Season 3

OCTOBER

14 MONDAY

Columbus Day
Indigenous Peoples' Day

15 TUESDAY

16 WEDNESDAY

CAMERA OBSCURA

In the opening movie scene from *The Mist* David Drayton is painting in his studio and the camera drifts from right to left. Many items and paintings appear within this short scene. Look closely and let's see what you discover.

There are two paintings above the desk in the very first shot. Can you describe them?

What's on the desk?

There's a framed painting on the wall referencing Frank Darabont's first Academy Award nominated film. Which film?

Who, or what, is in the framed wall painting?

What is David Drayton painting?

On the wall, in front of David Drayton (behind what he is painting), is a framed painting from what movie?

There is another painting, to the left of the painting on the wall, featuring a young girl lying down. What is this from?

As the family looks outside to the oncoming storm, in front of the picture window (in itself, its own sort of realistic painting), there is one more painting onscreen for only seconds. What is it a nod too?

OCTOBER

17 THURSDAY

18 FRIDAY

19 SATURDAY

20 SUNDAY

Answers:

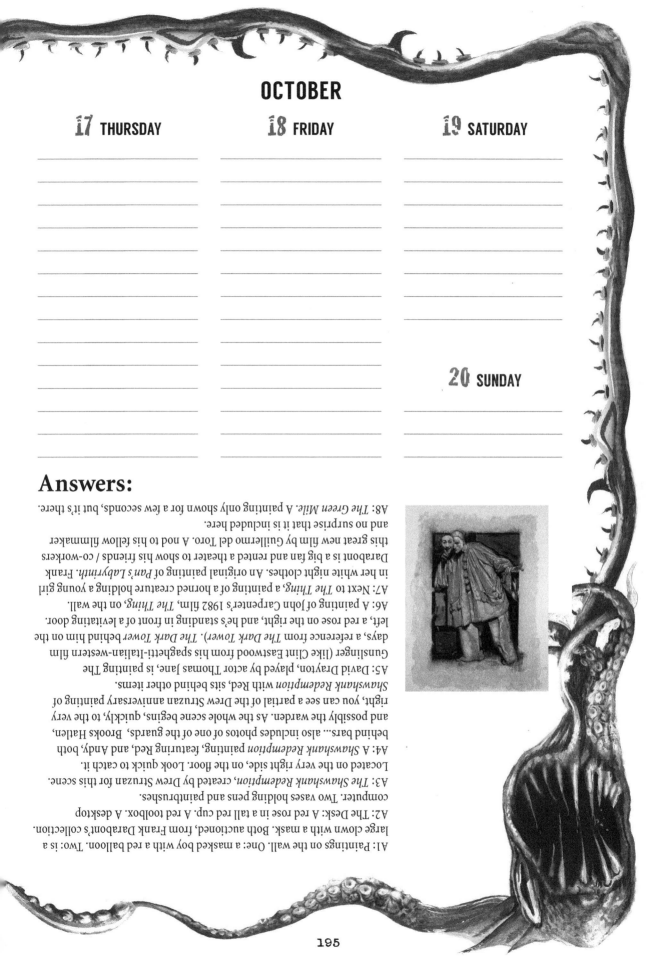

A1: Paintings on the wall. One: a masked boy with a red balloon. Two: is a large clown with a mask. Both auctioned, from Frank Darabont's collection.

A2: The Desk: A red rose in a tall red cup. A red toolbox. A desktop computer. Two vases holding pens and paintbrushes.

A3: *The Shawshank Redemption*, created by Drew Struzan for this scene. Located on the very right side, on the floor. Look quick to catch it.

A4: A *Shawshank Redemption* painting, featuring Red, and Andy, both behind bars... also includes photos of one of the guards, Brooks Hatlen, and possibly the warden. As the whole scene begins, quickly, to the very right, you can see a partial of the Drew Struzan painting of *Shawshank Redemption* with Red, sits behind other items.

A5: David Drayton, played by actor Thomas Jane, is painting The Gunslinger (like Clint Eastwood from his spaghetti-Italian-western film days, a reference from *The Dark Tower*). *The Dark Tower* behind him on the left, a red rose on the right, and he's standing in front of a levitating door.

A6: A painting of John Carpenter's 1982 film, *The Thing*, on the wall.

A7: Next to *The Thing*, a painting of a horned creature holding a young girl in her white night clothes. An original painting of *Pan's Labyrinth*. Frank Darabont is a big fan and rented a theater to show his friends / co-workers this great new film by Guillermo del Toro. A nod to his fellow filmmaker and no surprise that it is included here.

A8: *The Green Mile*. A painting only shown for a few seconds, but it's there.

OCTOBER

21 MONDAY

22 TUESDAY

23 WEDNESDAY

DARK FORCES "THE MOST IMPORTANT HORROR COLLECTION OF THE YEAR" – LOCUS MAGAZINE

Dark Forces: New Stories of Suspense and Supernatural Horror is an anthology of 23 original horror stories, first published by The Viking Press August 29th, 1980, and in the UK by Futura Publications on September 18th, 1980. The *Dark Forces* anthology was ground breaking and changed the course of the horror swell of fiction and success that was to follow it.

In his introduction Kirby McCauley explains the origins of *Dark Forces*. Kirby McCauley went to dinner with Anthony Cheetham, the publisher of Futura Publications Ltd in England. Cheetham suggested that since he had this portfolio of impressive authors, since he was their agent, that he recruit as many as possible to create a collection of "new stories of horror and the supernatural". Cheetham would then publish this new anthology. McCauley (also from the introduction) says that Cheetham "liked my only other anthology of original stories, Frights, and seemed to feel I was the person to do a more ambitious similar volume for him." He decided "to assemble [the] anthology with the same scope and dynamism of Harlan Ellison's *Dangerous Visions*, but in the supernatural horror field." Ellison's innovative 1967 anthology chose stories that were rooted in science fiction but took to new orchestrations to "break new ground, say and do things in new and varied and daring ways". Cheetham immediately grasped the

Dark Forces, Futura UK paperback 1986

196

24 THURSDAY

25 FRIDAY

26 SATURDAY

27 SUNDAY

concept and agreed to publish the book. McCauley "approached by letter or telephone near every writer living who had tried his or her hand at this type of story and whose writing" he liked. He also "deliberately sought variety, stories ranging wide across the horizon of fantasy fiction". He felt, "nothing seems...more boring than an anthology in one key, having similar backdrops or styles, or which are all variations on a narrow theme."

From one of his more successful clients, Stephen King, he pursued *The Mist*, which would close the anthology and he also took the "opportunity to meet Isaac Bashevis Singer", the Polish-born Jewish writer who won the Nobel Prize in 1978.

"I set out to offer as many of the subjects and moods and general directions the fantastic tale has tended traditionally to take as I could, but hopefully in imaginative, fresh ways."

Dark Forces won the World Fantasy Award for best Anthology/Collection in 1981 and Clive Barker, in *Faces of Fear*, said that reading the "great variation of horror stories" in the collection encouraged him to start writing the short stories that would come to make up his *Books Of Blood*. Kirby McCauley was born in Minnesota on 11th September 1941 and became a literary agent in the 1970s, representing the likes of Stephen King and George R. R. Martin. Helping to found the World Fantasy Convention in 1975, he also helped create the World Fantasy Awards and edited *Night Chills* (1975), *Frights* (1976) and *Dark Forces* (1980). He died on 30th August 2014, of renal failure associated with diabetes.

OCTOBER

28 MONDAY

_____

29 TUESDAY

_____

30 WEDNESDAY

_____

Constantine Nasr taking a spider web shower in the King Pharmacy.
The Mist set, 2007

KING PHARMA

What comic does David Drayton pull off the comic rack to take back to his son Billy?

Who is the creator?

David Drayton pulls the comic off the rack, right behind it is another comic. What is the title and issue number?

Who are the writers / creators of this comic?

Who created the cover art for this issue?

Bonus Questions: Can you name the comic series shown above and below the comic David Drayton pulls off the rack?

These comics are another nod to their creator. What is their name?

NOVEMBER

31 THURSDAY
Halloween

1 FRIDAY

2 SATURDAY

3 SUNDAY
Daylight Saving Time End

Answers:

A1: A *Hellboy* comic.

A2: Created by Mike Mignola and an obvious nod from director, Frank Darabont.

A3: *Bad Planet*, Issue No. 2.

A4: Written by Thomas Jane (David Drayton in *The Mist*) and Steve Niles.

A5: Bernie Wrightson!

A6: *The Goon.*

A7: This excellent series is by Eric Powell. There are two issues sitting right above and below the *Hellboy* comic David grabs. Eric Powell visited the set of *The Mist* and you can see him on the extra features of the DVD set, where he helps during the background of a scene.

Garbage Pail Kids card, "MistyHaze" 2019

NOVEMBER

4 MONDAY

5 TUESDAY
Election Day
(Go Vote!)

6 WEDNESDAY

THE MIST – ORIGINAL MOVIE ART BY DREW STRUZAN

Famed movie poster artist, Drew Struzan, was commissioned to create this original art for *The Mist* movie poster. It was auctioned and sold on April 25th, 2023, for $2,500. It is signed on the lower right hand side by the artist. This painting / poster was used extensively on posters, DVDs, BluRay, audio and a paperback release.

Drew Struzan (American, b. 1947)
The Mist, 2007
Mixed media on board
12 x 8 inches (30.5 x 20.3 cm)

7 THURSDAY

8 FRIDAY

9 SATURDAY

10 SUNDAY

The Mist paperback, 2007.

The Mist, Russia DVD

The Mist Collector's Edition, Blu Ray 2019

NOVEMBER

11 MONDAY
Veterans Day

12 TUESDAY

13 WEDNESDAY

THE MAJESTIC INTO *THE MIST*

In 2001 I went with a friend to see *The Majestic*, a new film directed by Frank Darabont. After the excitement of *The Shawshank Redemption* and *The Green Mile*, we couldn't wait to plunk down our bucks to purchase a ticket. *The Majestic* is a gorgeous effort. I can relate to it in so many ways, the time period was definitely Capraesque, Jim Carrey's heartfelt performance lightened up the screen, and this not being a comedy, about small-town life and the gambles anyone faces, no matter what the era. There's a turn in the story which, although expected, for some reason changed the feel of the film for me. I can't put my finger on it. I wasn't expecting a King adaptation, but then again all I knew from this director was Stephen King films. That still doesn't explain it, but for some reason it was just good, not great... but let's not get ahead of what I'm trying to express here, now some twenty-two years later. Stick with me.

After directing *The Green Mile* in 1999 Darabont then went straight into directing Michael Sloane's original script, *The Majestic*. Darabont had known Sloane since high school and had always loved this script. Darabont wanted to direct the film as he saw it as a "love letter" to works of Frank Capra and all the other movies he has loved throughout his life.

This 2001 American romantic drama starred Jim Carrey in the leading role. The film also features a who's who of actors: Bob Balaban, Brent Briscoe, Jeffrey DeMunn, Amanda Detmer, Allen Garfield, Hal Holbrook, Laurie Holden, Martin Landau, Ron Rifkin, David Ogden Stiers, and James Whitmore. He worked

The Majestic theatrical poster, signed by Frank Darabont. Warner Bros. 2001

NOVEMBER

14 THURSDAY

15 FRIDAY

16 SATURDAY

17 SUNDAY

with these actors frequently throughout his career. The film depicts a 1950s Hollywood screenwriter suspected of being a communist. After suffering amnesia as the result of a road accident, he is taken in by the residents of a small town, who mistake him for a local resident who went MIA while serving in the military during World War II. This film is one of the few which Frank Darabont directed, but did not write the screenplay.

He was a producer on *The Salton Sea* (2002 with Val Kilmer and Vincent D'Onofrio) and an executive producer on the film, *Collateral* (2004 with Tom Cruise and Jamie Foxx) however *The Mist* was the first film since *The Majestic* that found Darabont back in the seat as a director and screenwriter.

Film reviewer Roger Ebert awarded the film three and a half stars and praised the film and its ideals: "It flies the flag in honor of our World War II heroes, and evokes nostalgia for small-town movie palaces and the people who run them... Frank Darabont has deliberately tried to make the kind of movie Capra made, about decent small-town folks standing up for traditional American values. In an age of Rambo patriotism, it is good to be reminded of Capra patriotism - to remember that America is not just about fighting and winning, but about defending our freedoms." Ebert also praised Jim Carrey's performance stating that he "has never been better or more likable".

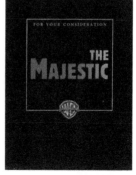

The Majestic, For Your Consideration Academy Award Screening DVD Warner Bros.

Roger Ebert had it right. I know because although I'd seen it one more time on cable (now streaming) back in the early 2000's, I hadn't seen it again... until two years ago. My wife and I were in the North Georgia mountains celebrating a late Christmas in a cabin (that had a record

NOVEMBER

18 MONDAY

19 TUESDAY

20 WEDNESDAY

Sand Pirates of the Sahara Poster
from *The Majestic*, 2001

player and records!), a small Christmas tree, with our son and his girl, down from Chicago for a few days. We are literally in the middle of "not much here," but. . .there was a thrift store, my Achilles heel. DVD hunting is my passion, looking for the forlorn, the odd TV seasons, horror and sci-fi. Upon this shelf of about thirty discs, I see this title, *The Majestic*, staring back at me. From the spine this DVD had a different look. Could it be the same film? I pulled it out and sure enough, same film, but one of the limited "For Your Consideration" discs that are sent only to the Academy members for Oscar consideration. These are simple productions only listing the film, the director, producers, cast, and crews that worked on the film, as directed by the rules of the Academy of Motion Pictures Arts and Sciences, the folks behind the Oscar Awards. I bought it. For a buck. It was a Darabont film and a no brainer. When we got back home we watched it again, after almost twenty years. And do you know what happened? I simply loved it. I embraced it like I had never seen it previously. What happened? I'd certainly reached a new pinnacle in life, raised a few wonderful young men, out in the world, with me now

NOVEMBER

21 THURSDAY

22 FRIDAY

23 SATURDAY

24 SUNDAY

closer to sixty than fifty. Whatever it was, I saw a film that is delightful, entertaining, a period picture that captured a time I had only seen in film, but here it was again. My perspective had obviously changed, and whatever that odd turn was back from the first viewing, it was completely gone. I was visiting an old friend that I look forward to seeing again. This time with my mom who will be eighty-three this year. I'm sure she'll love it too.

Frank Darabont has proven many times that he can make beautiful, wrenching, films, and Stephen King and his fans have benefitted from his work. After delving into other areas of film stories and producing Frank Darabont directed *The Mist*. Seven years after his last directed film, *The Majestic*, and if you've seen it, or if you're just discovering this lost gem here for the first time, I implore you to reach out and give it a viewing, on the biggest screen you can find. And if possible, see it with your partner and / or friends and family. I guarantee you a good time, there's a lot of life in this picture, and Jim Carrey is a delight. It is, it's simply, majestic.

Laurie Holden and Jim Carrey.
The Majestic, Warner Bros. 2001

NOVEMBER

25 MONDAY

26 TUESDAY

27 WEDNESDAY

KATIE, BAR THE DOOR!

Some facts you may not know, some of which have come to light just recently. Here we go!

It took a while to configure, but the loading dock effect of having the mist stay at the open roll-up door without spilling in "had to do with temperature in the room and air pressure," and they could control it by adjusting the temperature.

Jeffrey DeMunn, Melissa McBride, Laurie Holden, Juan Gabriel Pareja, Cheri Dvorak, Sam Witwer, Brandon O'Dell, Julio Cesar Cedillo, and Tiffany Morgan are all in *The Mist* and they also made their way into *The Walking Dead* (2010), courtesy of their *Mist* boss, Frank Darabont, who also adapted this series for television.

Chris Owens in *The Mist*, Dimension Films 2007.

NOVEMBER

28 THURSDAY
Thanksgiving

29 FRIDAY

30 SATURDAY

1 SUNDAY

Frank Darabont agreed to certain terms with the powers that be, to make his version of *The Mist*.

"I walked away from the $40 million budget, and the only person who stepped up and had the cojones to greenlight it was Bob [Weinstein]. I got a call from Bob and he said, 'I love your script, totally fine with the ending, but you gotta make it for this price,' which was a bit less than half of what the other guy was offering. So, I had that night of the soul where I'm going, 'Instead of paying myself my directing fee, I'll take scale. Instead of having some luxury of time to shoot, I'll have to shoot on half the schedule.' I've never, ever done a movie like that before." – Frank Darabont, slashfilm.com

The Mist, UK Steelbook set.

Director Frank Darabont originally wanted the film shown in black and white. The two-disc DVD/Blu-ray release contains Darabont's black-and-white version on the second disc.

DECEMBER

2 MONDAY   **3** TUESDAY   **4** WEDNESDAY

"WHAT IF GIANT BUGS STARTED TO FLY INTO THE GLASS."

Jake Tapper interviewed Stephen King on the ABC News Nightline program about *The Mist* in 2007. Here's a snippet of their *Mist* discussion.

JAKE TAPPER: How did the idea of "*The Mist*" come to you?

STEPHEN KING: "*The Mist*"? (Laughs) I answer these questions and I always sound totally mad, barking mad. There was a market, it is an actual market in Bridgeton, Maine, where my wife and I lived at that time. And I'd been blocked for some time. I'd written a very long novel called *The Stand*, and I'd finished it. And I couldn't seem to get anything else going. And about four months went by and I would try things, and they would die, and uh, I'd crumple up pages, and the wastebasket was full of paper, and the desk was bare. It was that kind of a situation. It was a writer's block.

Window bug, *The Mist*, Dimension Films 2007.

So, I was in the market one day, and uh, I was shopping, and I looked toward the front, and I saw the whole front of the market was plate glass. And what I thought of when I saw those big plate glass windows was, "What if giant bugs started to fly into the glass." (Laughs)

DECEMBER

5 THURSDAY

6 FRIDAY

7 SATURDAY

8 SUNDAY

TAPPER: That's what you saw?

KING: That's what I thought. That's what I thought. And I had no idea why. Probably because I saw too many movies when I was a kid.

But the story of "*The Mist*," in the background, there's this idea that the military has been fooling around with something that's too big for them, and has torn an actual hole in the fabric of reality, and these awful creatures from another dimension have come through.

In another part of the story, there's a religious zealot, Mrs. Carmody, who's in the market, and to begin with she's sort of a figure of fun. Because everybody's pretty well solemnly grounded, and nobody's worried about anything. But once the disaster strikes, Mrs. Carmody gets a weird power. And certainly we've seen this time and time again in our own lives, that as the situation worsens, in various parts of the world, the religious fanatics have a tendency to become more and more powerful.

So all of this stuff has resonance. That's one of the things that I've always liked about horror fiction, and about fiction in the fantastic, is that it does have a resonance.

DECEMBER

9 MONDAY

10 TUESDAY

11 WEDNESDAY

The Mist, Japan 2 Disc DVD, 2008

REMEMBER THOSE ALTERNATE ENDINGS FOR *THE MIST*? YEAH, ME NEITHER.

Here we are at the end of this year's Stephen King Annual, featuring *The Mist*. At this juncture why not discuss the ending of the *The Mist*, both Stephen King's original story ending and the shocking end of Frank Darabont's film version. If you have not seen the film yet, I recommend you do before continuing with this piece as the spoilers are going to fly.

In my research for this edition, reading the book, then watching the film several times, I was able to experience both versions with a new perspective. I've also picked up some new information on the way and I've discovered that there were alternate endings for the film that were explored but never used. Apparently they didn't work.

This was news to me. Alternate endings? Considering the film ending we received, I ponder what else was considered. A producer let is in with this quote from slashfilm.com in November 2022.

DECEMBER

12 THURSDAY

13 FRIDAY

14 SATURDAY

15 SUNDAY

Remember: spoilers ahead!

"I remember Frank and [editor] Hunter [Via] cut a few different things just to see how they would play, whether it's like the novella, [where] they just drive off into the mist and we don't know what happens. There was one that I swear to God was even worse. It was, you ended on Billy [Drayton, played by Nathan Gamble] waking up and saying 'Daddy?' and then it cuts to black and you hear a gunshot. And it was so awful. It was just so much worse. They did try a few different variations, but what we had worked best. It felt like the most complete story. It felt like the ending that the story needed to have." – Denise Huth, producer, *The Mist*

The actual ending has David Drayton making the decision, a pact with the rest of the adults in the vehicle, that he would execute the suicide for all of them. Including his young son, Billy. There aren't enough bullets for David to take his own life, and he finds himself with the horror of what he's done. Even with the knowledge that he was saving them all from the horrible Lovecraftian creatures in the mist. He saved them from excruciating pain. He exits the vehicle with a gut-wrenching scream, ready to embrace

DECEMBER

16 MONDAY

17 TUESDAY

18 WEDNESDAY

his death from whatever horror finds him first. Only he sees the mist clearing with the cavalry arriving in tanks and gas masks, flame throwers executing the nightmare creatures.

The lady in the grocery store, who left to save her kids, played by Melissa McBride, is now on the back of a military transport, with her kids, and she did the unthinkable... she survived in the mist. For her, all hope wasn't lost, which only throws into relief the utter folly and thudding finality of David Drayton's decision to give up hope.

This ending rocked most, if not all, audiences to the core. I dare say being a parent who's raised boys, this really took it out of me. I remember sitting in the theater, the credits rolling by, and I sat there, my wife by my side. If she, or any of our group would have spoken, or even touched me, I would have broken down crying. It had that kind of impact. Afterwards we all went to the bar in front of the theater and I ordered two whiskey shots, just for myself. I'll never forget that day. Never.

On *The Mist* set producer Denise Huth gave me the script, but she pointed out that the ending was not included. Now I knew why. To end the film on that note it had

DECEMBER

_____
_____
_____
_____
_____
_____
_____
_____
_____
_____
_____
_____
_____
_____
_____
_____
_____
_____
_____
_____
_____

_____
_____
_____
_____
_____
_____
_____
_____
_____
_____
_____
_____
_____
_____
_____
_____
_____
_____
_____
_____
_____

_____
_____
_____
_____
_____
_____

_____
_____
_____
_____
_____
_____
_____
_____

to be a surprise for everyone. Stephen King did approve the ending, in fact earlier in this tome it's mentioned that he wish he would have come up with that ending for his original story. Anyone who saw this movie in the theater during it's early run were fortunate. Once the ending started getting around, folks wouldn't likely be buying tickets to a film they heard had a . . . down ending. For Frank Darabont to stick to his guns and film what he knew this is how it had to end, you must give him, well, everything. I applaud his decision, and Stephen King's and Dimension Film, for supporting him.

Like Stephen King said about his novel, _Cujo_, when asked about the ending of that novel. He responded by saying he didn't know the kid was going to die. When he got to the end, the kid had to die. Of course, in the film you can't kill the kid, so he survived in the theatrical release. Reading a novel, bad and unfortunate events happen all the time, but if you want to sell tickets to a film, and keep them coming, you don't kill the kid.

Kudos to you, Frank Darabont. You shocked us all. Even the King.

DECEMBER

23 MONDAY

24 TUESDAY
Christmas Eve

25 WEDNESDAY
Christmas Day
Hanukkah begins

THINGS YOU MIGHT NOT KNOW ABOUT *THE MIST*

While researching *The Mist* I came across some interesting statements about the film. I had not come across some of these supposed facts previously so I thought I would explore and see what I could discover. *Horror News Network* noted a few items I was not aware of and with the help of Constantine Nasr (who worked on *The Mist*) he reached out to *The Mist* co-producer, Denise Huth, and CafeFX technician, Everett Burrell, to set the record straight on a few things.

Truth or...? Director Frank Darabont did not originally plan to include the giant, six-legged behemoth which walks over the car at the end, even though this is one of the novella's most popular scenes. Several CafeFX special effects technicians convinced him to put it in the film and it obviously made quite an impression on the audience... and the ground it sank into.

The Verdict Is: "That is true. I pushed Frank hard to keep it in and we did some tests. He loved it"
— Everett Burrell, CafeFX, *The Mist*.

DECEMBER

26 THURSDAY
Kwanzaa

27 FRIDAY

28 SATURDAY

29 SUNDAY

Truth or…? Frank Darabont originally wrote an opening scene showing the military scientist referenced to by Private Jessup accidentally opening the dimension portal that allows the creatures and the mist to enter our world. Over dinner, *Mist* actor Andre Braugher questioned Darabont whether this scene was necessary. After thinking about it for a week, Darabont was convinced to scrap the scene, leaving the nature of the mist more ambiguous.

The Verdict Is: "I don't remember the Andre part of it though it's possible. I do remember discussing it from a financial aspect. Frank wanted to have as many tanks and military vehicles he could get for the final scene and cutting the original opening scene helped get him a tank for the final scene." – Denise Huth

Truth or…? The original Stephen King novella was also one of the inspirations for the video game *Half-Life*(1998), where scientists at a top-secret military base are running experiments with inter-dimensional portals and open the flood gates to its hostile inhabitants.

The Verdict Is: On *Half-Life*: I discovered that the *Half-Life* creators have discussed in many interviews about its origins and that *The Mist* story was an influence, along with other ideas. Author Marc Laidlaw,

DECEMBER

30 MONDAY

31 TUESDAY
New Year's Eve

1 WEDNESDAY
New Year's Day

(The 37th Mandela, The Orchid Eater who signed novels of his for us in the past), helped create *Half-Life* and his interest and fiction in the Lovecraftian world in a couple of novels certainly adds credence to *The Mist* influence.

Truth or...? Frank Darabont had originally been offered twice the budget by a producer to make this film, but with one crippling caveat: Darabont would have to change his planned ending, a conclusion he'd personally envisioned and nursed for twenty years. In the end, he turned to another producer and made the movie for half the amount, but only after forfeiting his dirdctorial salary.

The Verdict Is: We could have had a higher budget if we changed the ending though I don't remember it being double. I don't think he completely forfeited his salary but he did not make what he typically made back then. – Denise Huth

Truth or...? At the end of the film, when the rescue truck with Melissa McBride passes by David, Frank Darabont originally wanted a second truck to pass by David. This one would have been filled with various people from the market, including Jim, Bud, Mr. Mackey, and most of Mrs. Carmody's ex-followers, indicating that they were rescued safely from the store and making David realize that he and his group should have never have even left the market in the first place.

JANUARY

2 THURSDAY
Hanukkah ends

3 FRIDAY

4 SATURDAY

5 SUNDAY

Unfortunately, most of the extras and other actors had already left because their parts were finished, so Darabont had to scrap this idea.

The Verdict Is: Originally, nobody survived. It was Jeff Demunn's idea to have Melissa McBride's character there with her children. I don't really remember him talking about having others there but as it wasn't part of the original script and we filmed the ending last, the rest of the cast had already been wrapped. – Denise Huth

Stephen King on the Set?: Frank Darabont had offered to cast Stephen King in a supporting role as the biker. However, Stephen King turned his offer down, but as you

The Mist by Aeron Alfrey

read earlier (from the King / Darabont interview), King almost surprised Frank on the set after the fact, but it was too long a trip (If you don't know by now, King prefers, if at all possible, to not fly the friendly skies). The role went to Brian Libby, who is every Frank Darabont film (but for certain Libby would have been in the film either way). Interesting note: In 2010 Stephen King played a biker named "Bachman", who's profession was as a "cleaner" (Who better to take care of an errant body here and there?).

Dedicated to

Stephen King

and

Frank Darabont

"Wherever there's fear, there's hysteria. Wherever there are people who whip up fear, for their own purposes, they will produce the hysteria, and they will try to do it again."
– DALTON TRUMBO, *Trumbo*

Every *Stephen King Annual* is dedicated to the writer that brought us all together here… Stephen King. He gave us a spectacular story that is "The Mist," over forty years ago. It still holds within it the explored human and moral implications when we are driven into unpredictable situations wherein we must make decisions, continuing one's personal survival. If you have a family, like an earthquake, that magnifies all responsibilities. He gave us a dilemma with monsters aplenty.

Frank Darabont brought *The Mist* even deeper into our lives, driving Stephen King's message home, making the ultimate sacrifice. How do you survive doing what you think is best, at any cost? Because of Frank Darabont we were able to live out this fantastic story on the big screen, and he gave us a helluva ending that not even Stephen King saw coming, but approved it.

Like it or loathe it, you won't ever forget it. That's the power of storytelling.

Every *Stephen King Annual* is a lot of work, work that I look forward to, every year. Thank you to the diligence and dedication of our writers to help bring this publication to fruition.

A thank you to my long-time partner in so many projects, the featured artist, Glenn Chadbourne. His covers for the *Stephen King Annual* have become legendary and everyone looks forward to his annual creations.

Our graphic designer, Bryan McAllister, creates the magic and wizardry to whip up our Annuals every year, especially the color electric you spun on the Extreme King title page. Wowee! Thank ya! Like a fellow brother in the trenches, he goes above and beyond the call of duty. Thank you, Bry.

Thank you to Laura McAllister for taking the time to proof-read this year's Annual. Laura, your insight was invaluable.

This edition is also dedicated to our new joys in our world:
Fenn, Luna, Pike, Olivia, Flora, and Elise.

To my wife, LeeAnn, who makes life a joy to share with, every day. ♥

CONTRIBUTORS:

Dave Hinchberger I devour everything. Whether it's movies or comic books, novels or theater, Rock n' Roll to Jazz. Before I was in "books" I managed record stores and then marketing at Polygram and Relativity Records for fifteen years. Growing up it was The Beatles, and rock music. At night, in the 70's, we'd tune into the *CBS Mystery Theater* on the car radio with my family on long car trips. The family huddled in behind mom and dad in the station wagon, as the fateful sound of the drum roll theme came echoing out of the tinny car speakers. Hairs raised on our necks. Experiencing *Planet of the Apes* in the theater with my dad, at the wide-eyed age of six. These are the sparks that have led us here! I've been operating The Overlook Connection Bookstore and Press, since 1987, and created The Stephen King Catalog to dedicate this area to everything Stephen King. I'm never bored. There isn't enough time for me to see, read, and experience what the creative world has to offer, but… I'm damn sure gonna try.

Glenn Chadbourne This amazing artist is well known in the horror world of writers, artists, and even in film (if you look close in Stephen King's *The Mist*, directed by Frank Darabont, you'll see Glenn's work). "Artist to the stars," we all call him. Illustrator of many novels and short story collections, but especially Stephen King special editions. He created a beautiful two-volume set, *The Secretary Of Dreams*, an illustrated Stephen King short story collection. Glenn is also the artist for the New Stephen King Cover Series that gives every Stephen King book a new cover (see ad within). You can see a whole category with hundreds of items from Glenn Chadbourne at StephenKingCatalog.com and you can visit with him at **glennchadbourne.com**.

Bryan McAllister has been bringing the visual design of OCP projects to life since 2002. A lifelong sci-fi fan, he honed his artistic abilities early, absorbing the gorgeous craftsmanship of *Star Wars*. Today, the man behind graphic design and illustration studio, Fine Dog Creative. He's also a devoted caver and serves on the board of directors of the Missouri Caves and Karst Conservancy, is a Life Member of the National Speleological Society - to which he was named Fellow in 2016. Inspired by the 70's TV series *The Land of the Lost* as a kid (remember those scary sleestaks?) he has discovered, mapped and surveyed caves across the United States including portions of Mammoth Cave (the longest known cave in the world). He lives in St. Louis with his lovely wife, Laura, their two children, Maya the wonder dog and two comical cats.

Bev Vincent, is the author of the just released *Stephen King: A Complete Exploration of his Work, Life and Influences, The Road to the Dark Tower, The Dark Tower Companion* and *The Stephen King Illustrated Companion*. Over 100 short stories, with appearances in *Doctor Who: Destination Prague, The X-files: The Truth Is Out There, Ellery Queen's, Alfred Hitchcock's* and *Cemetery Dance* magazines. He has been nominated for the Stoker (twice), Edgar, Ignotus and ITW Thriller Awards. In 2018, he co-edited the anthology *Flight or Fright* with Stephen King. He collaborated with Brian Keene on *Dissonant Harmonies*. More at **bevvincent.com** and Twitter **@BevVincent**.

(Continued)

The Dark Tower: The Gunslinger Born #7 Cover art, by Jae Lee 2007

CONTRIBUTORS:

Stephen R. Bissette, a pioneer graduate of the Joe Kubert School, was an instructor at the Center for Cartoon Studies (2005–2020) renowned for *Swamp Thing*, *Taboo* (launching *From Hell* and *Lost Girls*), '*1963*,' *S.R. Bissette's Tyrant®*, co-creating John Constantine, and creating the world's second '24-Hour Comic' (invented by Scott McCloud for Bissette). Comics creator (recently in *Spongebob Comics*, *Paleo*, *Awesome 'Possum*), illustrator (*Vermont Ghost Guide*, *Vermont Monster Guide*), author (*Teen Angels & New Mutants*, short fiction in *Hellboy: Odd Jobs*, *The New Dead*, *Mister October*, co-author of *Comic Book Rebels*, *Prince of Stories: The Many Worlds of Neil Gaiman*, *The Monster Book: Buffy the Vampire Slayer*), Bissette's latest includes co-authoring *Studio of Screams*, his sketchbooks *Brooding Creatures* and *Thoughtful Creatures*, the Electric Dreamhouse 'Midnight Movie Monograph' *David Cronenberg's The Brood*, and his book series *Cryptid Cinema™* and *Cryptid Cinema™: A Boggy Creek Primer*.

Pete Von Sholly has been drawing since childhood, mesmerized by the cult magazine *Famous Monsters of Filmland*. His fascination led to a long career as a Hollywood storyboard artist on over 100 feature films! *The Shawshank Redemption*, *The Green Mile*, *The Mist*, *The Mask*, *Darkman*, *Mars Attacks*, *Pumpkinhead*, one Jason from *Friday the 13th*, two Freddy Kruegers (3&4) and three *Chuckys*, (*Bride of*, *Seed of*, and *Curse of*)! And of course, comic books with John Stanley, Carl Barks and Jack Kirby also warped his life irreparably! He has churned out monster-filled graphic novels, model kits, trading cards published by Dark Horse, IDW, TwoMorrows, BOOM!, Kitchen Sink, etc. He has created lavishly illustrated editions classic horror books by H.P. Lovecraft, Joe R. Lansdale, Ramsey Campbell and Stephen King. Von Sholly's *Monsterbook* is a career overview in four volumes, on Amazon and through Bookland at **VonShollywood.net**

Stephen Spignesi is a retired Practitioner in Residence from the English Department at the University of New Haven and the author of more than 65 books. He is considered an authority on the work of Stephen King, the Titanic, the Beatles, and other pop culture and historical topics. His latest books are *Stephen King, American Master*, *Elton John: Fifty Years On*, and *Robin Williams, American Master*. He lives in New Haven, Connecticut.

Tyson Blue, a true *eminence grise* in the world of King scholarship, is one of the world's primary authorities on King's work and the media projects based thereon. He was a Contributing Editor for *Castle Rock: the Stephen King Newsletter* from 1985-1989, and his work has appeared in *Twilight Zone*, *Cemetery Dance*, *Midnight Graffiti* and many other magazines worldwide. He is the author of *The Unseen King*, and most recently edited *Hope and Miracles: The Shawshank Redemption and The Green Mile: Two Screenplays by Frank Darabont*, published in 2021 by Gauntlet Press. He lives near Rochester, NY with his wife, Janice, and Hank, their golden retriever.

Andrew J. Rausch is a popular culture writer and the author of nearly 50 books, including *The Stephen King Movie Quiz Book*, *The Wit & Wisdom of Stephen King*, and *Perspectives on Stephen King*. He lives in Independence, Kansas. He can be found at **authorandyrausch.wordpress.com**

(Continued)

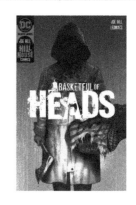
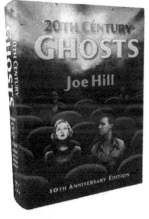

THE CAPE: FALLEN - VARIANT SET

Joe Hill First Printings, Comics,
Signed Limited editions available at:

StephenKingCatalog.com

CONTRIBUTORS:

Kevin Quigley is known for his monographic work on Stephen King (*The Stephen King Illustrated Movie Trivia Book*, *Chart of Darkness*, *Stephen King Limited*). He is the author of the novels *Meatball Express*, *I'm On Fire*, and *Roller Disco Saturday Night*, as well as the short story collections *Damage & Dread* and *This Terrestrial Hell*. His stories have appeared in the Cemetery Dance anthologies *Halloween Carnival* and *Shivers*, the bestselling *Shining in the Dark* anthology, the thriller collection *Death of a Bad Neighbour*, and Lawrence Block's upcoming *Playing Games*. He lives in Boston, Massachusetts with his husband, Shawn.

Anthony Northrup is the *Author of Stephen King Dollar Baby: The Book*, 2021 *Stephen King Dollar Baby: The Sequel*, coming in 2023 (Bear Manor Media), Currently adapting his story "Yardwork" as a screenplay for film director Rob Darren. Entertainment writer for the Tri-County Sun for over a decade, earning him two writer's awards. His "All Things King" Stephen King Fan Page (Facebook) of ten years is acknowledged in *Stephen King American Master*, by author Stephen Spignesi. Host/Co-Host of Stephen King Dollar Baby Film Fests: Crypticon MN, (2014/15) SK Rules: DB1 Worldwide Online (2021), SKR: DB2 Alternating Currents, Davenport, IA (2022), "Long Live the King" DBFF Brazil (2022) Anthony currently resides in North Dakota with his wife Gena.

Ariel Bosi was born and lives in Buenos Aires, Argentina. He's the author of *Todo sobre Stephen King* (2016, Penguin Random House) and *Edición limitada* (2020, RdlM Ediciones). He's been a constant reader since 1996 and has worked in the publishing field, focusing on Stephen King promotional campaigns for the Spanish publisher since 2010. Currently, he hosts *La Corte del Rey*, a podcast about Stephen King's works and life for Penguin Random House, and *Los Tesoros del Rey*, a newsletter about King's works, all available in Spanish for Constant Readers in Spain and Latin America. He's attended red carpet events and press junkets of Stephen King adaptations as an influencer and has personally met his favorite author on several occasions. See his published work: *Todo sobre Stephen King:*
penguinlibros.com/ar/biografias/135313-libro-todo-sobre-stephen-king-9788401346958
and Edición limitada:
restaurantdelamente.com/4227-edicion-limitada-nueva-edicion-a-bosi-y-p-tarantino.html

L.L. Soares is a marooned time traveler from the year 2317, trying to find a way home. In the meantime, he tells stories. His books include the novels *Life Rage* (2012 Bram Stoker Award-winner for First Novel), *Rock 'n' Roll*, *Hard*, *Buried in Blue Clay*, and *Teach Them How to Bleed*, and a new career-spanning story collection, *Something Blue and Other Colorful Deaths*. His short fiction has appeared in dozens of magazines and anthologies, including *Gothic.net*, *Cemetery Dance*, *Zippered Flesh Vol. I-III*, and *Wicked Sick*. For more than a decade, he co-wrote the Stoker-nominated movie review column *Cinema Knife Fight*. He lives in the Boston area with his wife and their pet iguana, Osiris, King of the Dead. To keep up on his endeavors (and to find out if he ever gets back to this own time), please go to **www.llsoares.com**

Constantine Nasr is the award-winning filmmaker and producer behind *The Manhunt for Whitey Burger*, *Public Enemies: The Golden Age of the Gangster Film*, *Shadows of the Bat: The Cinematic Saga of the Dark Knight*, *The Summers of IT*, and *Walking the Mile*. He is the author of *Roger Corman: Interviews*, has contributed numerous essays to film journals like *Little Shoppe of Horrors* and *Video Watchdog*, and has recorded over 40 audio commentaries on classic cinema and animation.

(Continued)

CONTRIBUTORS:

Noah Mitchell has been reading King since 1980 and collecting since 1985. He has an extensive King collection that includes first US and UK editions, signed limited and lettered editions, and first appearances of short stories. He has an enormous home library that includes impressive collections of many other writers such as Joe Hill, Clive Barker, Dean Koontz, Ed Gorman, Jack Ketchum, Shirley Jackson, Robert McCammon, Peter Straub, Dan Simmons, F Paul Wilson, and others. Facebook friends from across the country have traveled to New York to tour his home library.

Diana Petroff has been an avid Stephen King reader for decades, and, while relatively new to the rare collecting world, has dedicated years to learning the idiosyncrasies of rare book collecting with a concentration on Stephen King. This love of rare books has led her into the world of publishing. She currently works with Alex Berman, the founder of Phantasia Press in the production and design of limited editions. Phantasia marked Stephen King's entry into the signed/limited market in 1980 with one of the most coveted collectibles: the lettered "asbestos" *Firestarter*.

THE DARK TOWER - ORIGINAL LITHOGRAPH.
THE LITTLE SISTERS OF ELURIA.
Based on Stephen Kings original *Dark Tower* story.
By Artist Erik Wilson

This Signed Limited Lithograph is the only COLOR version published of this original art!

Artist Erik Wilson was commissioned by Stephen King to produce an original artwork for his novella, THE LITTLE SISTERS OF ELURIA, from the *Dark Tower* universe. It was published in black and white in the LEGENDS book. However, the work was originally produced by the artist in color! The Overlook Connection Press published this as a color lithograph and is produced with the artist permission.

LITHOGRAPH FEATURES:

- **The only color version produced of this artwork**
- **Printed on acid-free card stock in four-color**
- SIGNED and numbered by artist Erik Wilson
- **Limited to a numbered 1 of 500 copies**
- **This is a movie-sized poster suitable for framing, measuring 17 x 24 inches**
- **This poster is mailed rolled and kept protected in plastic.**

This movie-sized poster will look great in your Stephen King Library at home. We also have a lettered remarqued version with Erik Wilson's own *Gunslinger* drawn on 1 of 52 copies!

Order at StephenKingCatalog.com

Stephen King Artwork Portfolios
Signed and Numbered by the Artists.

Available at **StephenKingCatalog.com**

BIBLIOGRAPHY, END NOTES, IMAGES

PAGE: 1 Stephen King Catalog, 2010 unpublished cover. Photos courtesy of Frank Darabont / Dimension Films 2007

PAGE: 2 *Dark Forces* Lettered Edition cover. Art by Bernie Wrightson. Lonely Road Books 2007

PAGE: 6 "The Monsters Are Due on Maple Street" monologue 1962 Rod Serling, *The Twilight Zone*, CBS

PAGE: 6 Stephen King *Mist* quote, *The Mist*, Scribners, Pg 105. 2018

PAGE: 12, 15 *The Mist* computer game artwork, 1985 Angelsoft

PAGE: 13 *The Mist* computer game screen artwork & text, 1985 Angelsoft

PAGE: 13-15 Martyn Carroll, "The Making of Stephen King's The Mist:" Oct. 2020. gamesradar.com

PAGE: 15 The Development of *Half-Life*, 2020 arcadology.net

PAGE: 16,17,18,19,20,21,22, 24, 25,26, 27. On the set *Mist* photos 2007 Dave Hinchberger.

PAGE: 17 Photo of Frank Darabont 2007 Frank Darabont

PAGE: 18 *Pan's Labyrinth* Blu-ray cover art 2016 Criterion.

PAGE: 18 *Castle Rock Weekly, The Mist* movie prop newspaper. 2007 Dimension Films.

PAGE: 21 *The Mist* screenplay, signed for Dave Hinchberger on the set of *The Mist*. 2007 Dave Hinchberger.

PAGE: 22 *Them!* Movie poster art 1954 Warner Bros.

PAGE: 24 Chris Owens 2007 Frank Darabont, Dimension Films.

PAGE: 25 King's Pharmacy set photos, *The Mist*. 2007 Dave Hinchberger.

PAGE: 28 Marcia Gay Harden 2007 Frank Darabont, Dimension Films.

PAGE: 29 *The Complete Idiot's Guide: The Book of Revelation* cover. 2002

PAGE: 29 *Lord of the Flies* by William Golding, first UK hardcover. 1954 Faber and Faber, London.

PAGE: 31 *The Painted Veil*, DVD cover art 2007 Warner Bros.

PAGE: 33 *Bad Planet* No. 2 cover 2006 Bernie Wrightson and Image Comics.

PAGE: 33 *Alien Pig Farm* No. 1 cover 2007 William Stout and Image Comics.

PAGE: 34, 35, 36 Photo 2007 Frank Darabont, Dimension Films.

PAGE: 38 1. The word count here doesn't permit anything further on this point. I don't adhere to any particular faith or doctrine, but I read plenty of theological texts; if you're interested, start at https://www.ligonier.org/learn/articles/two-important-words-good-friday-expiation-and-propitiation and go from there. 2023 Stephen R. Bissette

PAGE: 38 2. In genre terms, just as King's novella and Darabont's film owe an obvious debt to everything from H.P. Lovecraft's "From Beyond" (written in 1920, published 1934) to René Ray 1956 serial teleplay and novel *The Strange World of Planet X* (US title for the 1957 feature film version: COSMIC MONSTERS; a debt acknowledged by Darabont via a line spoken by Andre Braugher as Brent Norton), Darabont's finale owes a clear debt to John Farrow's harrowing *Five Came Back* (1939; in which there are only two bullets, not three, in the chamber) and Terence Fisher's *Island of Terror* (1966). In the latter film, Edward Judd almost pulls the trigger to mercy-kill Carole Gray (before the bone-devouring "silicates" get her) when Peter Cushing nods in assent. Being a 20th century Brit, not 21st century American, Judd doesn't. Note Darabont reveals the worried mother (Melissa McBride) from the market, she who no one will accompany—she doesn't capitulate to fear—riding in the military caravan, safe with the two children she risked her life to rescue. There is a choice. 2023 Stephen R. Bissette

PAGE: 38 Photo 2007 Frank Darabont, Dimension Films.

PAGE: 40 *Dark Forces* cover art, 1980 Viking

PAGE: 40 *Different Seasons* cover art, 1982 Viking

PAGE: 41 *Cycle of the Werewolf* trade paper, 2019 Gallery 13

PAGE: 41 *Skeleton Crew* cover art, 1985 Putnam.

PAGE: 41 *The Bachman Books* cover art, 1986 NEL

PAGE: 42 *The Bachman Books* cover art, 1986 Signet

PAGE: 42 Stephen King *Short Fiction* set: *The Mist, Apt Pupil, The Body, The Sun Dog* 2021 Scribner

PAGE: 42 *Four Past Midnight* cover art, 1990 Viking

PAGE: 43 *Colorado Kid* cover art, 2017 PS Publishing

PAGE: 43 *The Mist* movie cover art, 2007 Signet

PAGE: 44 *Skeleton Crew* Lettered cover art, 2015 Pete Von Sholly and PS Publishing

PAGE: 44 *Creepy* No. 1 cover art, 1964 Jack Davis and Warren Publishing Corp.

PAGE: 44 Susan Malerstein-Watkins, Frank Darabont photo 1999 Pete Von Sholly

PAGE: 45 Pete Von Sholly's Altar of Monsters photo 1999 Pete Von Sholly

PAGE: 45 *Classics Not Illustrated* cover art of *The Mist* by 1999 Pete Von Sholly

PAGE: 46 *Skeleton Crew* unpublished art 1999 Pete Von Sholly

PAGE: 46 *Classics Not Illustrated* cover art of *The Stand* by 1999 Pete Von Sholly

PAGE: 48-56 *The Missed* comic text and art 1999 Pete Von Sholly

PAGE: 58 *The Shawshank Redemption* UK Blu-ray Steelbook 2012

PAGE: 58 *The Mist* DVD Cover art 2021

PAGE: 58 *The Punisher* DVD Cover art 2004 Lionsgate

PAGE: 58 *'Salem's Lot* TV Series, 2004 Warner Bros.

PAGE: 59 *Infamous* DVD 2010 Warner Bros.

PAGE: 59 *The Mist* TV Series, 2017 Spike TV, Dimension Television

PAGE: 59 *The Walking Dead* Season eleven trading card, 2021 AMC

PAGE: 60 *Evil Dead Rise* UK DVD, 2023 StudioCanal

PAGE: 60 *The Mist* TV Series, 2017 Spike TV, Dimension Television

PAGE: 61 *The Mist / 1408* Blu-ray 2010 Alliance

PAGE: 61 Marcia Gay Harden, *The Mist* 2007 Frank Darabont, Dimension Films

PAGE: 61, 62, 63, 64 *The Mist* TV Series, 2017 Spike TV, Dimension Television

PAGE: 64 Frank Darabont e-mail, 2007 Glenn Chadbourne

PAGE: 66-73 *The Mist Centipede* storyboard art 2007 Pete Von Sholly

PAGE: 74-78 Photos 2007 Constantine Nasr, Denise Huth, Juan Melchor.

PAGE: 76 Food House Photo, Denise Huth 2007

PAGE: 80 Group photo, Alliance Theatre, 2023 Dave Hinchberger

PAGE: 80, 81 *The Shining* Opera photos, 2023 Atlanta Opera

PAGE: 82, 84 *Holly* hardcover art, 2023 Scribners US

PAGE: 82 *Holly* hardcover art, 2023 Heyne, Germany

PAGE: 83 *Holly* hardcover art, 2023 Hodder & Stoughton. UK.

PAGE: 83 *Holly* hardcover art, 2023 Armada. Romania.

PAGE: 84 talkingscaredpod.com logo 2023.

PAGE: 84 Stephen & Tabitha King photo, 2023 mainelibraries.org/kings-interview.

PAGE: 85 S.A. Cosby, *All the Sinners Bleed* cover art, Flatiron Books 2023.

PAGE: 85 *Pet Sematary: Bloodlines* movie art, 2023 Paramount Pictures.

PAGE: 85 *King on Screen* DVD art, 2023 Dark Star Pictures.

PAGE: 85 *Le Talisman (The Talisman)* by Stephen King and Peter Straub,

BIBLIOGRAPHY, END NOTES, IMAGES

1987 LGF - Livre de Poche.

PAGE: 86 Photos from *The Mist* set 2007 David Schow.

PAGE: 88 *The Monkey* logo, 2023 Spencer Sherry.

PAGE: 88 *Stephen King Dollar Baby the Book* dollar image, 2022 Anthony Northrup.

PAGE: 89 *The Monkey* film images, 2023 Spencer Sherry.

PAGE: 90 *The Monkey* movie poster, 2023 Spencer Sherry.

PAGE: 92 *University of Maine Alumni Association* cover, Fall 1989.

PAGE: 92 *King's Garbage Truck* logo, *The Maine Campus*, July 11, 1969.

PAGE: 92 *Slade* No 2 of 8, *Maine Campus* Vol. 78, June 18, 1970.

PAGE: 93 *Different Seasons*, Stephen King. NAL 1983 Signet paperback.

PAGE: 93 *King's Garbage Truck* logo, *The Maine Campus*, 1969.

PAGE: 93 *Frankenstein Meets the Wolf Man* movie poster. 1943 Universal.

PAGE: 94 *Startling Mystery Stories*, No 12, 1969.

PAGE: 94 *'Salem's Lot*, Stephen King. Signet Paperback cover art 1976.

PAGE: 95 *The Running Man*, Stephen King (as Richard Bachman), NAL Signet 1977.

PAGE: 95 Stephen King photograph, 1969. *Hearts in Suspension*, University of Maine Press 2016.

PAGE: 96 *Hearts in Suspension* cover art, 2016 University of Maine Press.

PAGE: 99 *VQR* cover, *Virginia Quarterly Review* Spring 2016.

PAGE: 100 *Harper's* cover March, 2020 Harper's.

PAGE: 101 *Esquire* cover, Oct / Nov 2020 Esquire.

PAGE: 101 *Red Screen* artwork, Humble Bundle ebook, September, 2021

PAGE: 102 *Finn* artwork, May 2022 Scribd

PAGE: 103 *McSweeney's No. 66* cover art, May 2022 McSweeney's.

PAGE: 105 *Skeleton Crew* cover art, Stephen King. 1985, June, Putnam.

PAGE: 105 *Skeleton Crew* cover art, Stephen King. 1985 MacDonald, UK.

PAGE: 105 *Skeleton Crew* Limited cover art, Stephen King. Scream Press, Oct. 1985.

PAGE: 105 *Skeleton Crew* Lettered cover art, Stephen King. Scream Press, Oct. 1985.

PAGE: 106 *The Art of Skeleton Crew*. 1985 Scream Press.

PAGE: 106 *Skeleton Crew* Limited signature page, Stephen King. Oct. 1985 Scream Press.

PAGE: 106 *Skeleton Crew* Anniversary Edition Lettered (green cover), PS Publishing.

PAGE: 106 *Skeleton Crew* Anniversary Edition Limited (blue & black-red covers), 2016 PS Publishing UK.

PAGE: 106 *Dark Forces* hardcover art, 1980 Viking Press.

PAGE: 106 *Dark Forces* hardcover art, 1980 MacDonald, UK.

PAGE: 107 *Dark Forces*, Lettered Edition, 2006 Lonely Road Books.

PAGE: 107 *Dark Forces*, Limited Edition, 2006 Lonely Road Books.

PAGE: 107 *Ubris*, *University of Maine literary magazine*, Spring 1968.

PAGE: 107 *Gallery Magazine*, November 1980.

PAGE: 107 *The Monkey*, Stephen King, pull-out booklet, November 1980, *Gallery Magazine*.

PAGE: 107 *Gallery Magazine*, November 1982.

PAGE: 107 *The Raft*, Stephen King, pull-out booklet, November 1982, *Gallery Magazine*.

PAGE: 107 *Startling Mystery Stories* #12, 1969.

PAGE: 108 *Terrors*, Playboy Paperbacks 1982.

PAGE: 108 *Rolling Stone Magazine* July 19 - August 2, 1984.

PAGE: 108 *Redbook Magazine* May 1984.

PAGE: 108 *Twilight Zone Magazine* June 1981.

PAGE: 108 *Ellery Queen's Mystery Magazine* December 1980.

PAGE: 108 *Playboy* January 1983.

PAGE: 108 *Shadows 4*, Doubleday 1981.

PAGE: 108 *Weirdbook #19* - Spring 1984.

PAGE: 109 *Shadows*, Doubleday 1978.

PAGE: 109 *Yankee Magazine* October 1983.

PAGE: 109 *New Terrors 2*, Pan Books 1980.

PAGE: 109 *Weird Tales* Fall 1984.

PAGE: 109 *The Magazine of Fantasy & Science Fiction* June 1984.

PAGE: 109 *Yankee Magazine* November 1981.

PAGE: 108 Stephen King quote, *Danse Macabre*, Everest House 1981.

PAGE: 114 Stephen King quote, *The Mist*, Scribners 2019.

PAGE: 114-115 Wikipedia.com 2023.

PAGE: 116 Chris Owens in t-shirt 2007 Frank Darabont, Dimension Films.

PAGE: 116 Chris Owens artwork on back of t-shirt 2002 Glenn Chadbourne.

PAGE: 128, 184, 188 Stephen King *The Mist*, 2018 Scribner.

PAGE: 118-119 Blockbuster press release, 2008.

PAGE: 118, 119 *The Mist* Blockbuster exclusive DVD, 2008 Dimension films, Blockbuster.

PAGE: 122 "Meet the Draytons", photo 2007 Dimension Films.

PAGE: 124, 125 *The Mist* TV Series, 2017 Spike TV, Dimension Television.

PAGE: 132, 133 *The Mist* license plate and photo, 2023 propstoreauction.com.

PAGE: 146 Frank Darabont, Chris Owens, Thomas Jane, *The Mist*. 2007 Dimension Films

PAGE: 156, 157 *The Mist* series, Nova Scotia, 2016. unravelhalifax.ca, Atlantic.ctvnews.ca, atlasofwonders.com

PAGE: 164, 165 "Stephen King on *The Mist*. Stephen King on killer clowns, 'Stranger Things,' and his secrets for scaring you silly", Nick Schager, Writer September 6, 2017, Yahoo.com/entertainment.

PAGE: 169 University of Maine logo 2023.

PAGE: 172, 173 *The Mist* screen art and disc. 1985 Angelsoft

PAGE: 175 *For A Few Dollars More* movie poster. 1965 United Artists.

PAGE: 186 Brian Libby as the prisoner in Frank Darabont's first film, "The Woman in The Room" 1983 Frank Darabont, Stephen King.

PAGE: 188 *Christina's World* 1948 Andrew Wyeth.

PAGE: 189 Olson House photo, Farnsworth Art Museum 2023.

PAGE: 190, 191 WKIT, WZON logos 2023 Stephen and Tabitha King.

PAGE: 194, 195 2007 Drew Struzan paintings, auctioned at HA.com from Frank Darabont's collection.

PAGE: 214-216 *The Mist* on set photos, 2007 Constantine Nasr.

PAGE: 217 *The Mist* artwork Aeron Alfrey.

PAGE: 219 *The Mist* movie theater newspaper ad, *Atlanta Journal-Constitution* 2007.

PAGE: 219 Thanks to Ross Perry for supplying that wonderful color ad of theater showings for *The Mist*.

PAGE: 232 *The Mist*, 2007 Frank Darabont, Dimension Films.

Calendar Border Art © 2023 Glenn Chadbourne.

Glenn Chadbourne art on pages © 2023
3, 4, 5, 86, 104, 117, 127, 130, 131, 138, 155, 161, 162, 163, 166, 167, 170, 174, 183, 197, 211, 213, 232

2024 Stephen King Catalog Annual: *The Mist*.

© 2023 by Overlook Connection Press.

Published © 2023 by Overlook Connection Press. PO Box 1934, Hiram, Georgia 30141

OverlookConnection.com StephenKingCatalog.com

First Printing ISBN: 978-1-62330-706-6